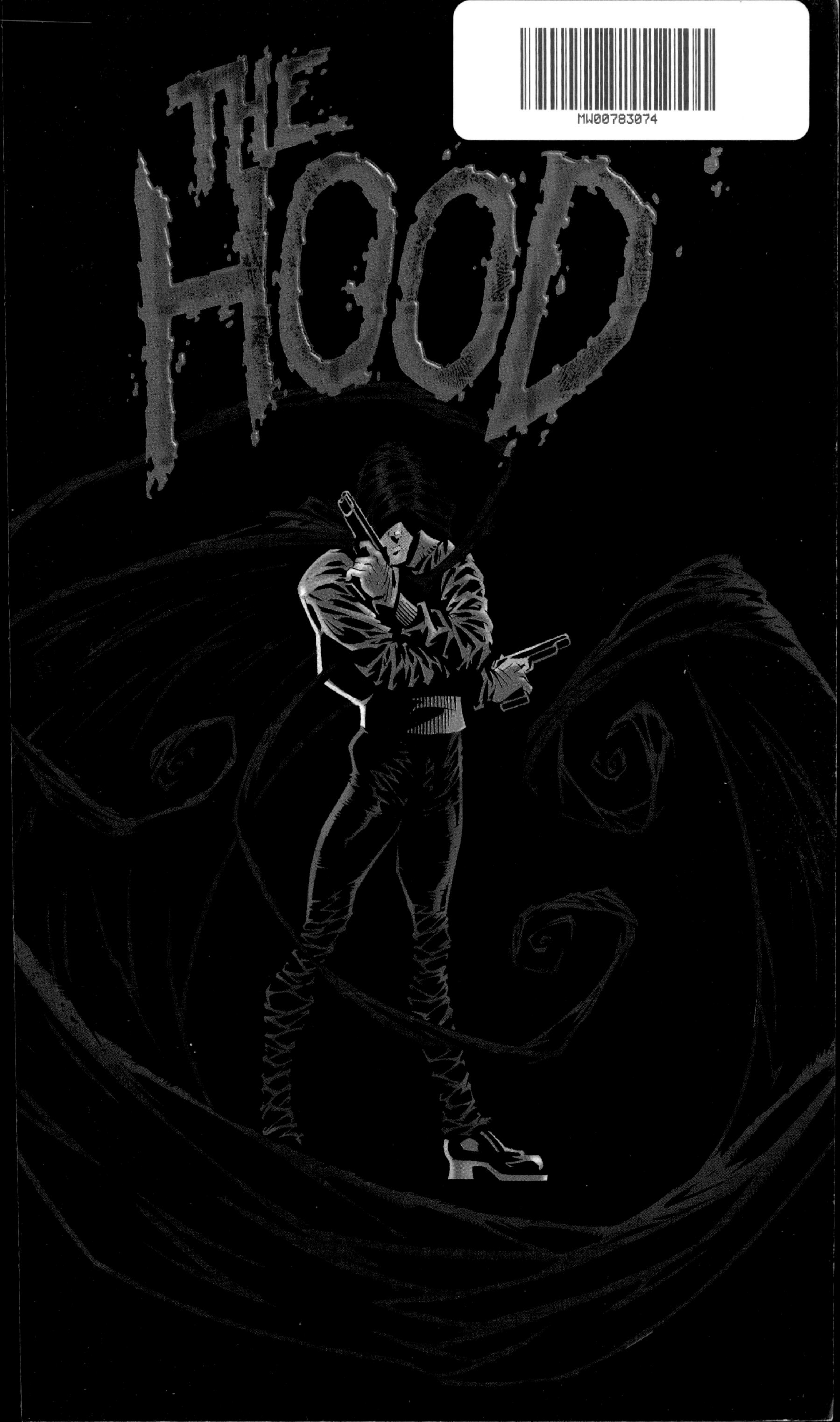
THE HOOD

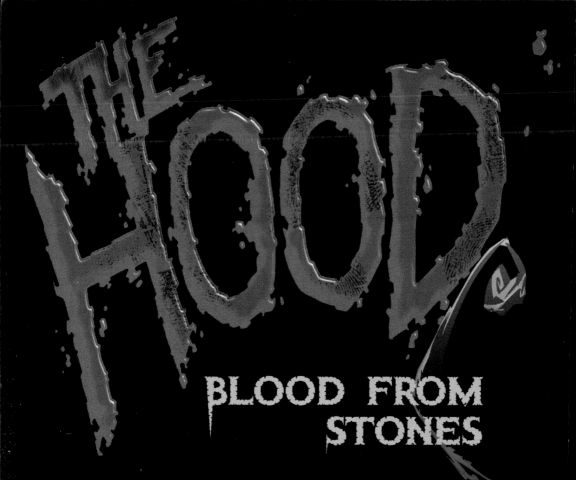

# THE HOOD

## BLOOD FROM STONES

**WRITER**
Brian K. Vaughan

**PENCILER**
Kyle Hotz

**INKER**
Eric Powell

**COLORIST**
Avalon Studios' Brian Haberlin

**LETTERERS**
Randy Gentile & Dave Sharpe

**ASSISTANT EDITORS**
Marc Sumerak & Andy Schmidt

**EDITOR**
Tom Brevoort

**EDITOR IN CHIEF**
Joe Quesada

**PRESIDENT**
Bill Jemas

**THE HOOD VOL. 1: BLOOD FROM STONES.** Contains material originally published in magazine form as THE HOOD #1-6. First printing 2003. ISBN# 0-78
5. Published by MARVEL COMICS, a division of MARVEL ENTERTAINMENT GROUP, INC. OFFICE OF PUBLICATION: 10 East 40th Street, New York, N
Copyright © 2002 and 2003 Marvel Characters, Inc. All rights reserved. $14.99 per copy in the U.S. and $24.00 in Canada (GST #R127032852);
Agreement #40668537. All characters featured in this issue and the distinctive names and likenesses thereof, and all related indicia are trademarks c
Characters, Inc. No similarity between any of the names, characters, persons, and/or institutions in this magazine with those of any living or dead p
institution is intended, and any such similarity which may exist is purely coincidental. **Printed in Canada.** STAN LEE, Chairman Emeritus. For inf
regarding advertising in Marvel Comics or on Marvel.com, please contact Russell Brown, Executive Vice President, Consumer Products, Promotions a
Sales at 212-576-8561 or rbrown@marvel.com

10 9 8 7 6 5 4 3 2 1

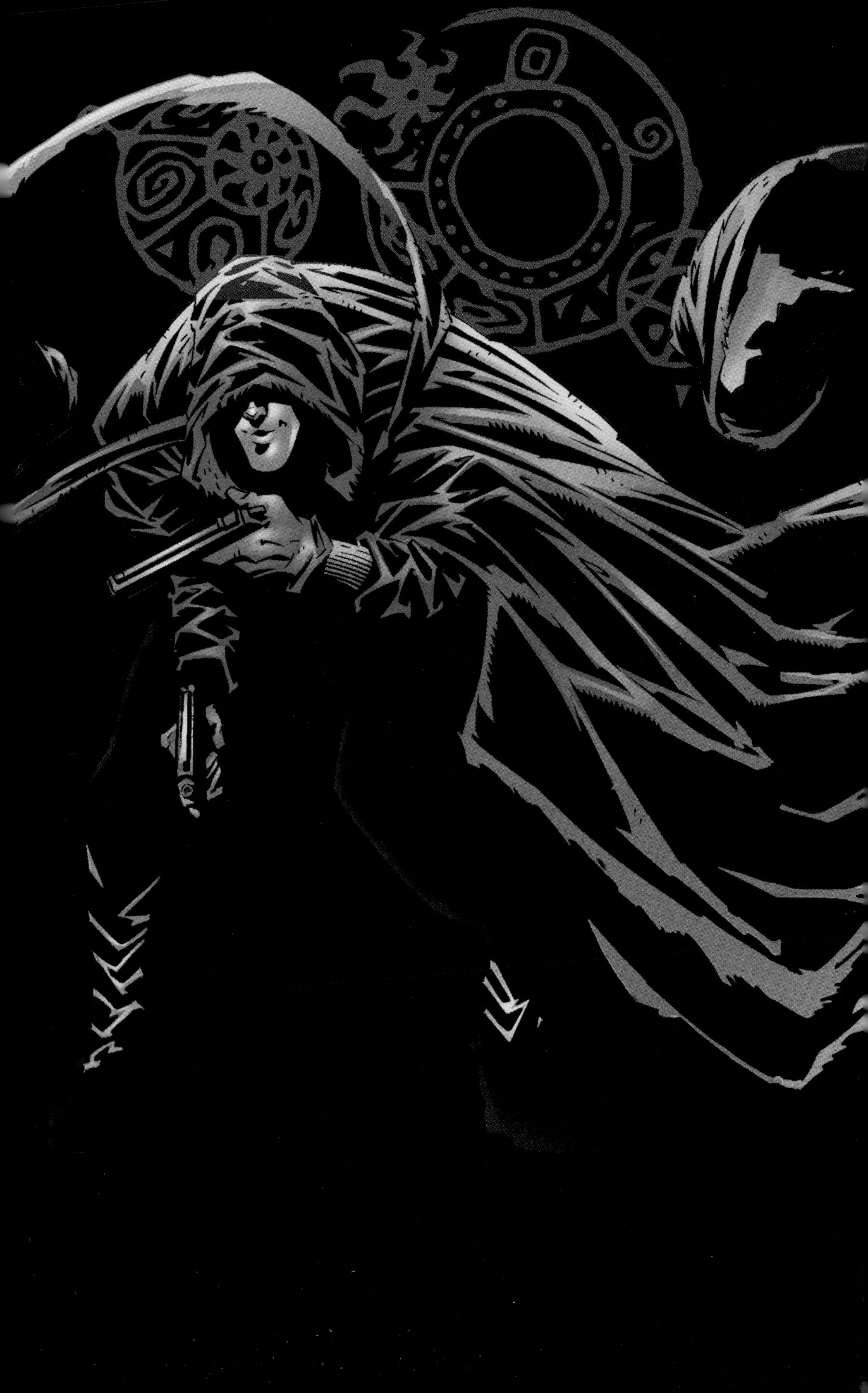

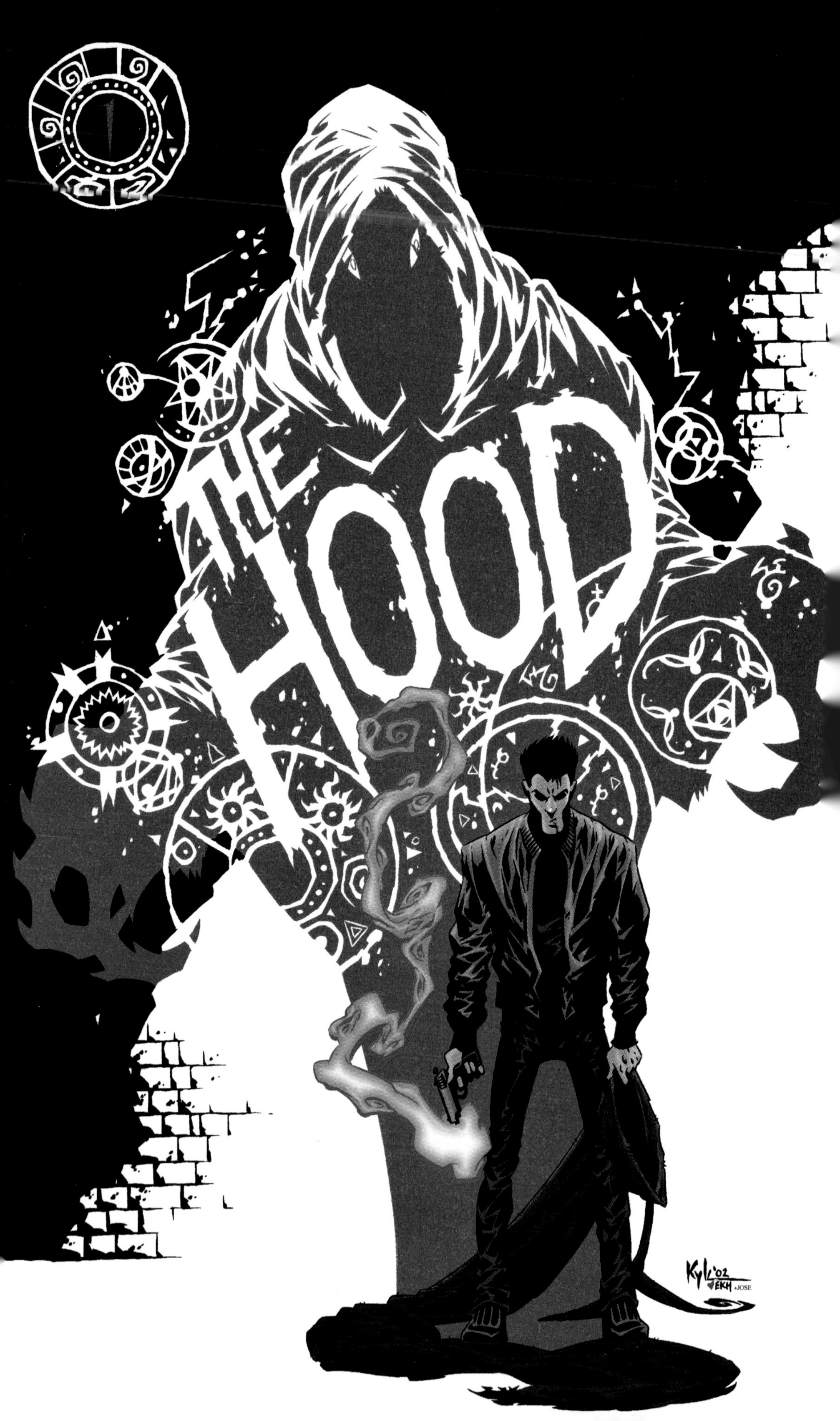
THE HOOD
Kyle '02
EKH
+JOSE

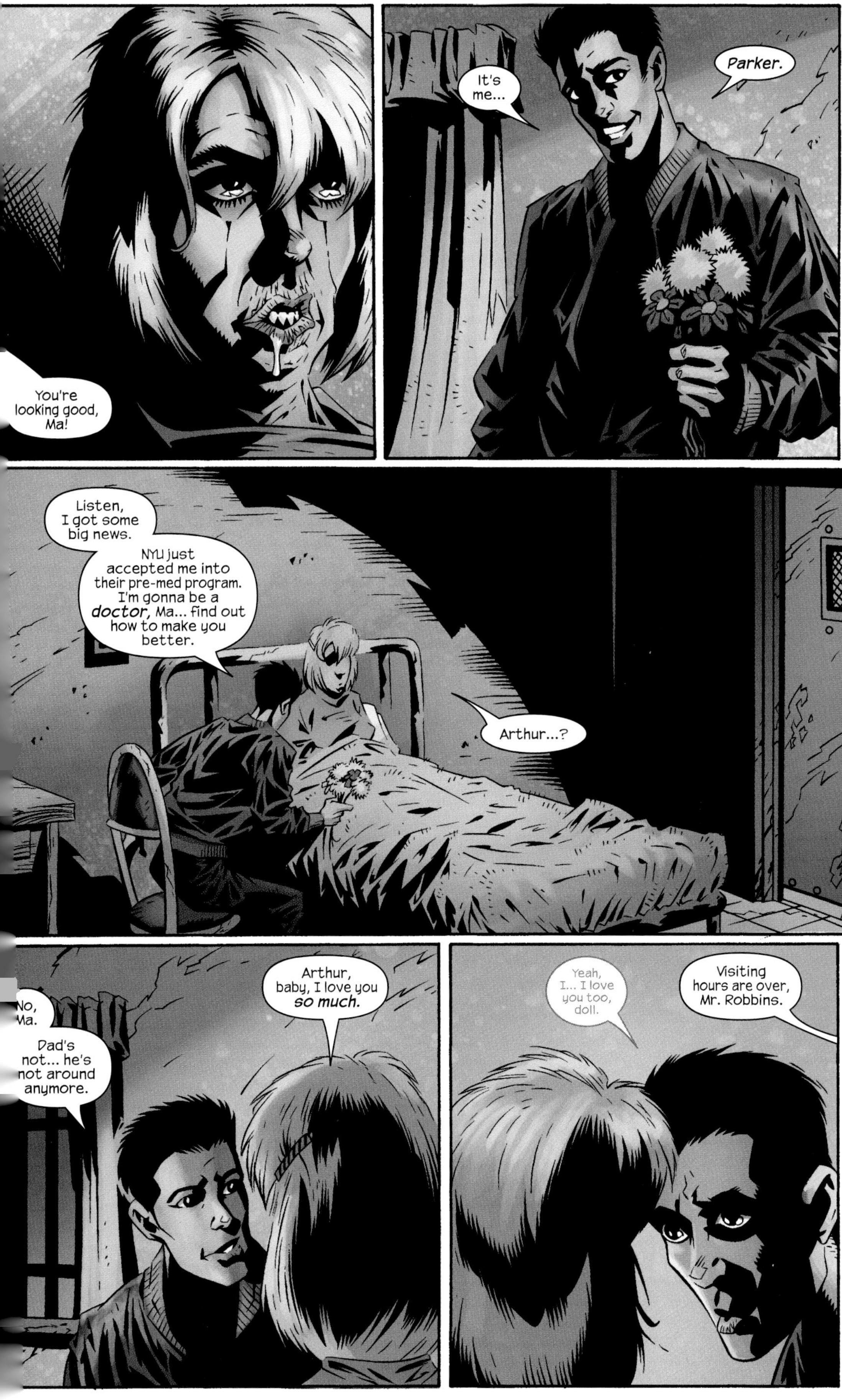
You're looking good, Ma!
It's me...
Parker.
Listen, I got some big news.
NYU just accepted me into their pre-med program. I'm gonna be a doctor, Ma... find out how to make you better.
Arthur...?
Arthur, baby, I love you so much.
No, Ma.
Dad's not... he's not around anymore.
Yeah, I... I love you too, doll.
Visiting hours are over, Mr. Robbins.

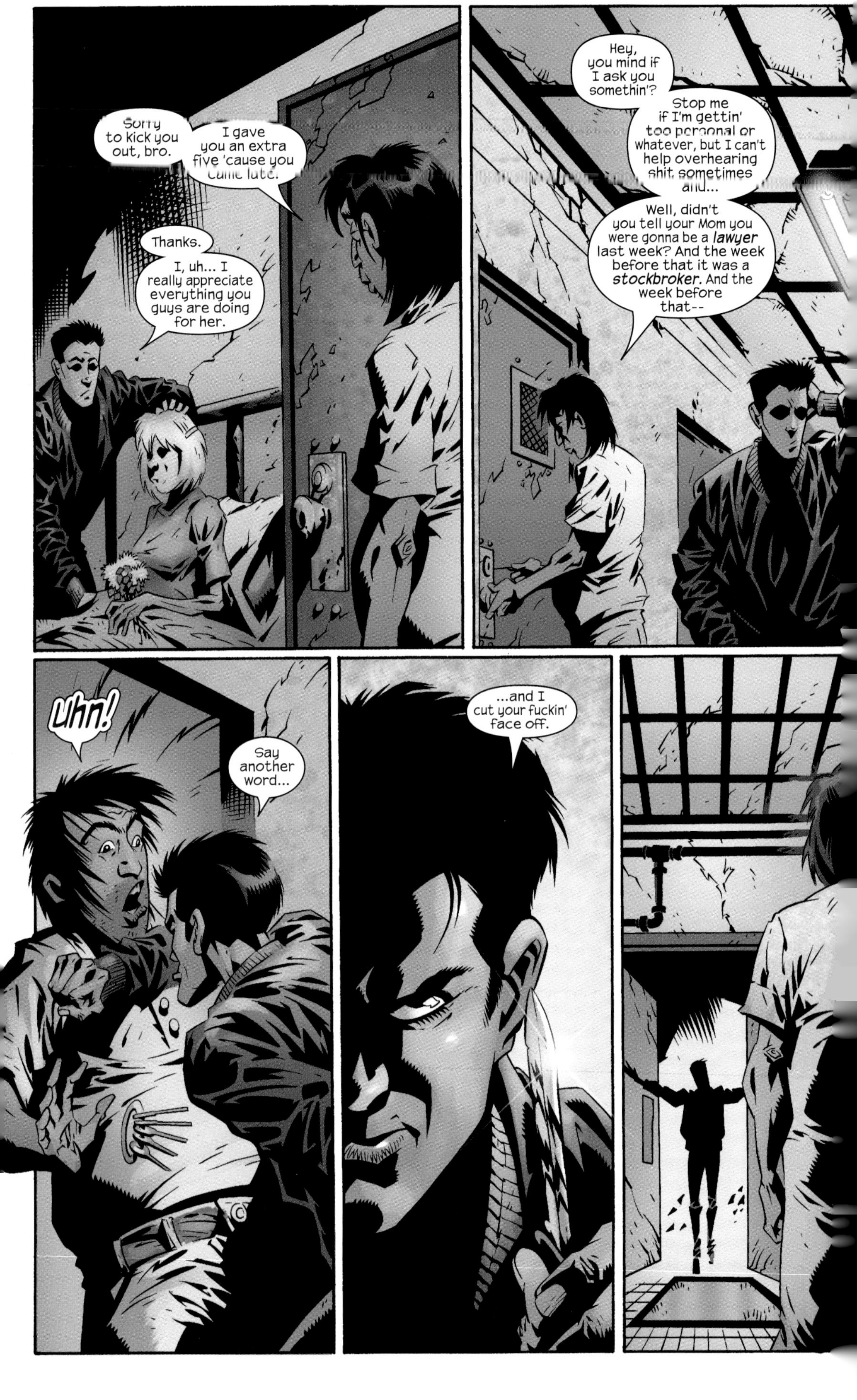
Sorry to kick you out, bro.
I gave you an extra five 'cause you came late.
Thanks.
I, uh... I really appreciate everything you guys are doing for her.
Hey, you mind if I ask you somethin'?
Stop me if I'm gettin' too personal or whatever, but I can't help overhearing shit sometimes and...
Well, didn't you tell your Mom you were gonna be a lawyer last week? And the week before that it was a stockbroker. And the week before that--
Uhn!
Say another word...
...and I cut your fuckin' face off.

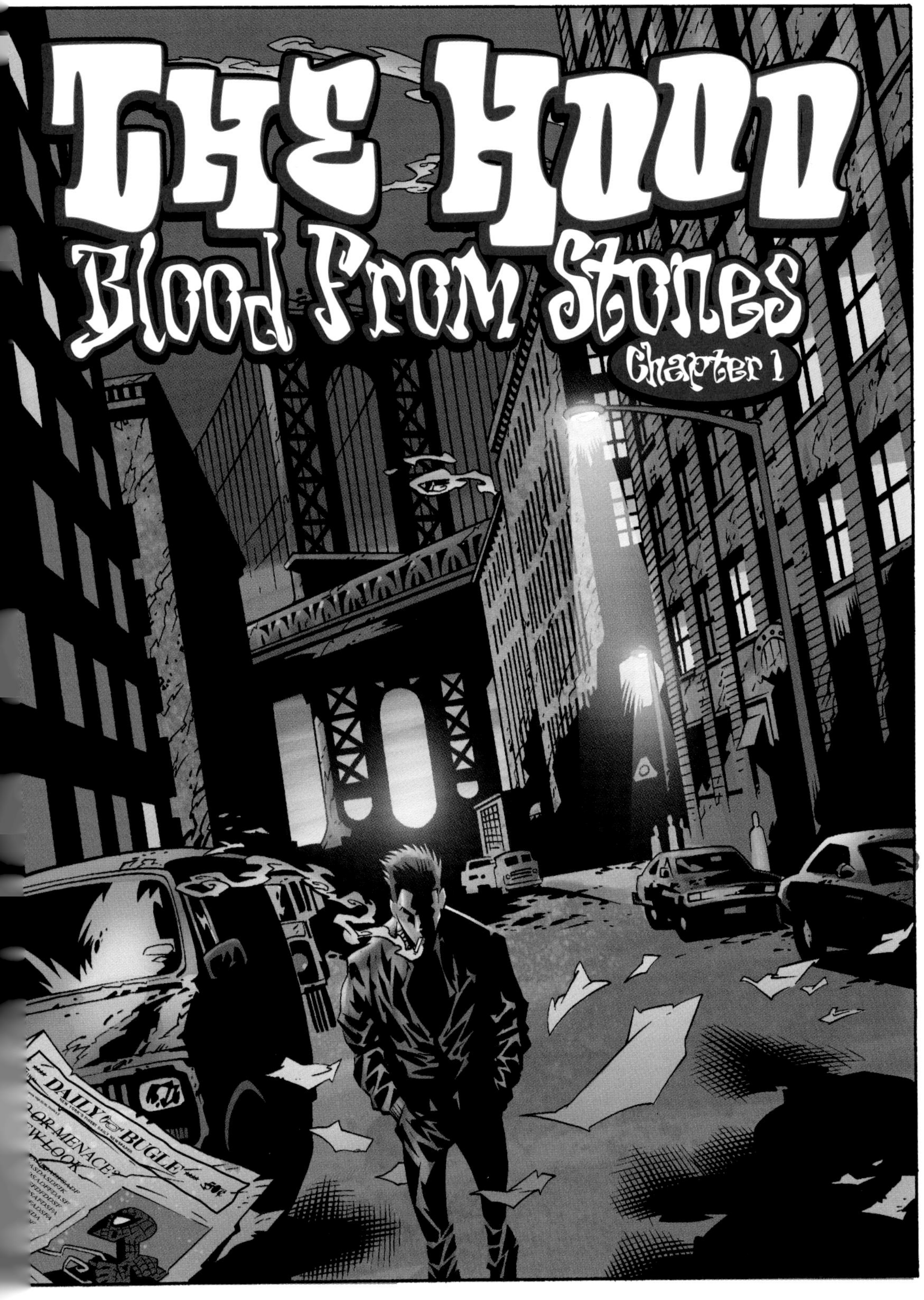
THE HOOD
Blood From Stones
Chapter 1
DAILY BUGLE

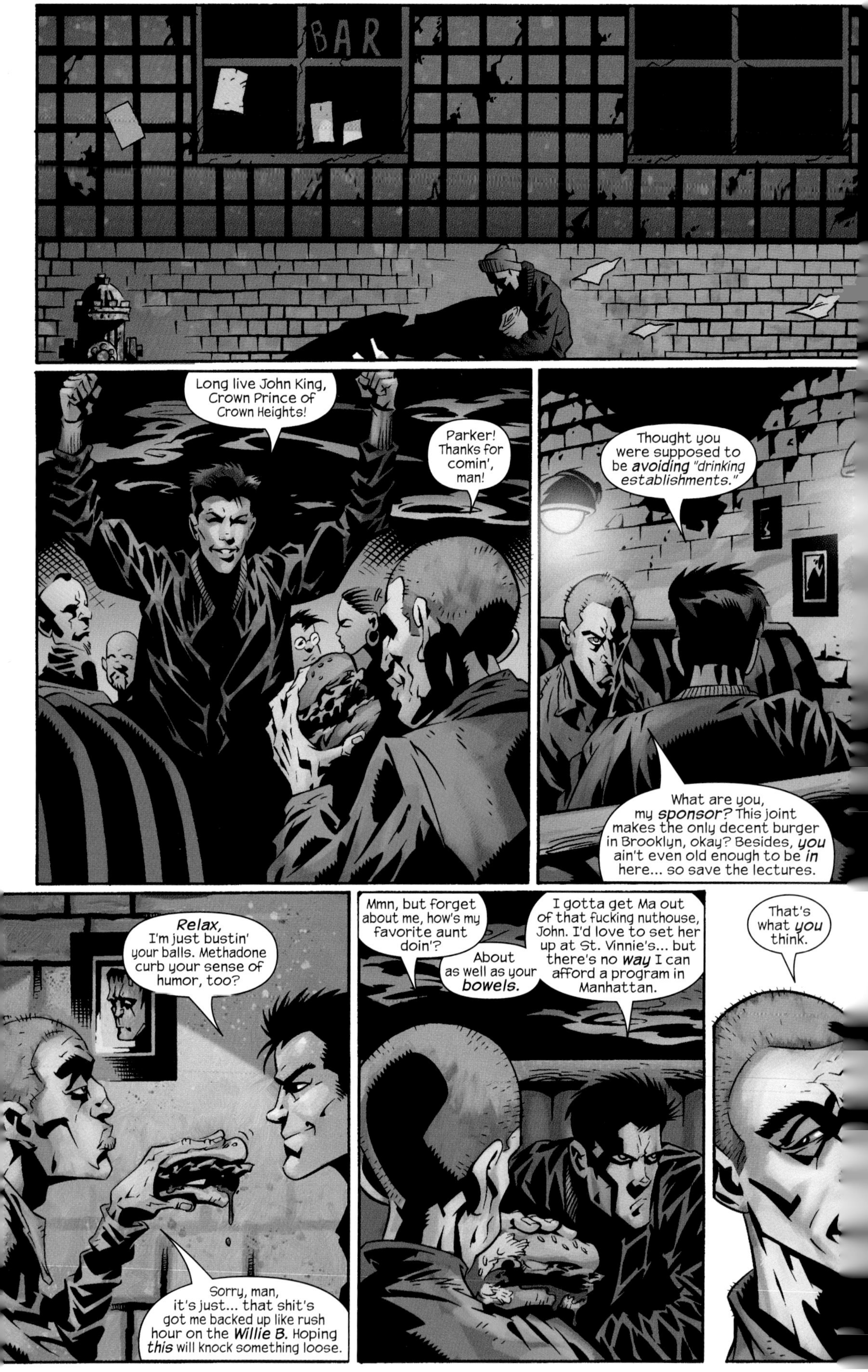
BAR
Long live John King, Crown Prince of Crown Heights!
Parker! Thanks for comin', man!
Thought you were supposed to be *avoiding* "drinking establishments."
What are you, my *sponsor?* This joint makes the only decent burger in Brooklyn, okay? Besides, *you* ain't even old enough to be *in* here... so save the lectures.
*Relax,* I'm just bustin' your balls. Methadone curb your sense of humor, too?
Sorry, man, it's just... that shit's got me backed up like rush hour on the *Willie B.* Hoping *this* will knock something loose.
Mmn, but forget about me, how's my favorite aunt doin'?
About as well as your *bowels.*
I gotta get Ma out of that fucking nuthouse, John. I'd love to set her up at St. Vinnie's... but there's no *way* I can afford a program in Manhattan.
That's what *you* think.

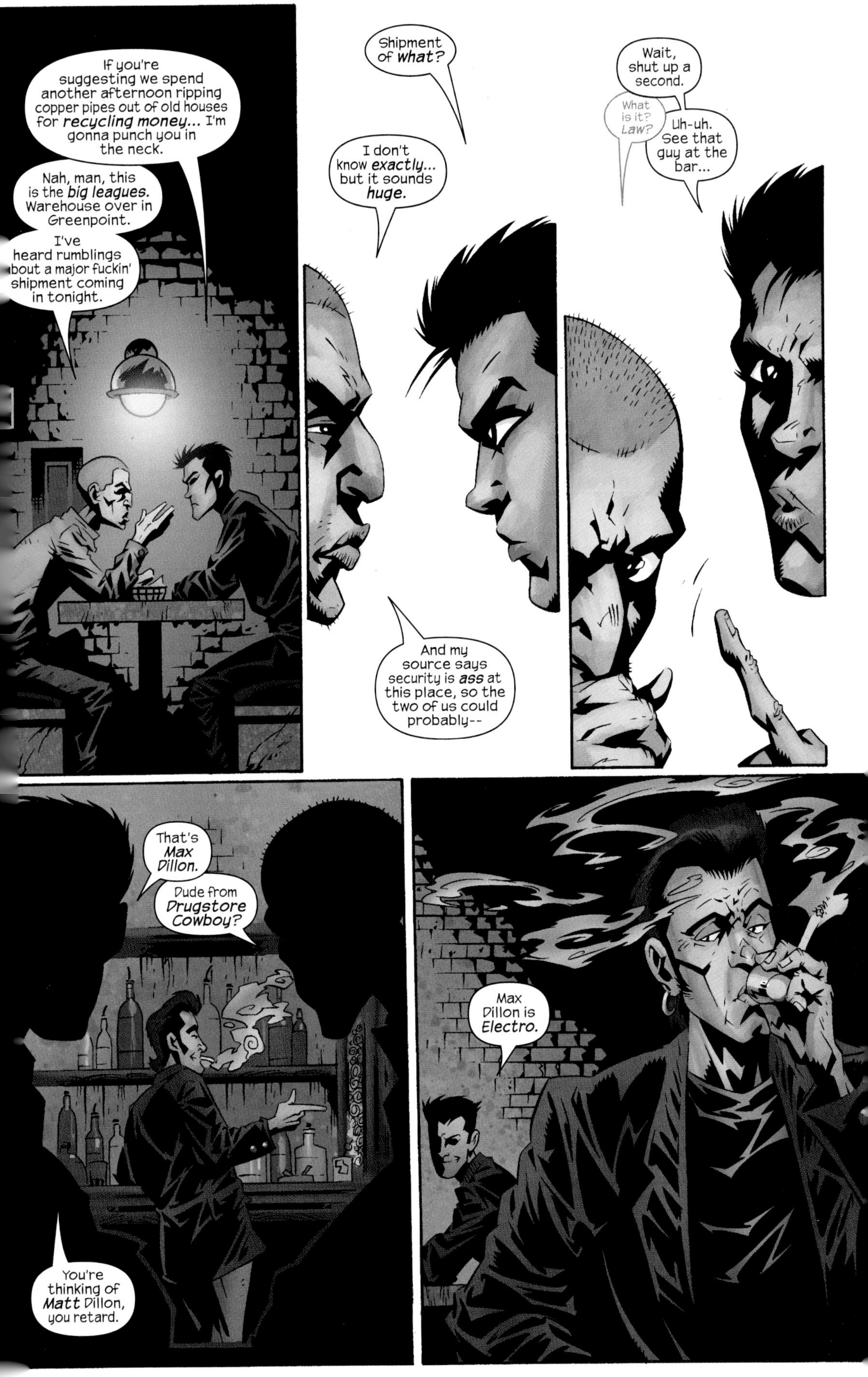

If you're suggesting we spend another afternoon ripping copper pipes out of old houses for recycling money... I'm gonna punch you in the neck.
Nah, man, this is the big leagues. Warehouse over in Greenpoint.
I've heard rumblings bout a major fuckin' shipment coming in tonight.
Shipment of what?
I don't know exactly... but it sounds huge.
And my source says security is ass at this place, so the two of us could probably--
Wait, shut up a second.
What is it? Law?
Uh-uh. See that guy at the bar...
That's Max Dillon.
Dude from Drugstore Cowboy?
You're thinking of Matt Dillon, you retard.
Max Dillon is Electro.

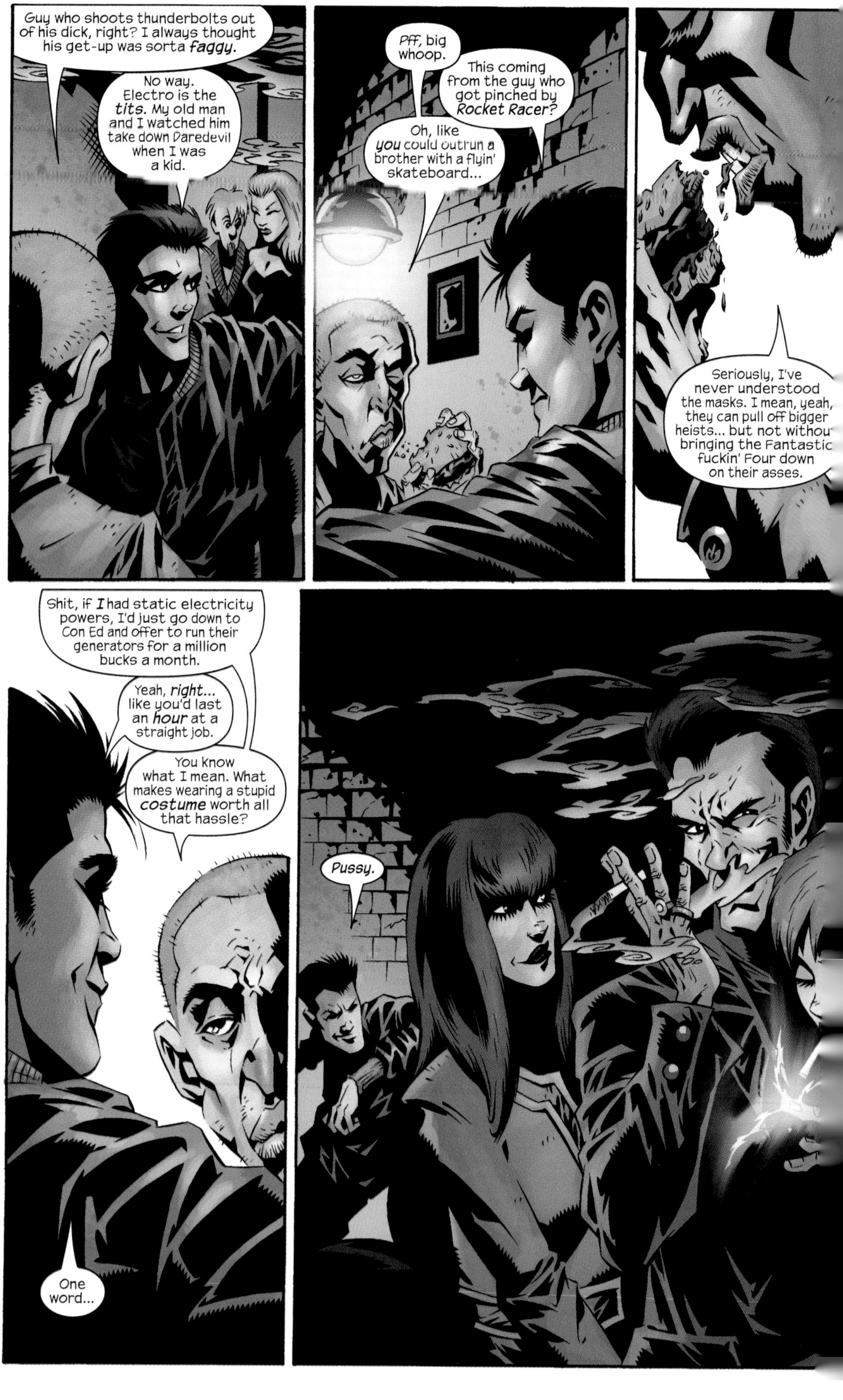

Guy who shoots thunderbolts out of his dick, right? I always thought his get-up was sorta faggy.
No way. Electro is the tits. My old man and I watched him take down Daredevil when I was a kid.
Pff, big whoop.
This coming from the guy who got pinched by Rocket Racer?
Oh, like you could outrun a brother with a flyin' skateboard...
Seriously, I've never understood the masks. I mean, yeah, they can pull off bigger heists... but not withou bringing the Fantastic fuckin' Four down on their asses.
Shit, if I had static electricity powers, I'd just go down to Con Ed and offer to run their generators for a million bucks a month.
Yeah, right... like you'd last an hour at a straight job.
You know what I mean. What makes wearing a stupid costume worth all that hassle?
One word...
Pussy.

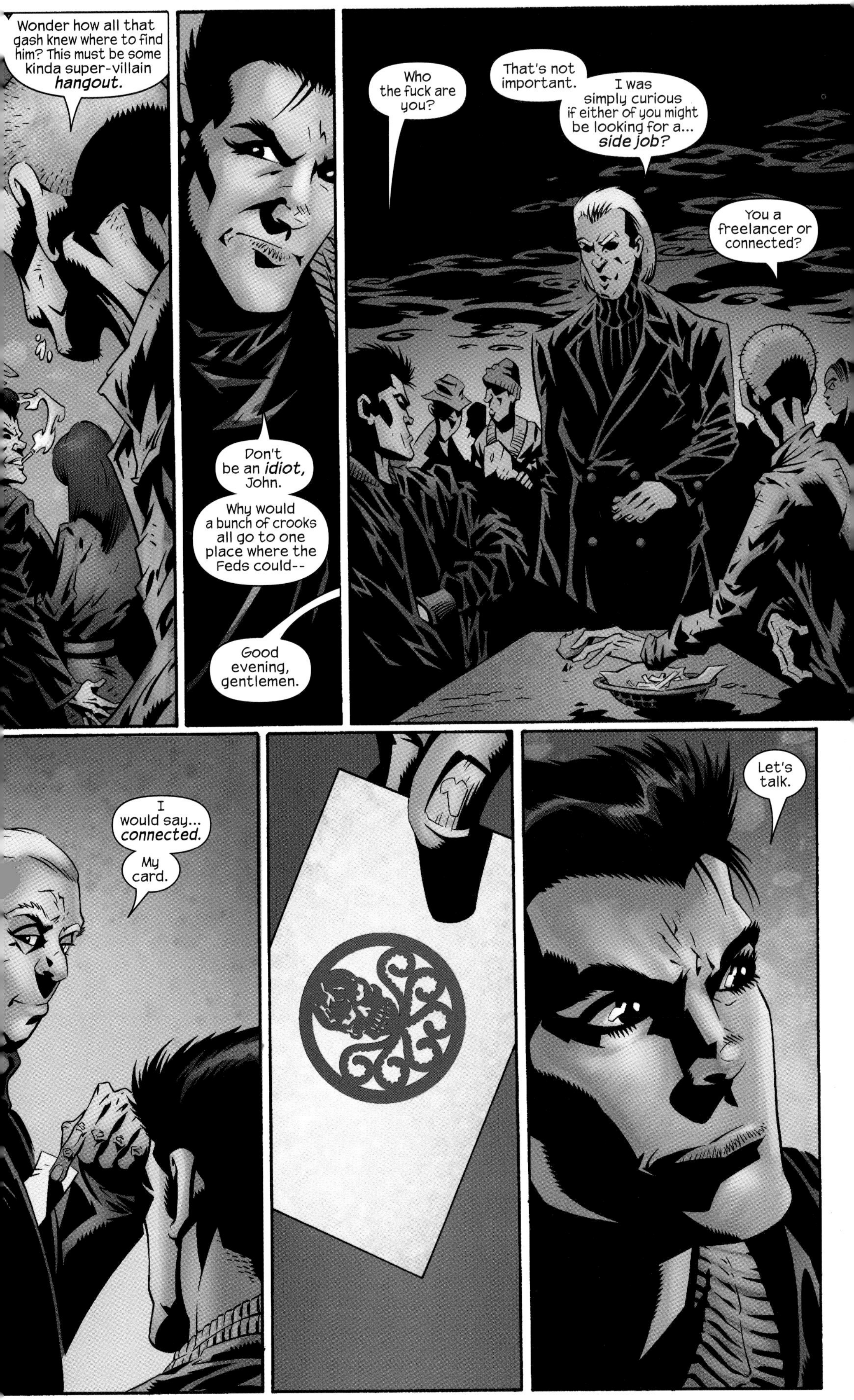
Wonder how all that gash knew where to find him? This must be some kinda super-villain *hangout.*
Don't be an *idiot,* John.
Why would a bunch of crooks all go to one place where the Feds could--
Good evening, gentlemen.
Who the fuck are you?
That's not important.
I was simply curious if either of you might be looking for a... *side job?*
You a freelancer or connected?
I would say... *connected.*
My card.
Let's talk.

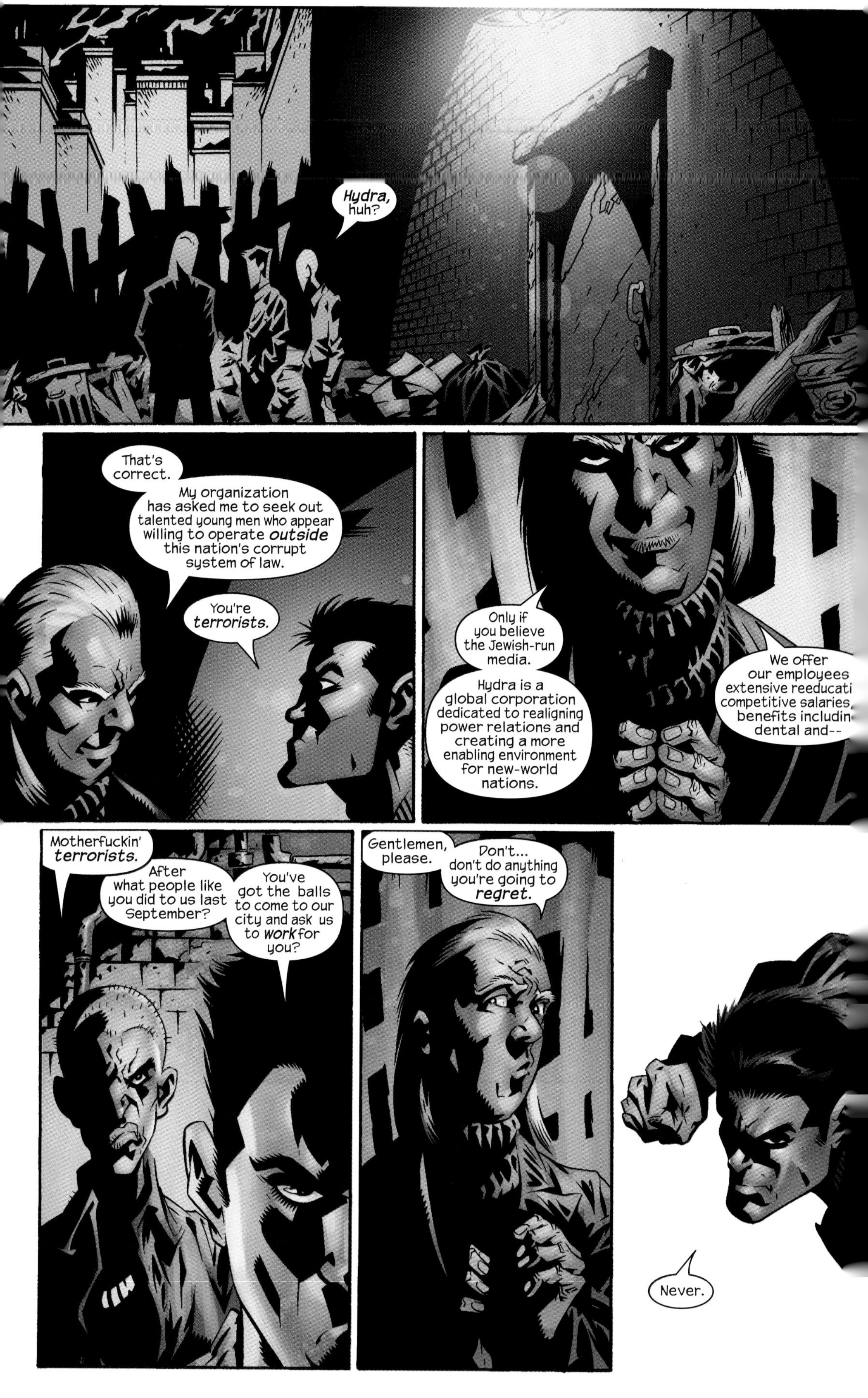
Hydra, huh?
That's correct.
My organization has asked me to seek out talented young men who appear willing to operate outside this nation's corrupt system of law.
You're terrorists.
Only if you believe the Jewish-run media.
Hydra is a global corporation dedicated to realigning power relations and creating a more enabling environment for new-world nations.
We offer our employees extensive reeducati competitive salaries, benefits includin dental and--
Motherfuckin' terrorists.
After what people like you did to us last September?
You've got the balls to come to our city and ask us to work for you?
Gentlemen, please.
Don't... don't do anything you're going to regret.
Never.

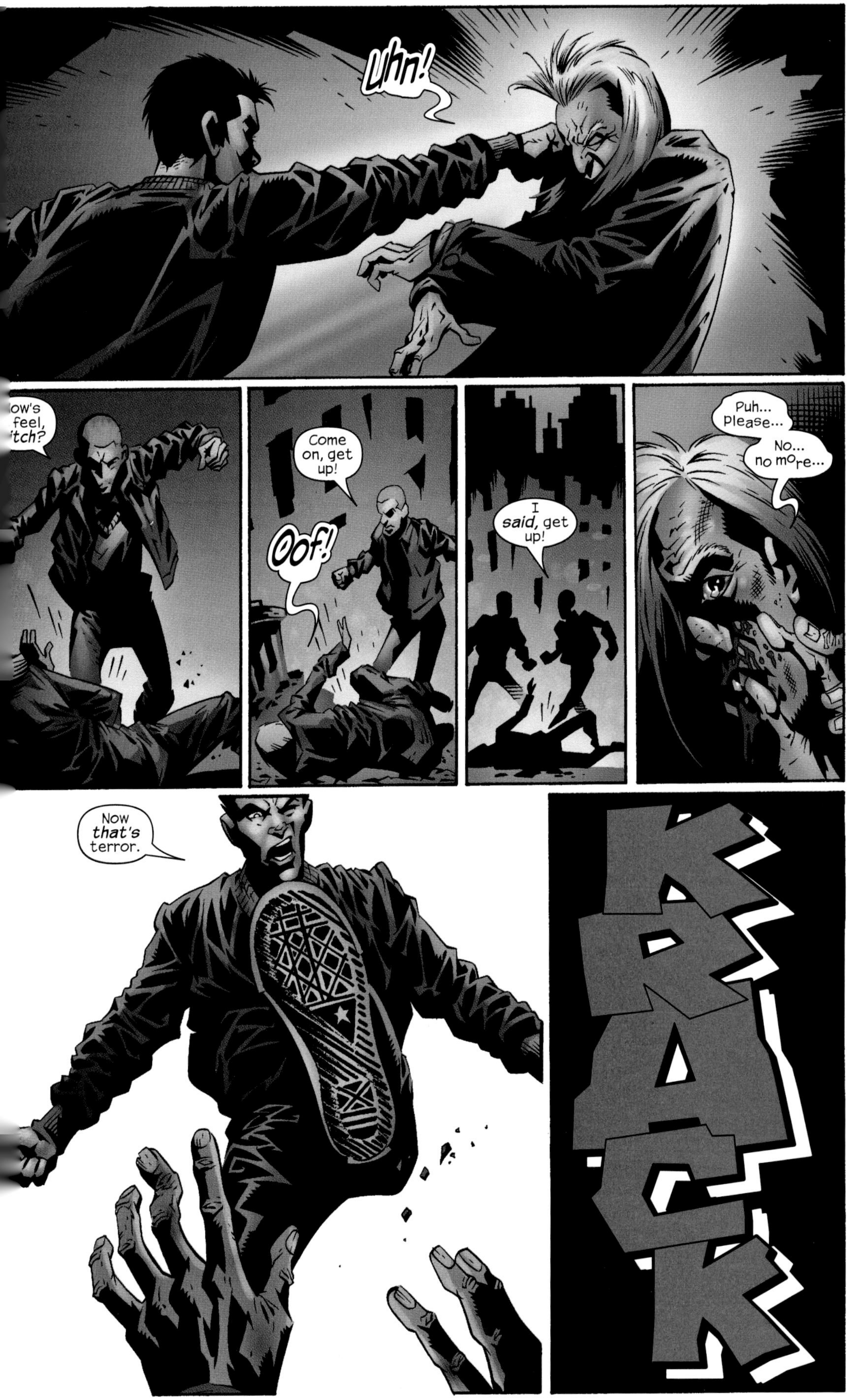
Uhn!
ow's feel, itch?
Come on, get up!
Oof!
I said, get up!
Puh... please...
No... no more...
Now that's terror.
KRACK

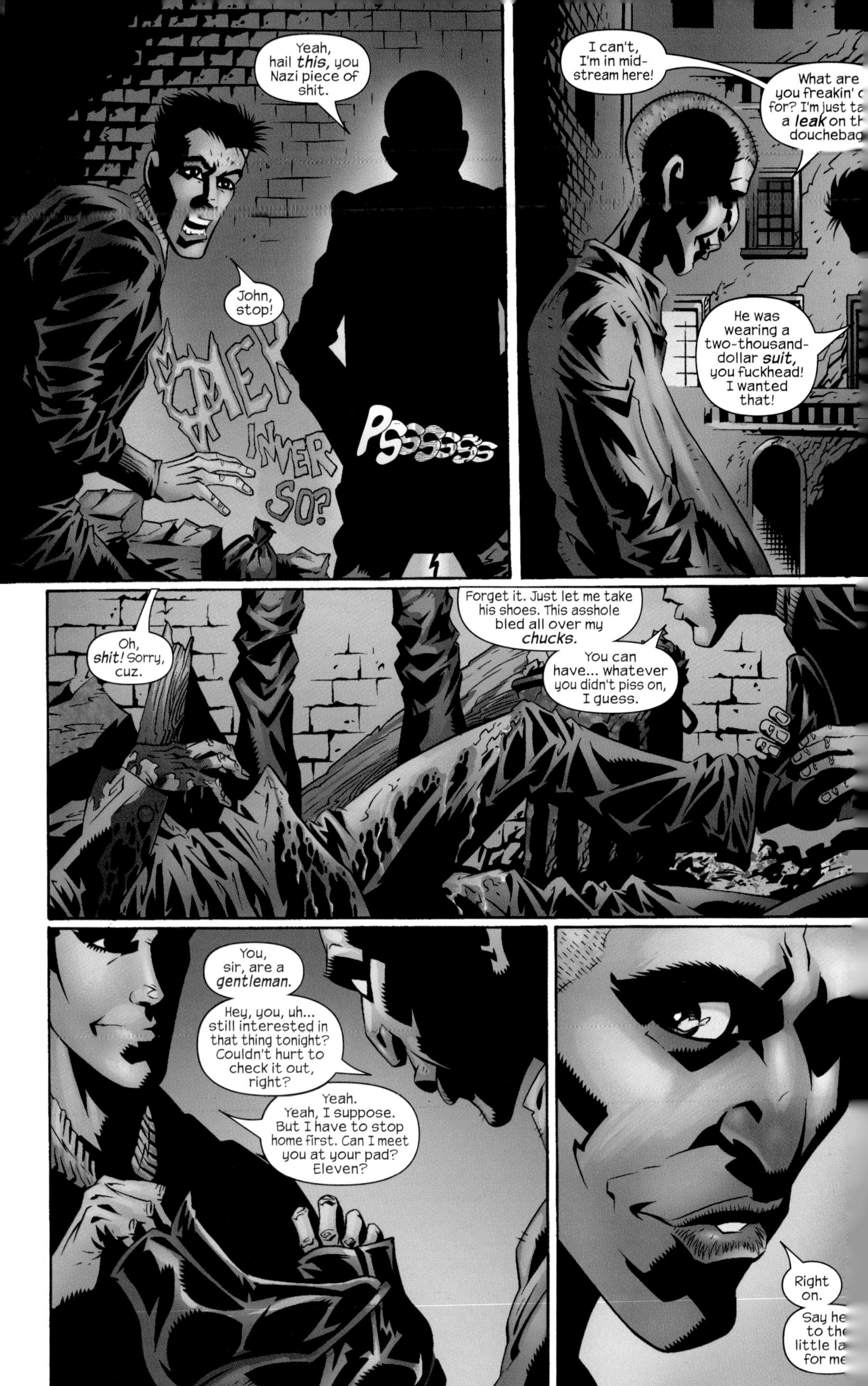
Yeah, hail *this,* you Nazi piece of shit.
John, stop!
PSSSSSS
I can't, I'm in mid-stream here!
What are you freakin' c for? I'm just ta a *leak* on th douchebag
He was wearing a two-thousand-dollar *suit,* you fuckhead! I wanted that!
Oh, *shit!* Sorry, cuz.
Forget it. Just let me take his shoes. This asshole bled all over my *chucks.*
You can have... whatever you didn't piss on, I guess.
You, sir, are a *gentleman.*
Hey, you, uh... still interested in that thing tonight? Couldn't hurt to check it out, right?
Yeah. Yeah, I suppose. But I have to stop home first. Can I meet you at your pad? Eleven?
Right on.
Say he to the little la for me

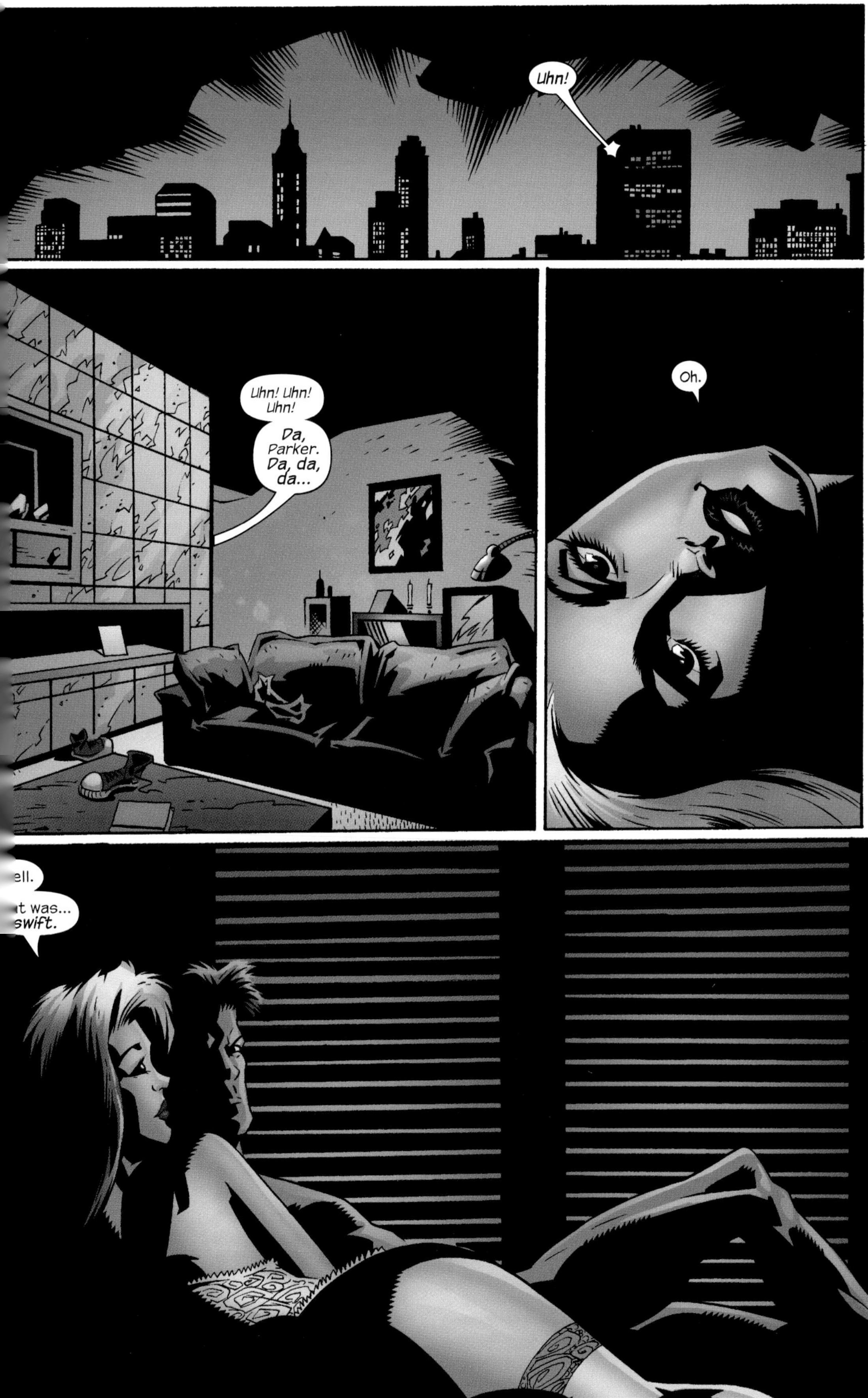
Uhn!
Uhn! Uhn! Uhn!
Da, Parker. Da, da, da...
Oh.
ell.
t was... swift.

You have been ready to *explode* since you walked through that door, no? What has you in such a state?

I dunno. *Nothing.* Listen, I... I should probably get back to Brooklyn, Gro.

Do not be embarrassed, Parker. You are *young...*

I'm not *embarrassed.*

I just have shit to do, okay?

Mm... I will never understand why a handsome child like you has to come to someone like me.

So I don't have to put up with *small talk* after sex.

Your money's on the dresser.

Spokoinoi nochi.

And see yo tomorrow

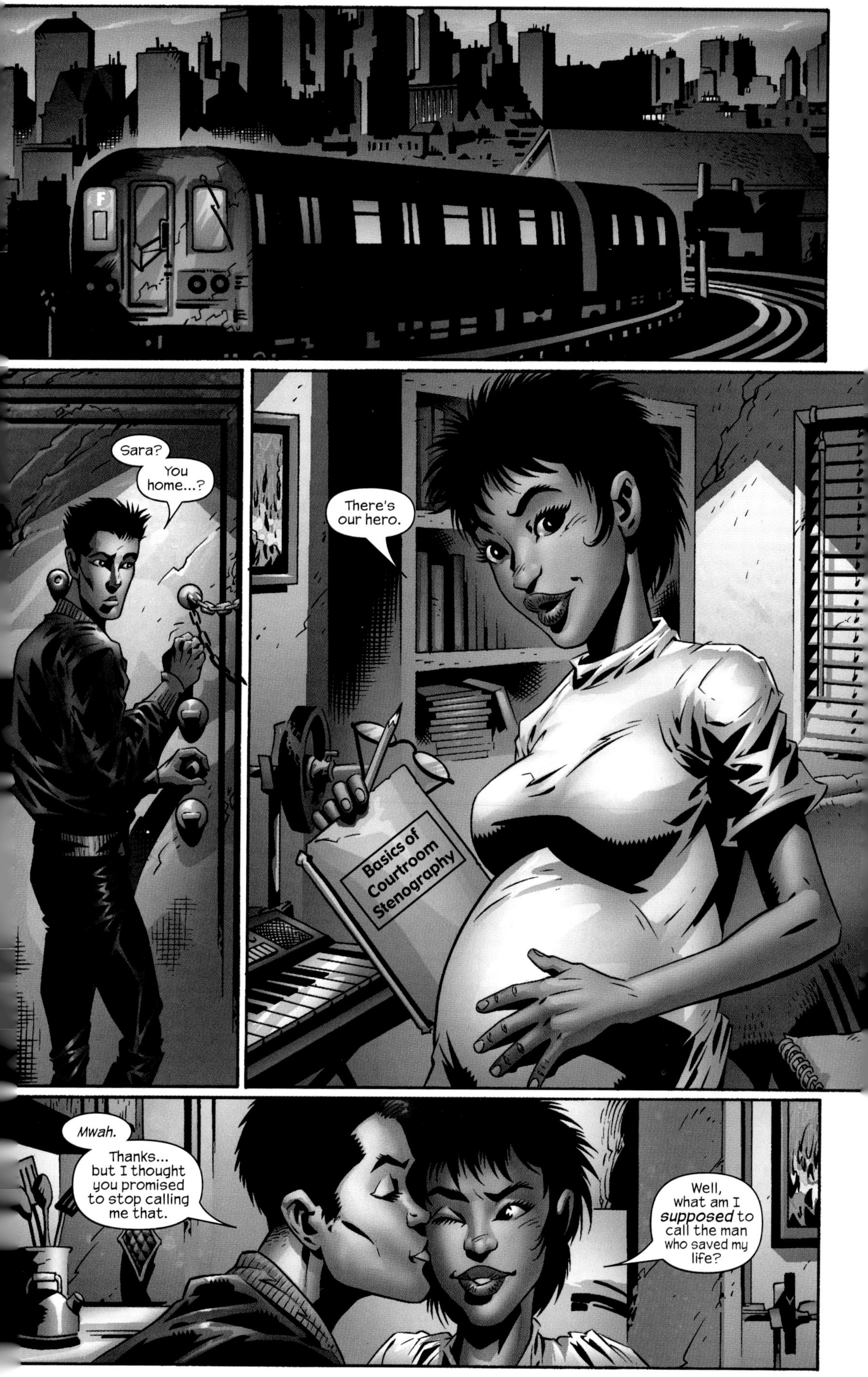
F
Sara? You home...?
There's our hero.
Basics of Courtroom Stenography
Mwah.
Thanks... but I thought you promised to stop calling me that.
Well, what am I *supposed* to call the man who saved my life?

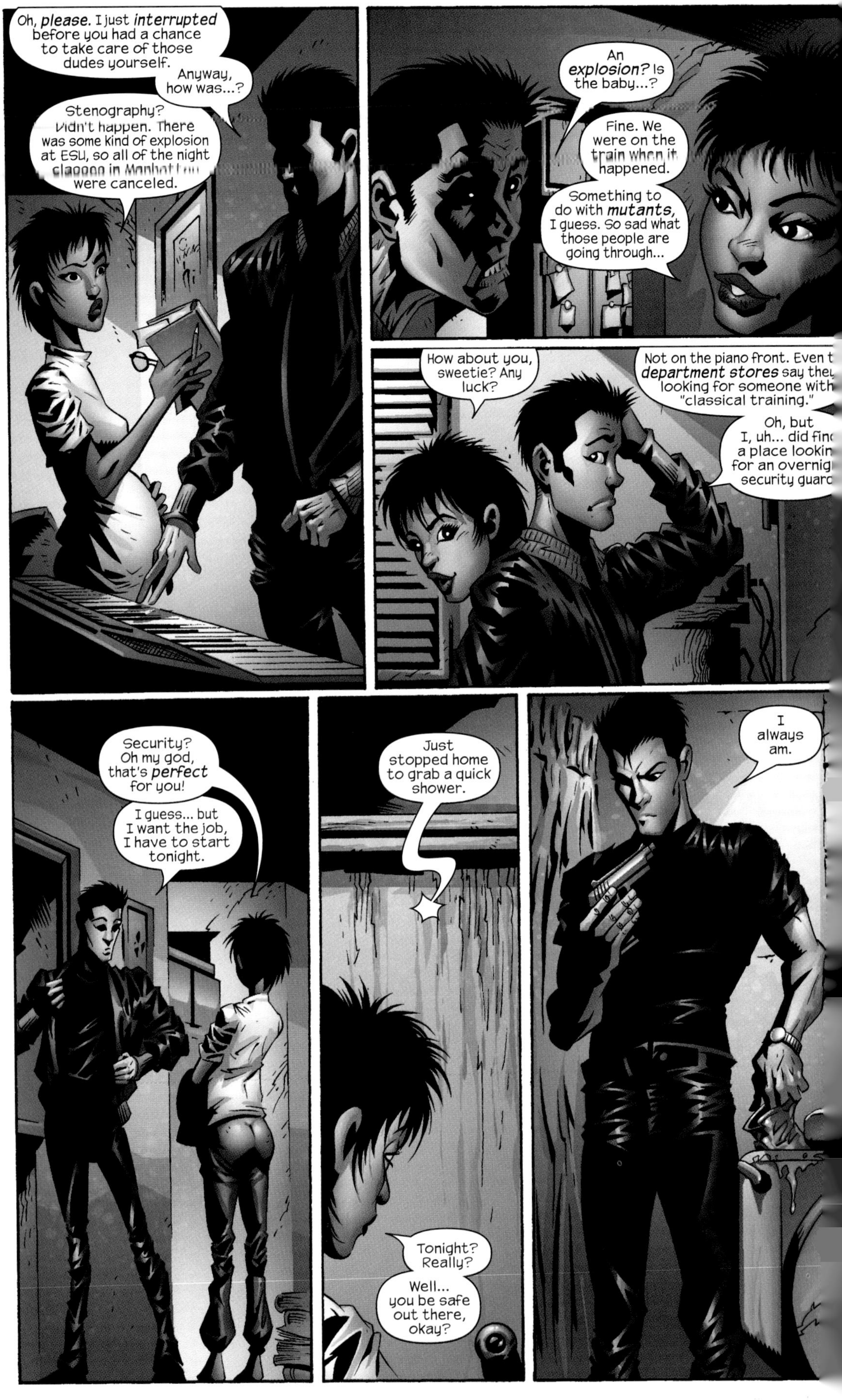
Oh, *please.* I just *interrupted* before you had a chance to take care of those dudes yourself.
Anyway, how was...?
Stenography? Didn't happen. There was some kind of explosion at ESU, so all of the night classes in Manhattan were canceled.
An *explosion?* Is the baby...?
Fine. We were on the train when it happened.
Something to do with ***mutants,*** I guess. So sad what those people are going through...
How about you, sweetie? Any luck?
Not on the piano front. Even t
*department stores* say the
looking for someone with
"classical training."
Oh, but I, uh... did fin
a place lookin
for an overnig
security guar
Security? Oh my god, that's *perfect* for you!
I guess... but I want the job, I have to start tonight.
Just stopped home to grab a quick shower.
Tonight? Really?
Well... you be safe out there, okay?
I always am.

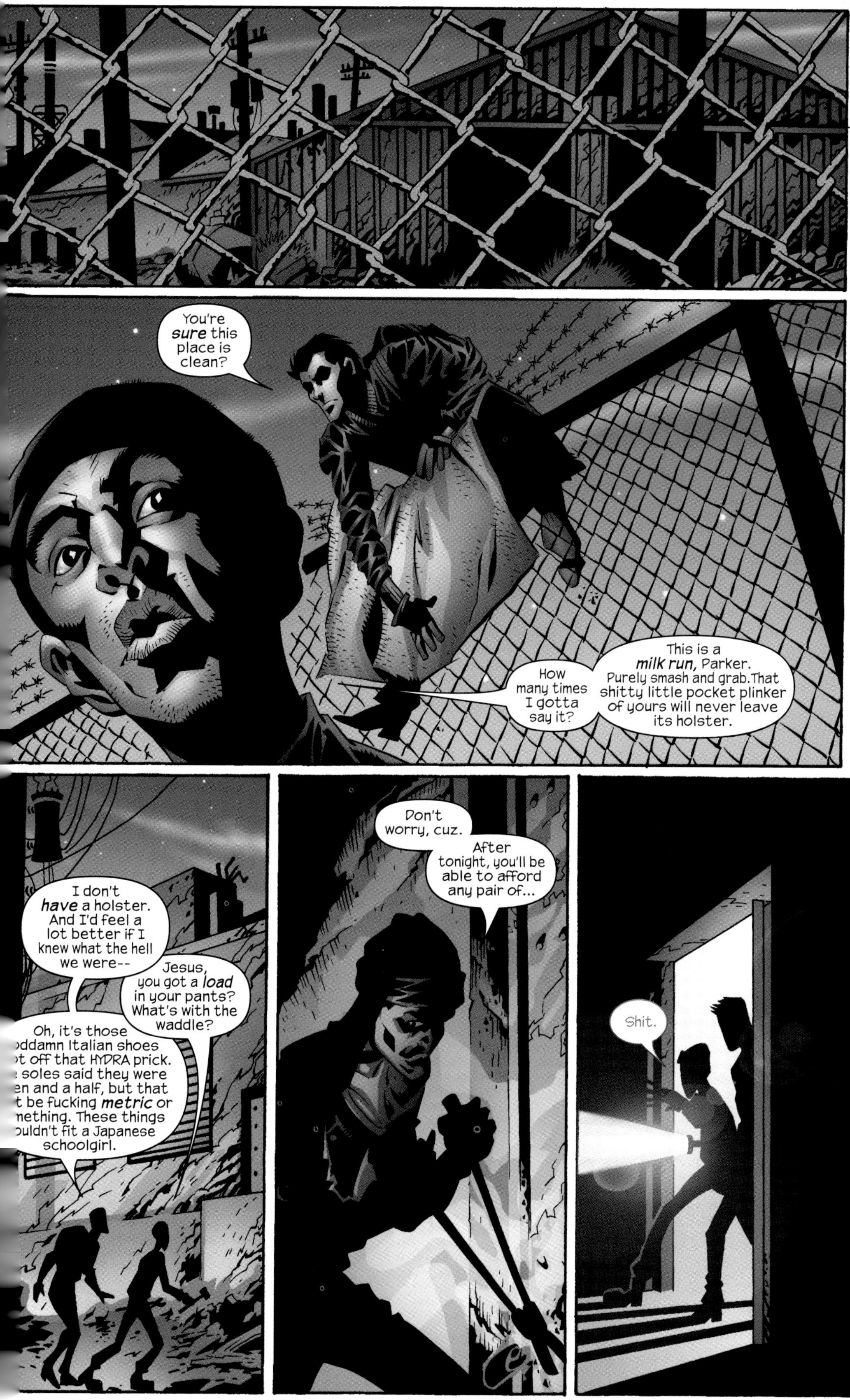
You're sure this place is clean?
How many times I gotta say it?
This is a milk run, Parker. Purely smash and grab. That shitty little pocket plinker of yours will never leave its holster.
I don't have a holster. And I'd feel a lot better if I knew what the hell we were--
Jesus, you got a load in your pants? What's with the waddle?
Oh, it's those oddamn Italian shoes ot off that HYDRA prick. e soles said they were en and a half, but that t be fucking metric or mething. These things ouldn't fit a Japanese schoolgirl.
Don't worry, cuz.
After tonight, you'll be able to afford any pair of...
Shit.

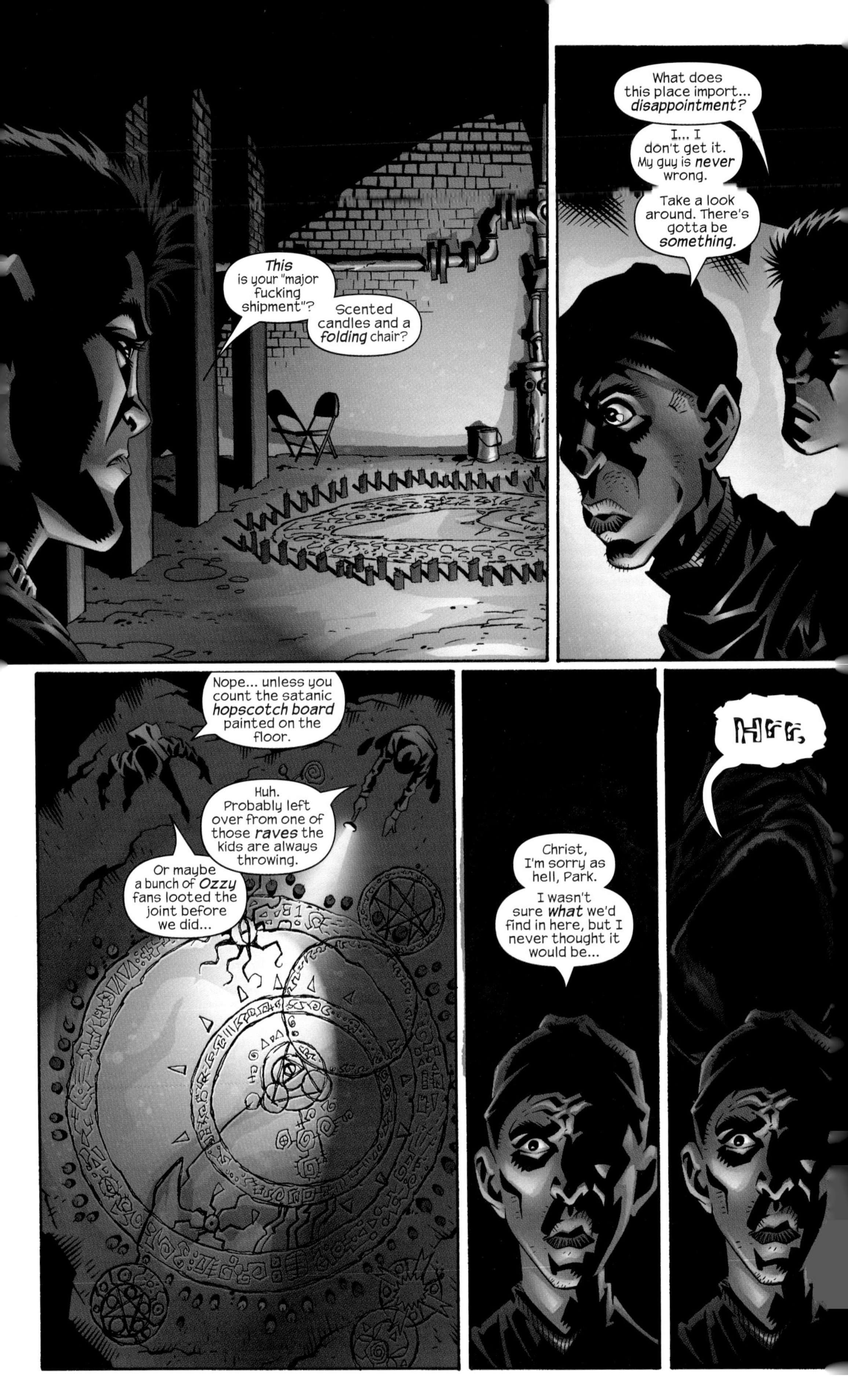
This is your "major fucking shipment"?
Scented candles and a folding chair?
What does this place import... disappointment?
I... I don't get it. My guy is never wrong.
Take a look around. There's gotta be something.
Nope... unless you count the satanic hopscotch board painted on the floor.
Huh. Probably left over from one of those raves the kids are always throwing.
Or maybe a bunch of Ozzy fans looted the joint before we did...
Christ, I'm sorry as hell, Park.
I wasn't sure what we'd find in here, but I never thought it would be...
Hrr.

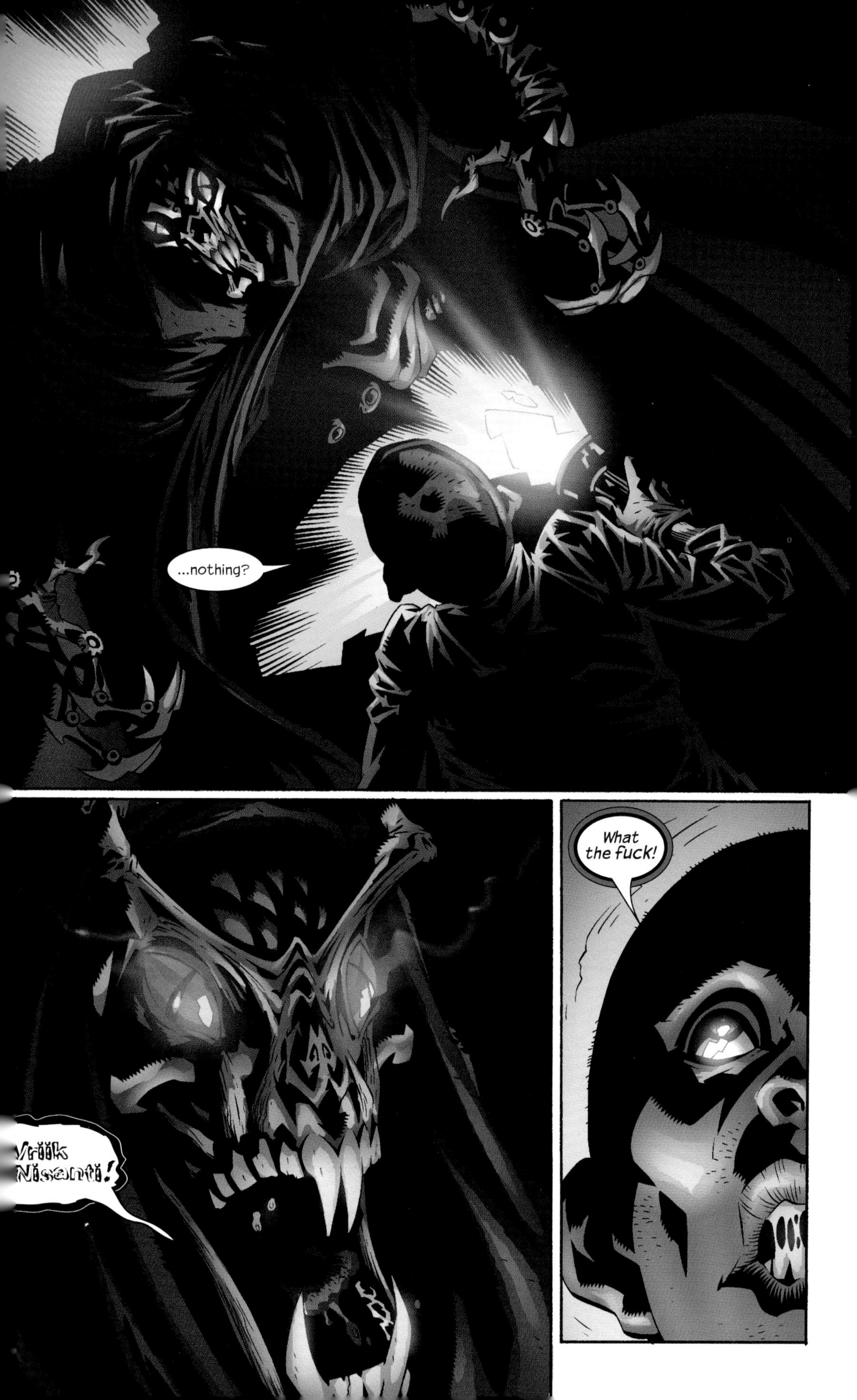
...nothing?
Vriik Nisanti!
What the fuck!

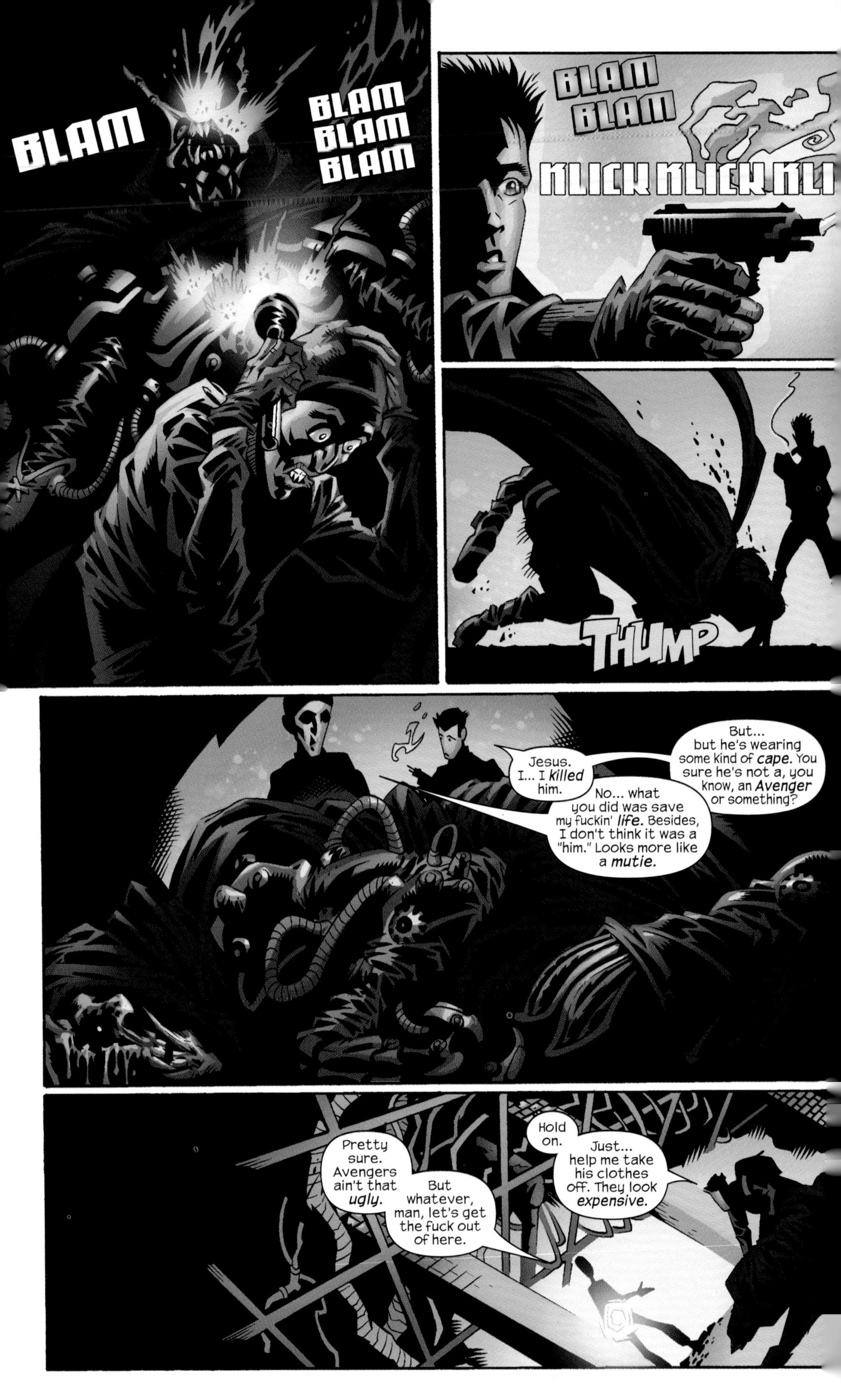
BLAM
BLAM BLAM BLAM
BLAM BLAM
KLICK KLICK KLI
THUMP
Jesus. I... I killed him.
But... but he's wearing some kind of cape. You sure he's not a, you know, an Avenger or something?
No... what you did was save my fuckin' life. Besides, I don't think it was a "him." Looks more like a mutie.
Pretty sure. Avengers ain't that ugly.
But whatever, man, let's get the fuck out of here.
Hold on.
Just... help me take his clothes off. They look expensive.

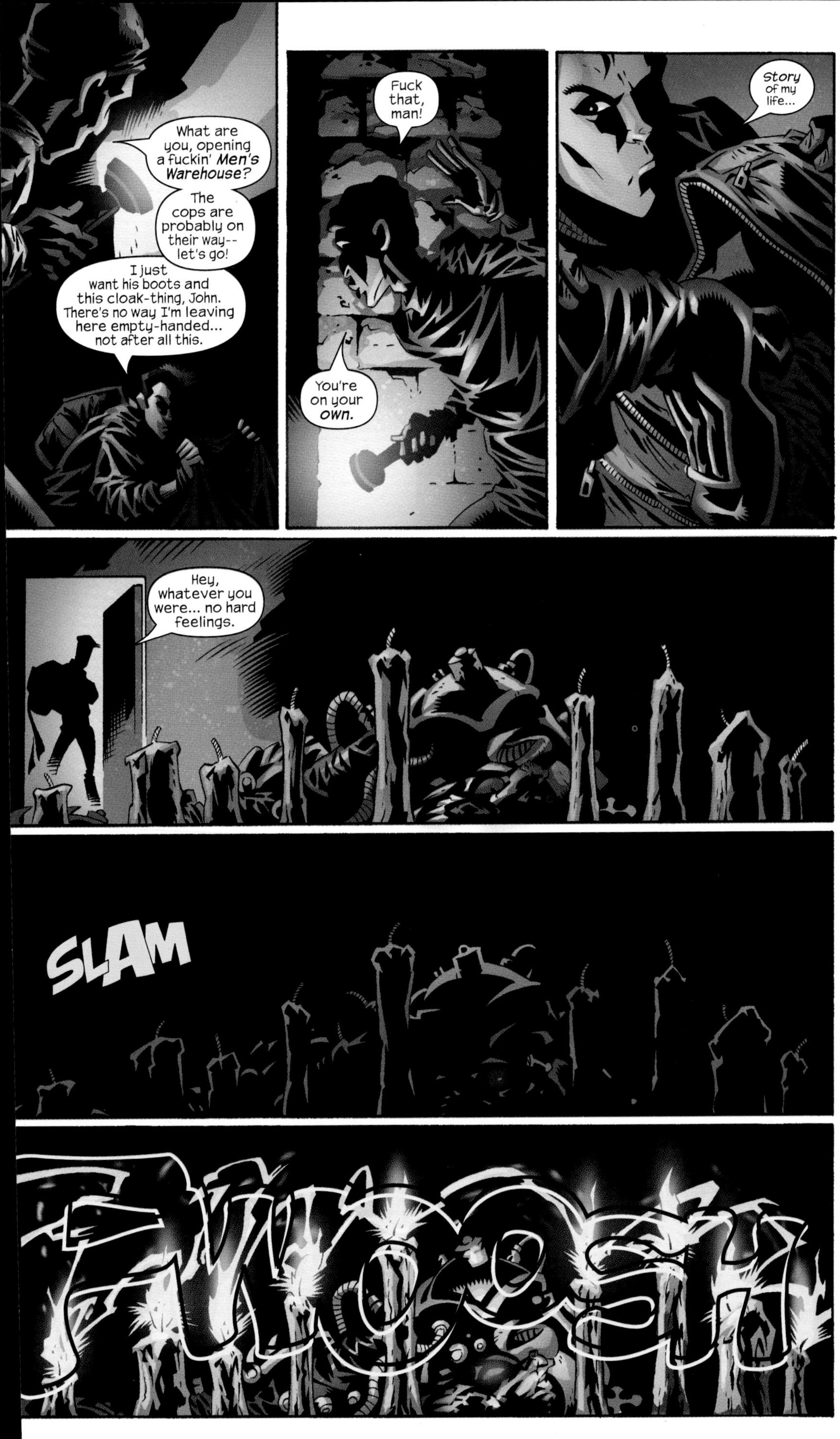
What are you, opening a fuckin' *Men's Warehouse*?
The cops are probably on their way-- let's go!
I just want his boots and this cloak-thing, John. There's no way I'm leaving here empty-handed... not after all this.
Fuck that, man!
You're on your ***own.***
Story of my life...
Hey, whatever you were... no hard feelings.
SLAM

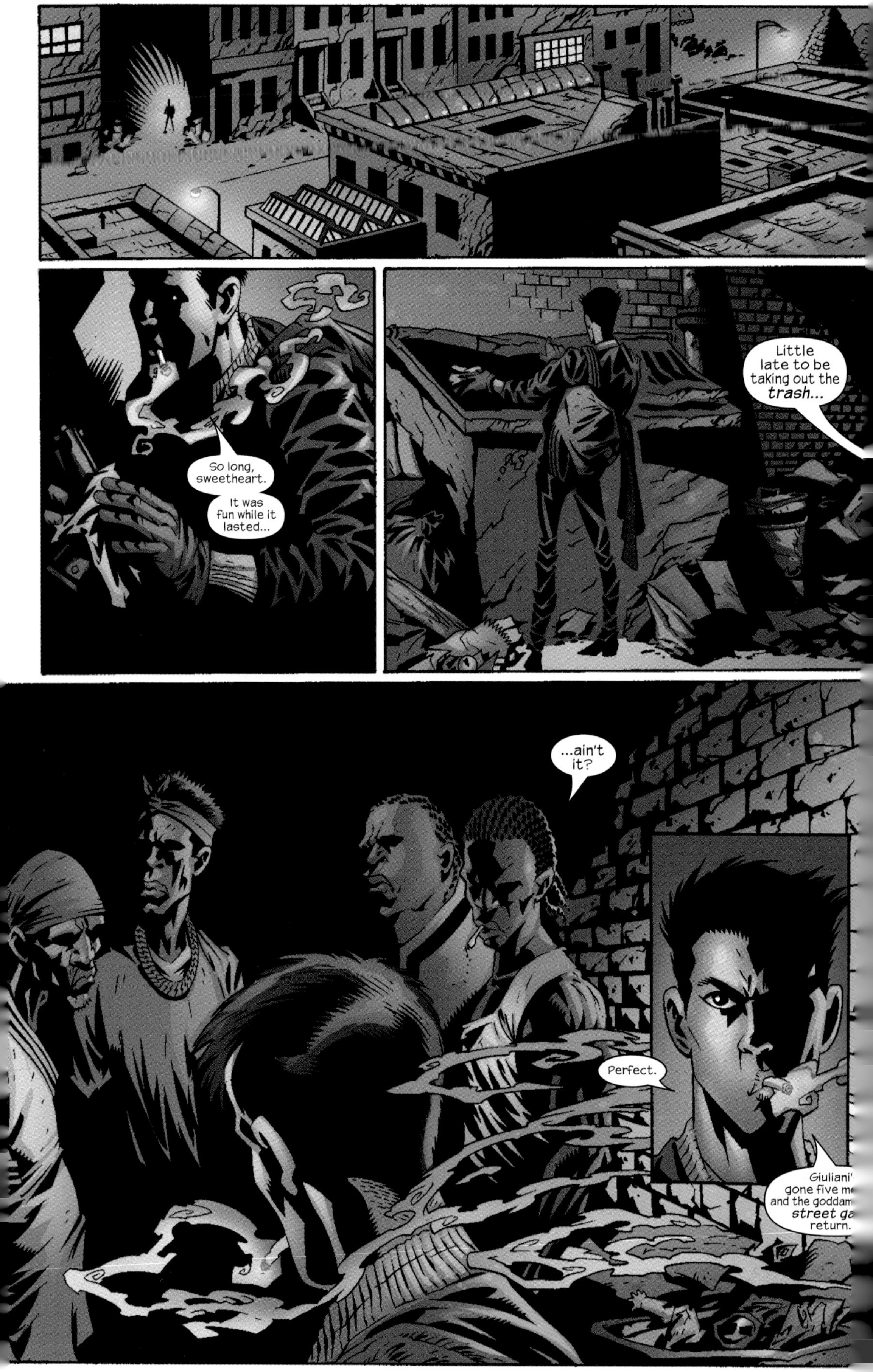

So long, sweetheart.
It was fun while it lasted...
Little late to be taking out the *trash...*
...ain't it?
Perfect.
Giuliani' gone five m and the goddam *street ga* return.

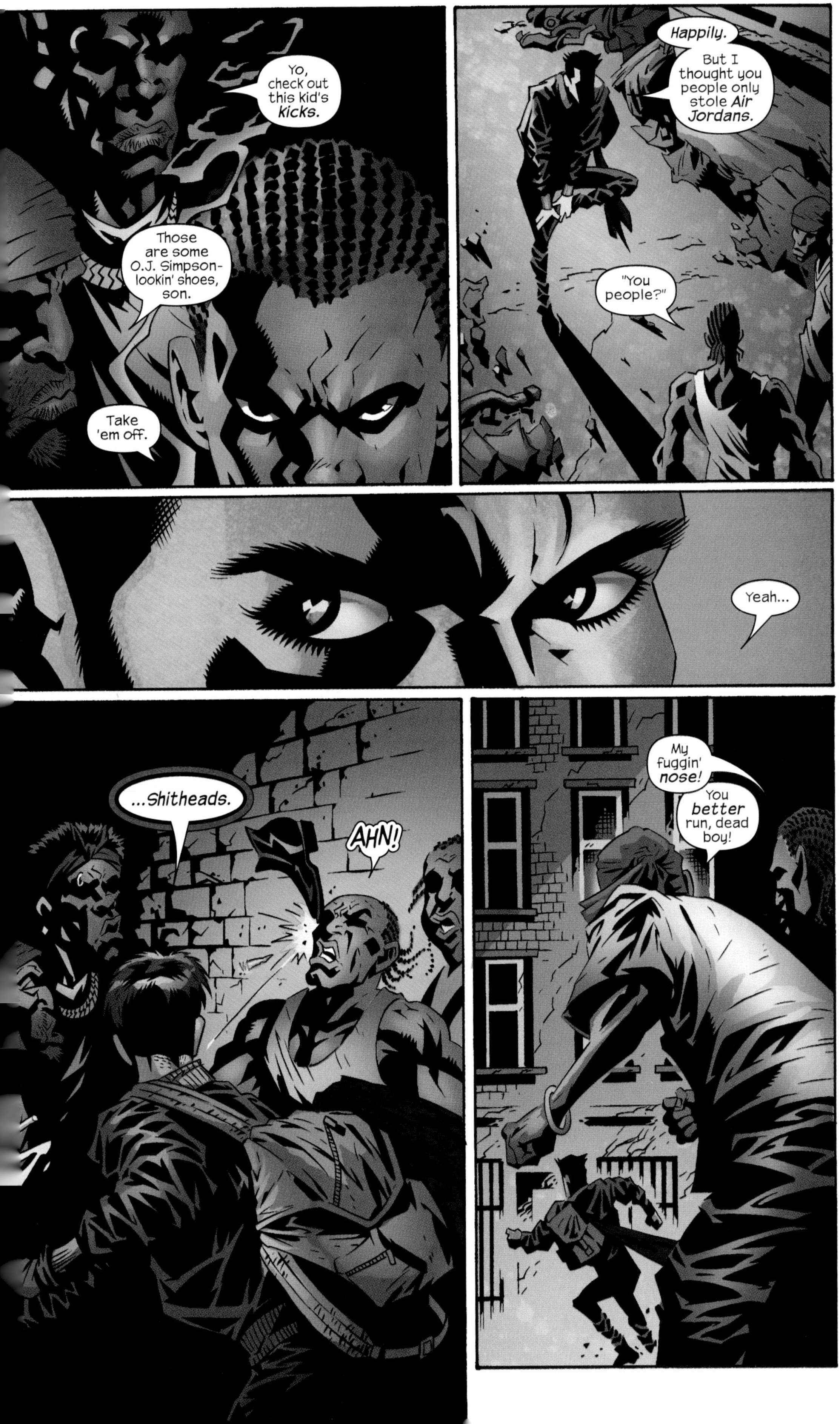
Yo, check out this kid's kicks.
Those are some O.J. Simpson-lookin' shoes, son.
Take 'em off.
Happily.
But I thought you people only stole Air Jordans.
"You people?"
Yeah...
...Shitheads.
AHN!
My fuggin' nose!
You better run, dead boy!

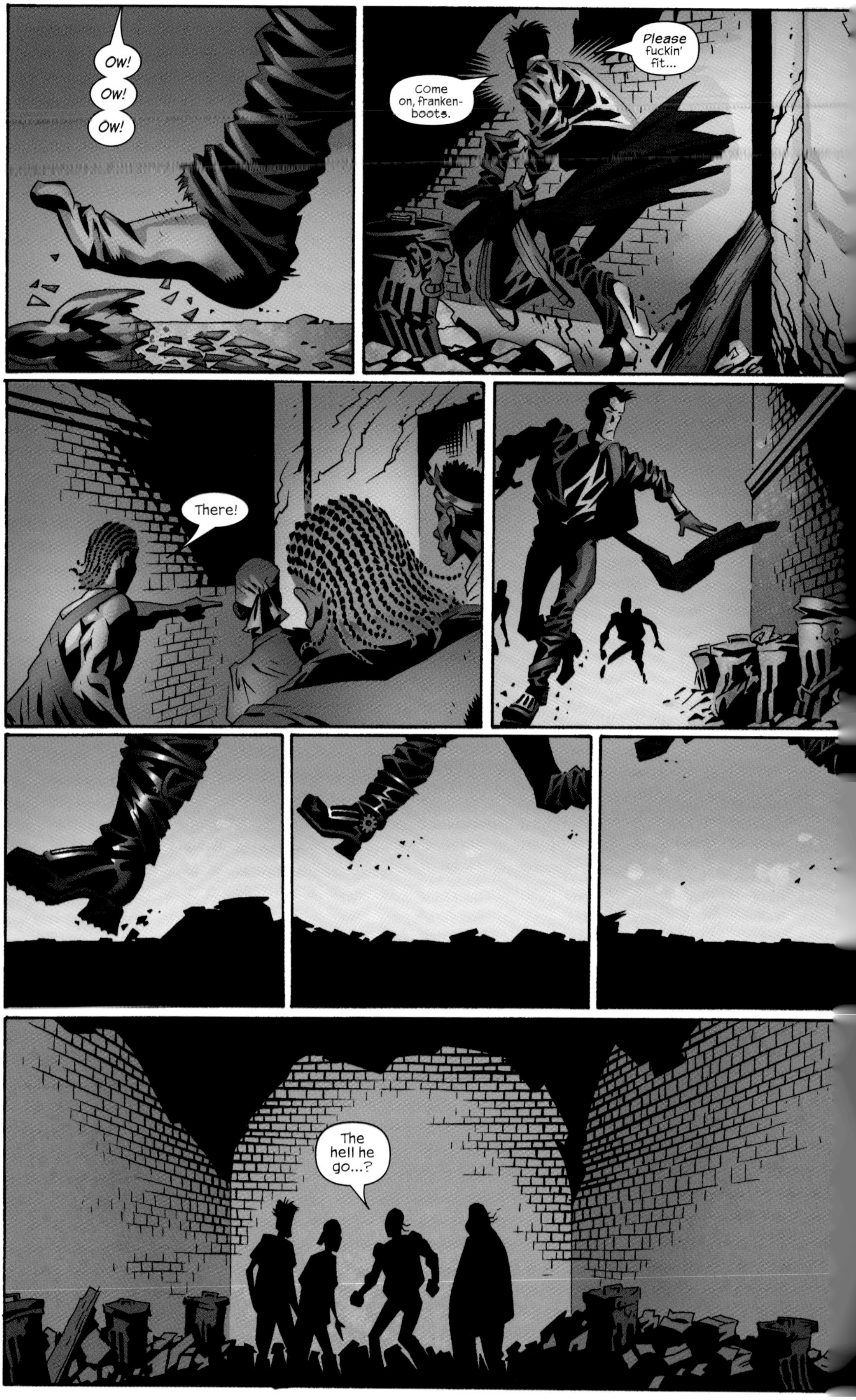
Ow!
Ow!
Ow!
Come on, franken-boots.
Please fuckin' fit...
There!
The hell he go...?

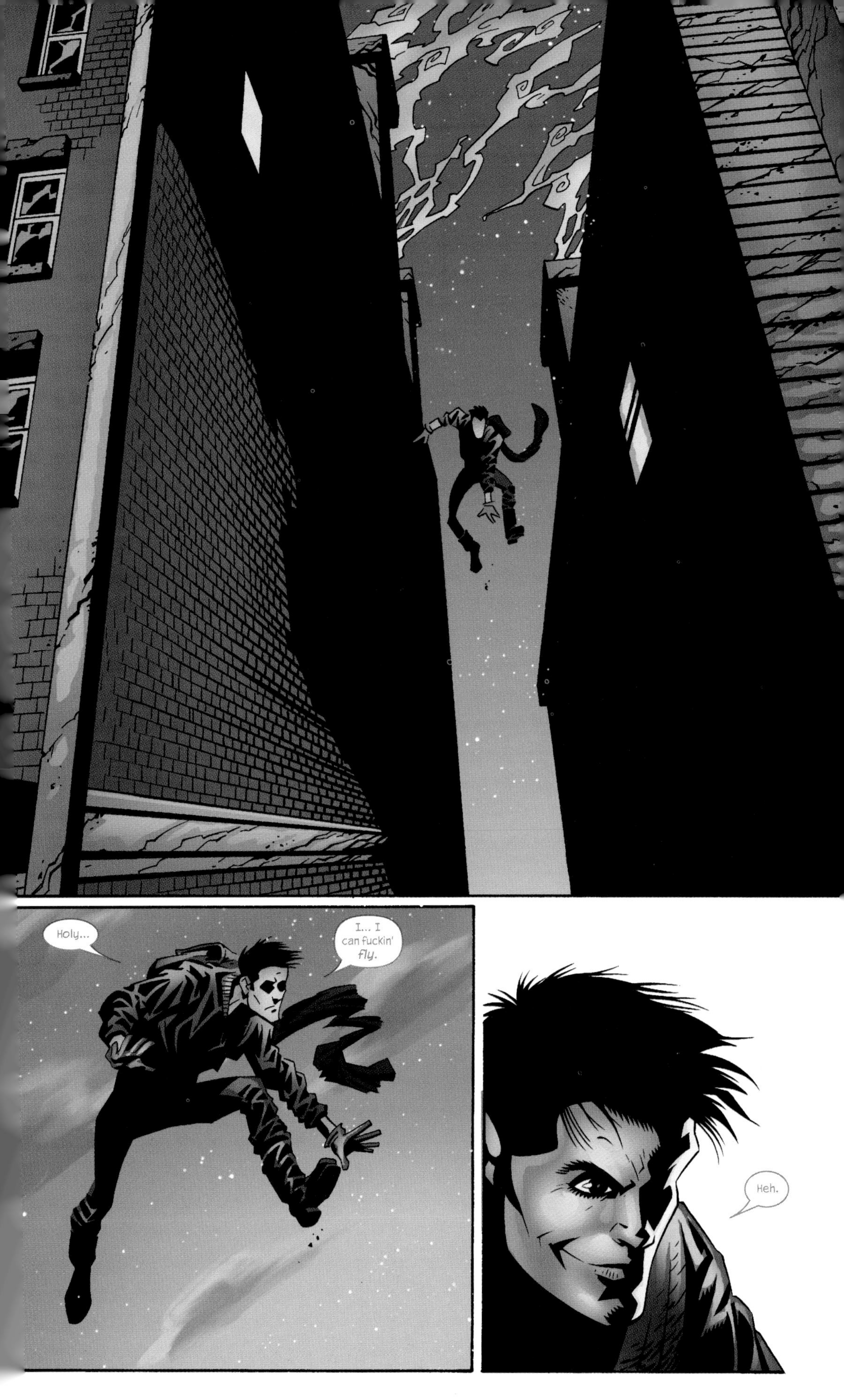
Holy...
I... I can fuckin' fly.
Heh.

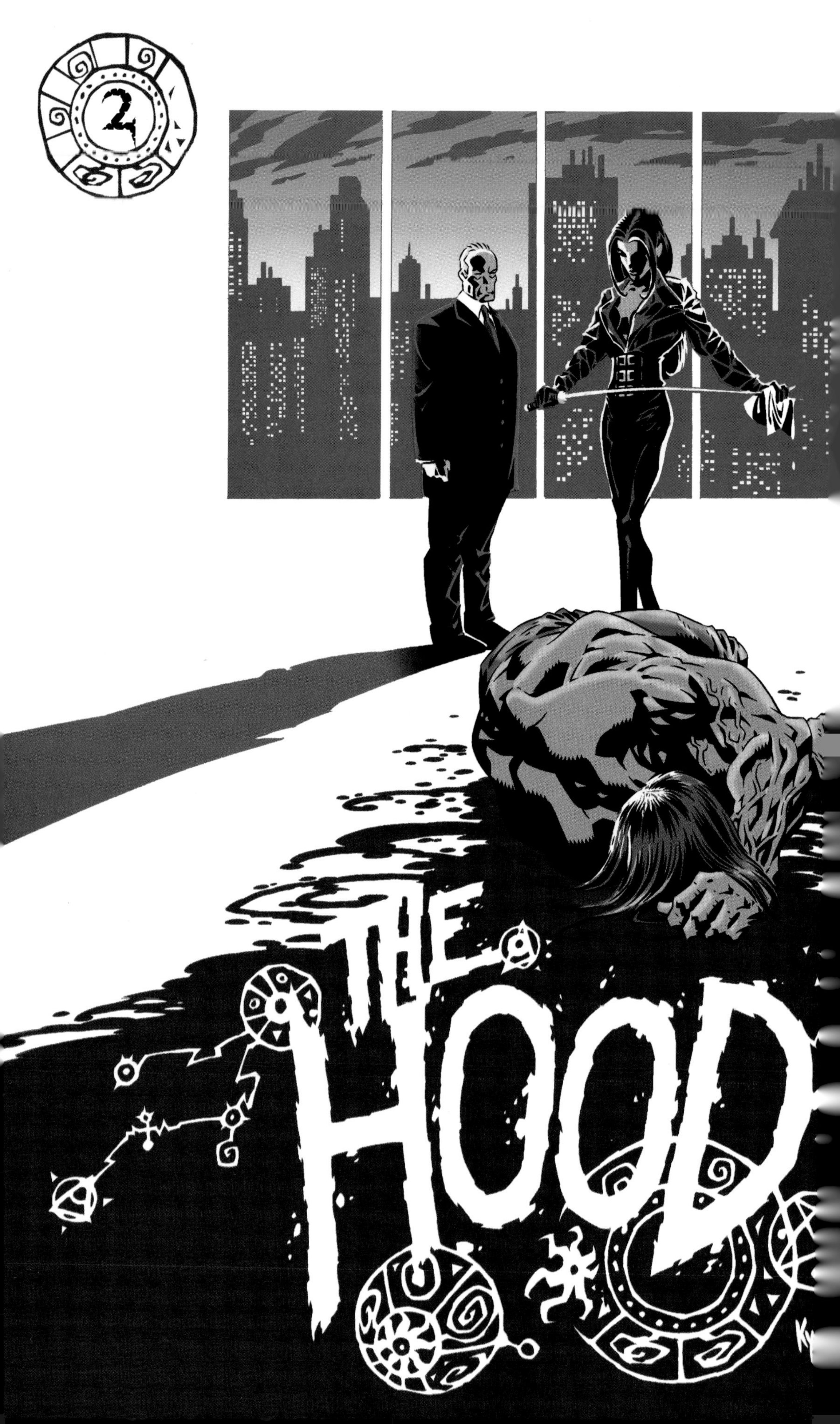
2
THE HOOD

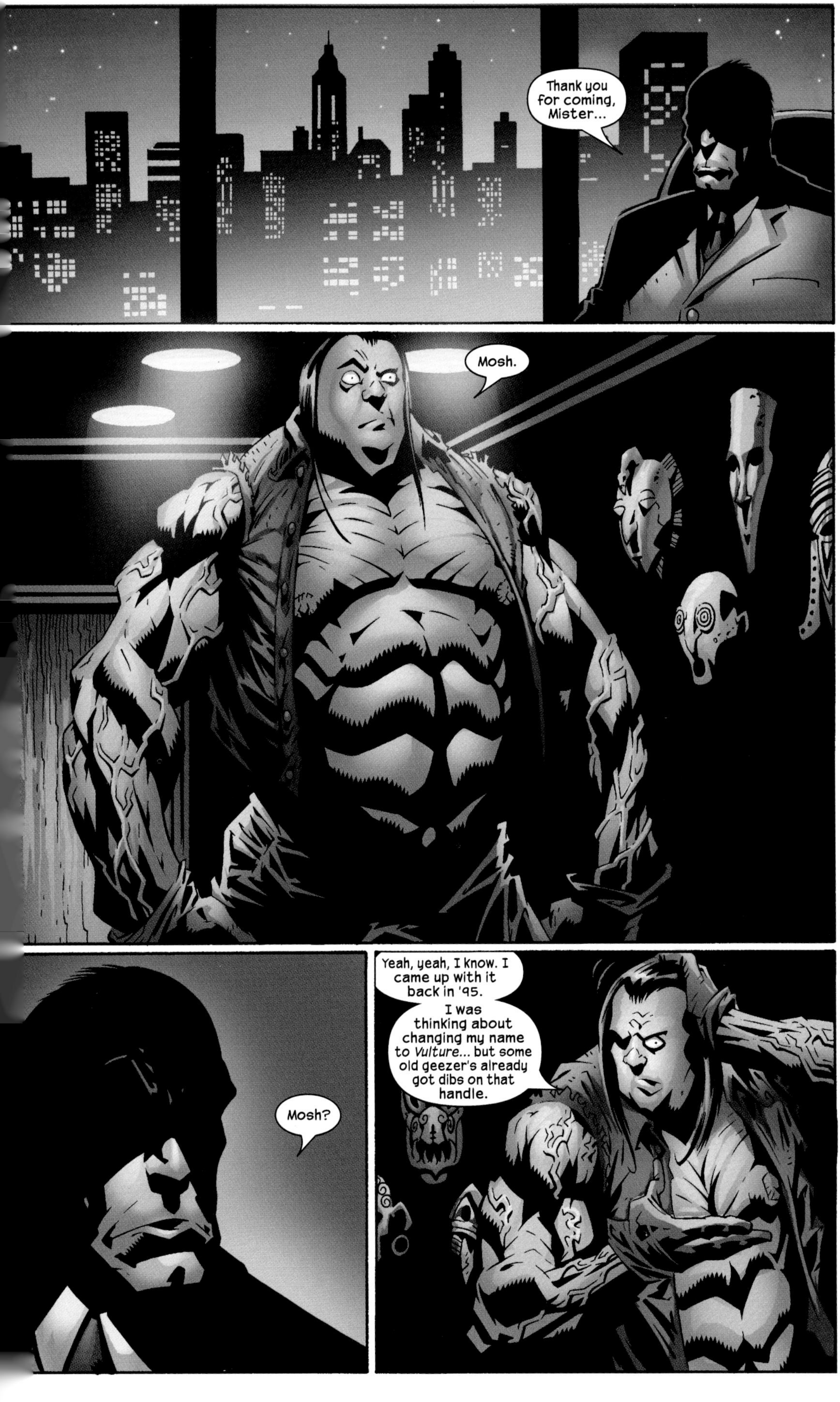
Thank you for coming, Mister...
Mosh.
Mosh?
Yeah, yeah, I know. I came up with it back in '95.
I was thinking about changing my name to *Vulture*... but some old geezer's already got dibs on that handle.

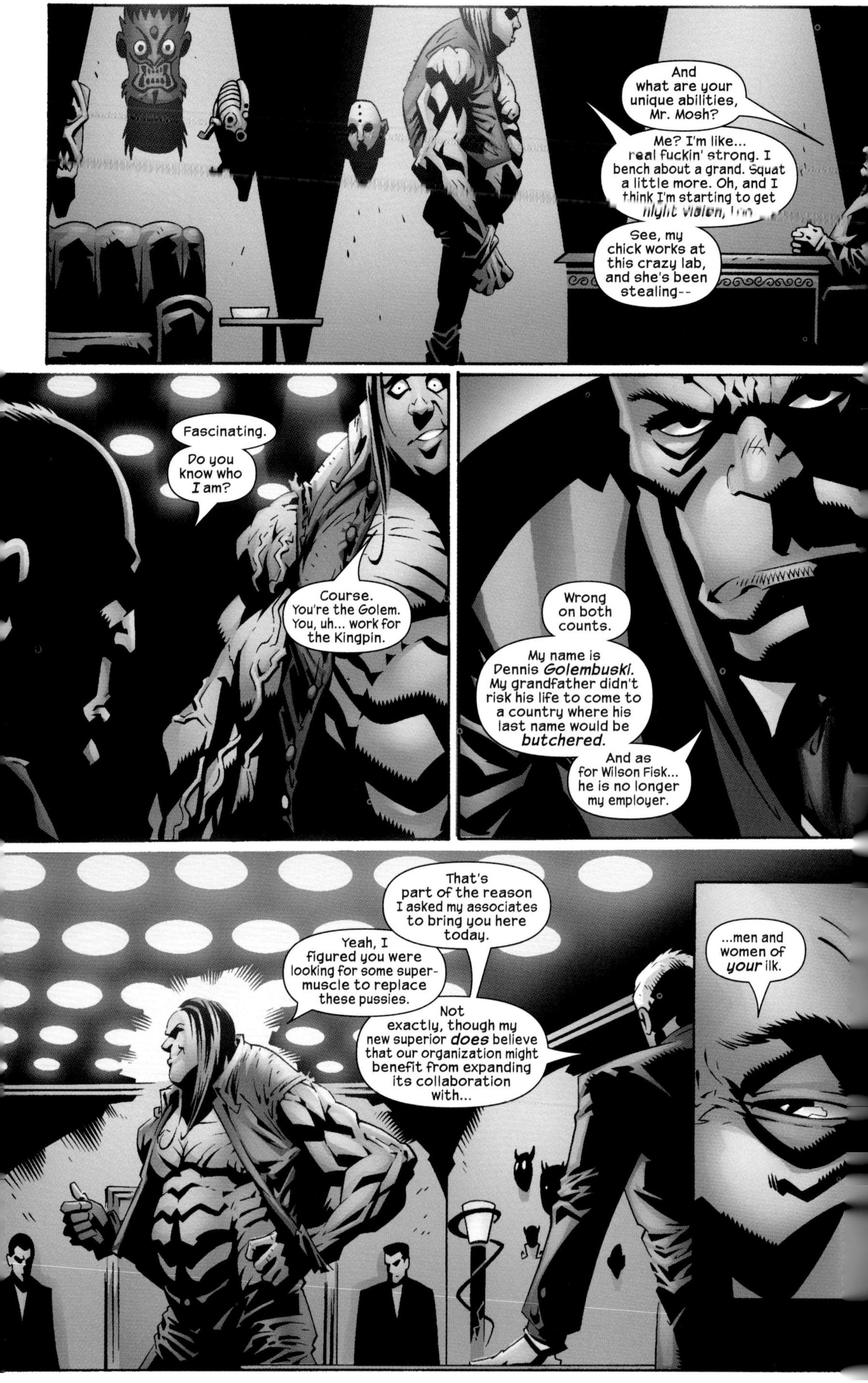
And what are your unique abilities, Mr. Mosh?
Me? I'm like... real fuckin' strong. I bench about a grand. Squat a little more. Oh, and I think I'm starting to get
See, my chick works at this crazy lab, and she's been stealing--
Fascinating.
Do you know who *I* am?
Course. You're the Golem. You, uh... work for the Kingpin.
Wrong on both counts.
My name is Dennis *Golembuski.* My grandfather didn't risk his life to come to a country where his last name would be *butchered.*
And as for Wilson Fisk... he is no longer my employer.
Yeah, I figured you were looking for some super-muscle to replace these pussies.
That's part of the reason I asked my associates to bring you here today.
Not exactly, though my new superior *does* believe that our organization might benefit from expanding its collaboration with...
...men and women of *your* ilk.

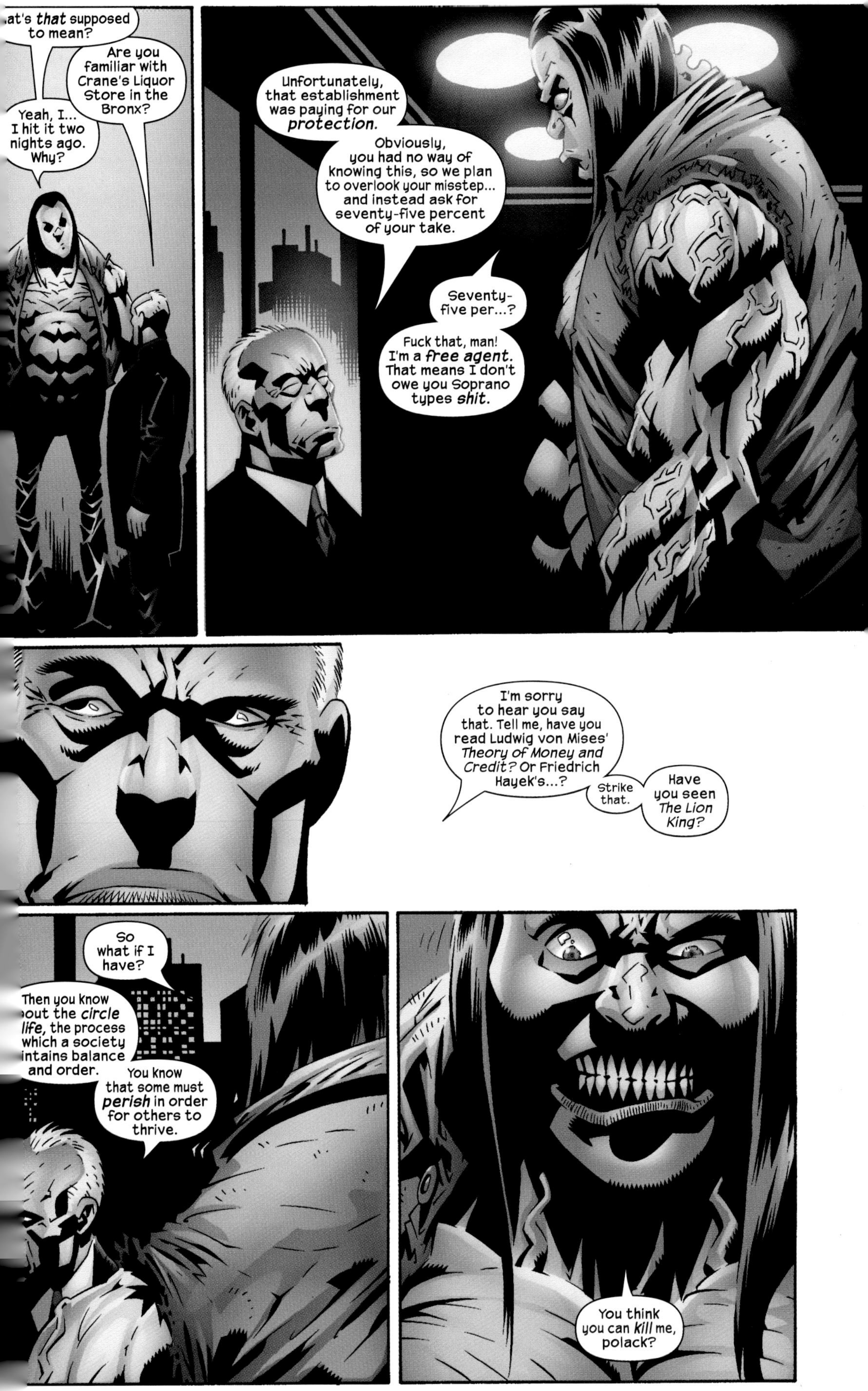

at's *that* supposed to mean?
Are you familiar with Crane's Liquor Store in the Bronx?
Yeah, I... I hit it two nights ago. Why?
Unfortunately, that establishment was paying for our *protection*.
Obviously, you had no way of knowing this, so we plan to overlook your misstep... and instead ask for seventy-five percent of your take.
Seventy-five per...?
Fuck that, man! I'm a *free agent*. That means I don't owe you Soprano types *shit*.
I'm sorry to hear you say that. Tell me, have you read Ludwig von Mises' *Theory of Money and Credit*? Or Friedrich Hayek's...?
Strike that.
Have you seen *The Lion King*?
So what if I have?
Then you know out the *circle life*, the process which a society intains balance and order.
You know that some must *perish* in order for others to thrive.
You think you can *kill* me, polack?

No.
But I'm confident that my new friend *Madam Rapier* can.

Rapier, huh?
Bring it on, bitch. I wouldn't mind getting raped by a broad like y--

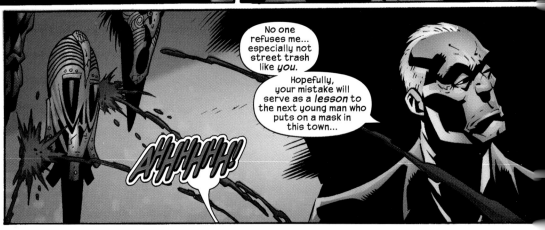

No one refuses me... especially not street trash like *you*.
Hopefully, your mistake will serve as a *lesson* to the next young man who puts on a mask in this town...

AHHHHHH!

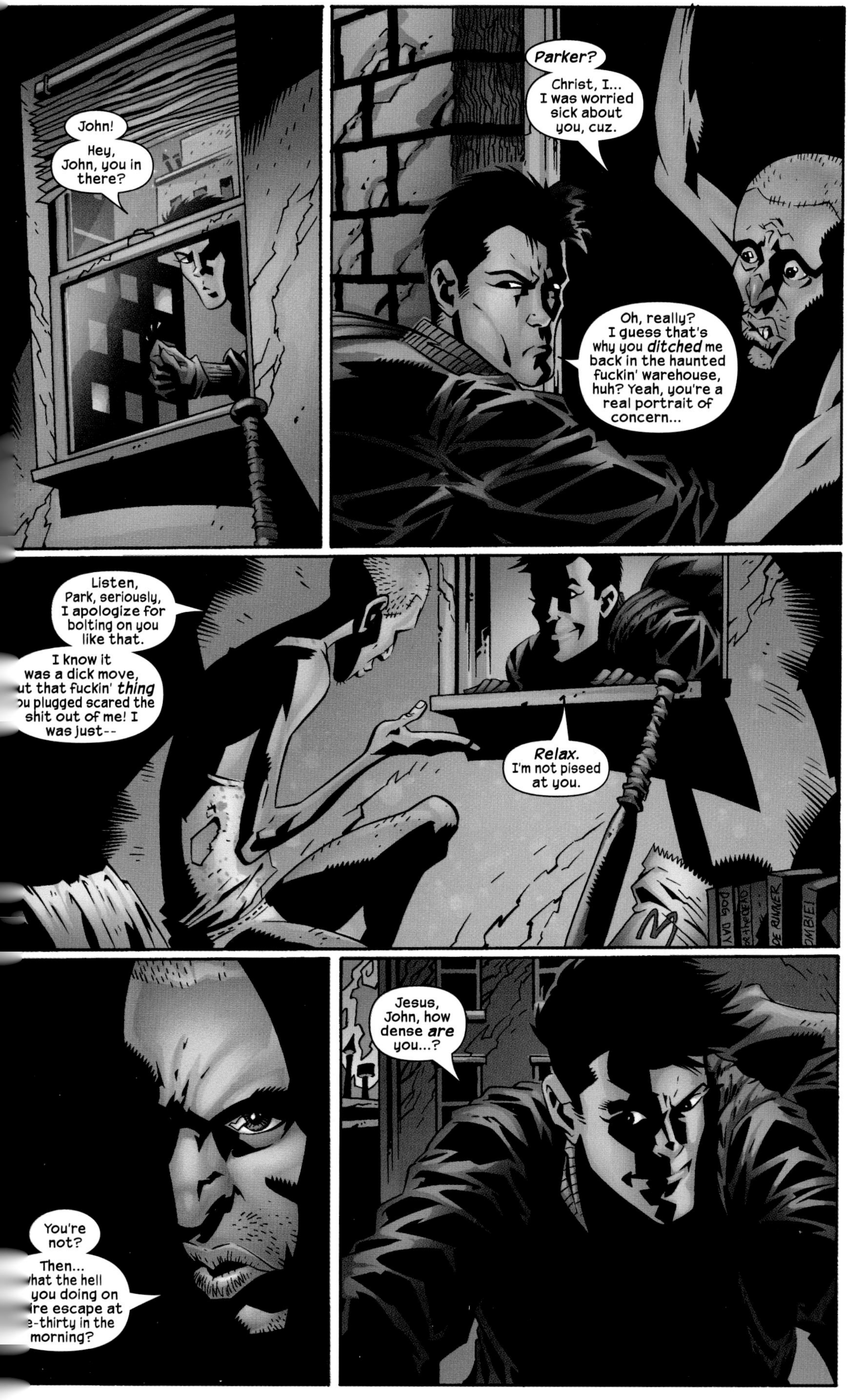
John!
Hey, John, you in there?
Parker?
Christ, I... I was worried sick about you, cuz.
Oh, really? I guess that's why you *ditched* me back in the haunted fuckin' warehouse, huh? Yeah, you're a real portrait of concern...
Listen, Park, seriously, I apologize for bolting on you like that.
I know it was a dick move, ut that fuckin' *thing* ou plugged scared the shit out of me! I was just--
*Relax.* I'm not pissed at you.
DOG DAY
You're not?
Then... hat the hell you doing on ire escape at -thirty in the morning?
Jesus, John, how dense *are* you...?

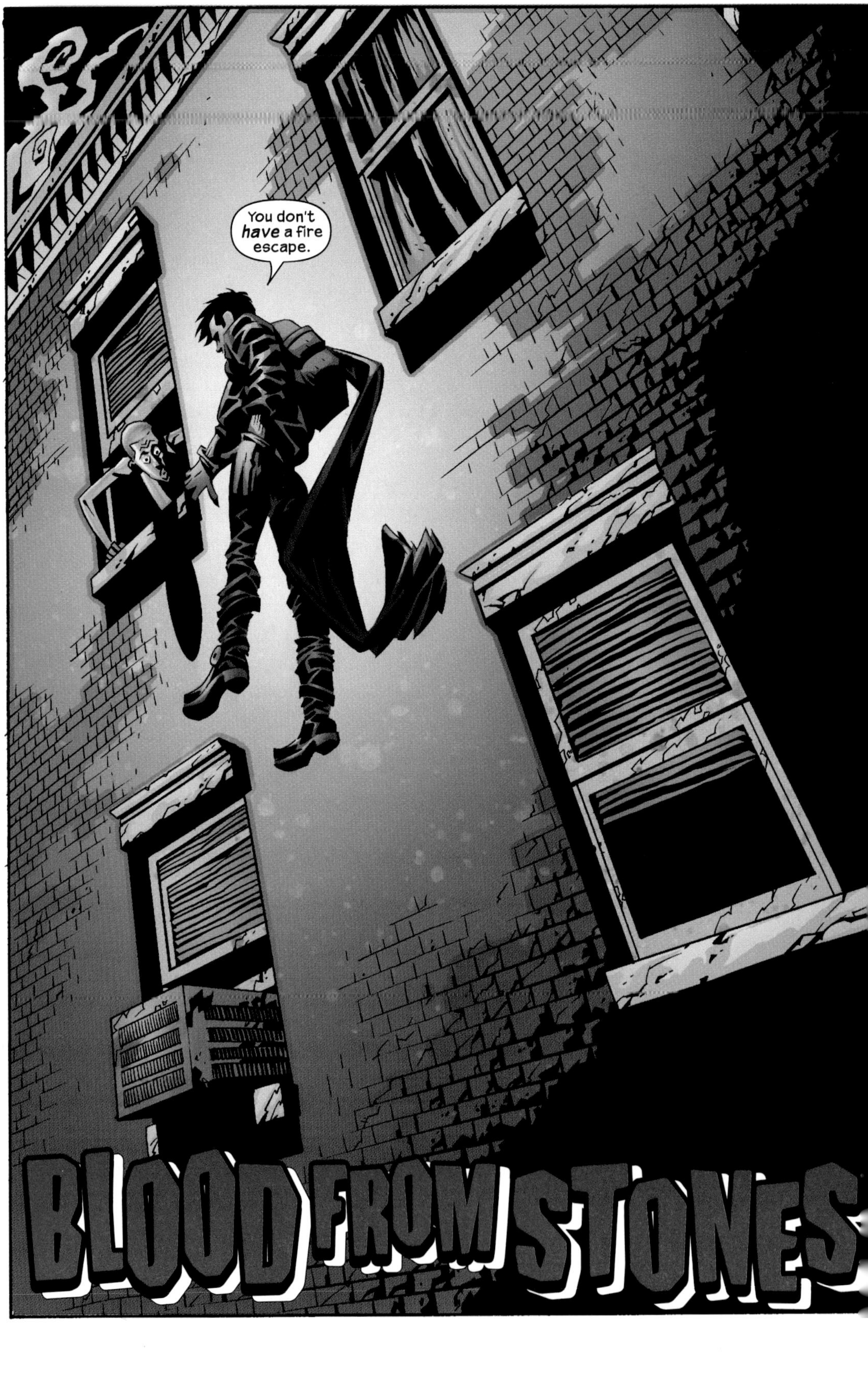
You don't *have* a fire escape.
BLOOD FROM STONES

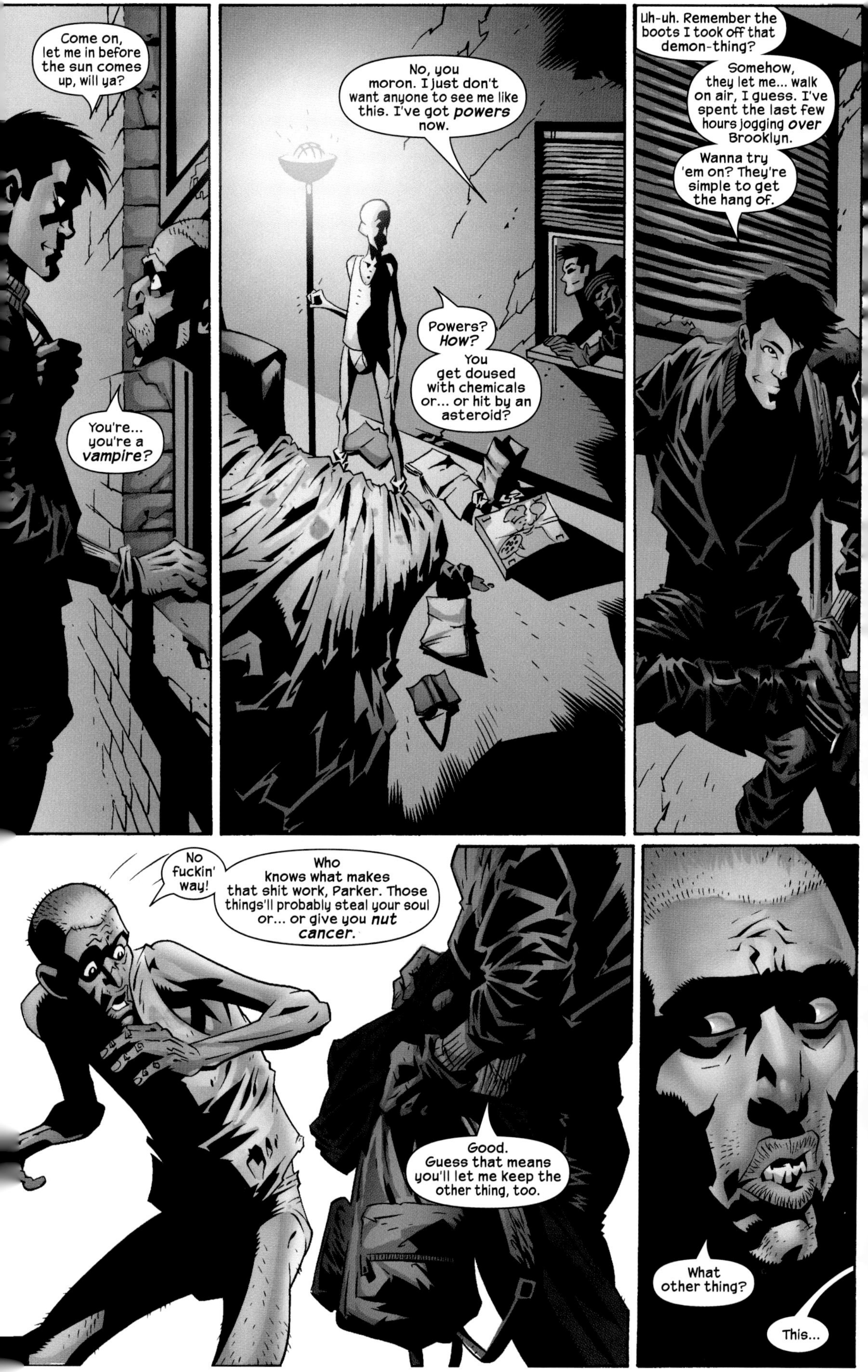
Come on, let me in before the sun comes up, will ya?
You're... you're a *vampire*?
No, you moron. I just don't want anyone to see me like this. I've got *powers* now.
Powers? *How?*
You get doused with chemicals or... or hit by an asteroid?
Uh-uh. Remember the boots I took off that demon-thing?
Somehow, they let me... walk on air, I guess. I've spent the last few hours jogging *over* Brooklyn.
Wanna try 'em on? They're simple to get the hang of.
No fuckin' way!
Who knows what makes that shit work, Parker. Those things'll probably steal your soul or... or give you *nut cancer*.
Good. Guess that means you'll let me keep the other thing, too.
What other thing?
This...

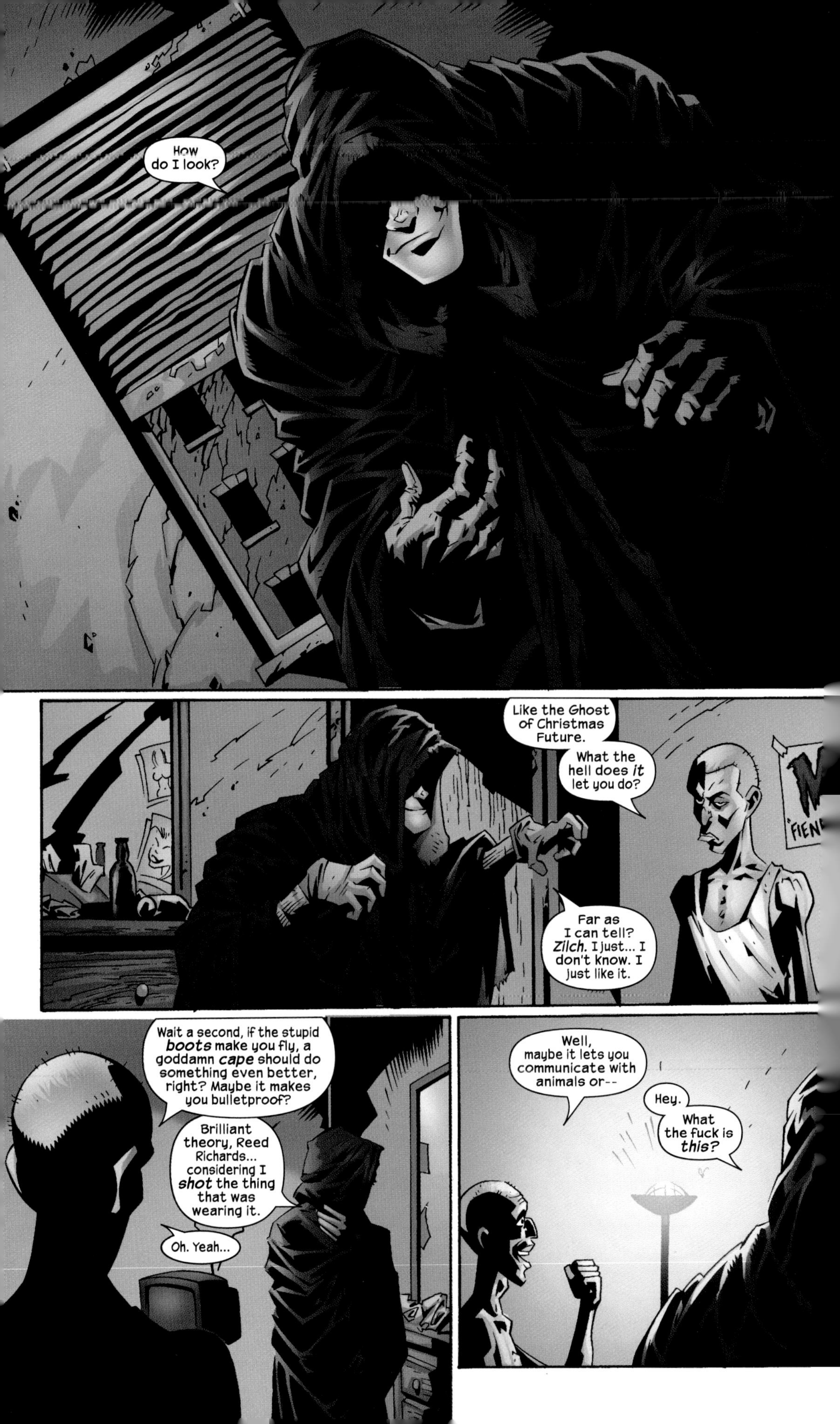

How do I look?
Like the Ghost of Christmas Future.
What the hell does *it* let you do?
Far as I can tell? *Zilch.* I just... I don't know. I just like it.
FIEN
Wait a second, if the stupid *boots* make you fly, a goddamn *cape* should do something even better, right? Maybe it makes you bulletproof?
Brilliant theory, Reed Richards... considering I *shot* the thing that was wearing it.
Oh. Yeah...
Well, maybe it lets you communicate with animals or--
Hey. What the fuck is *this?*

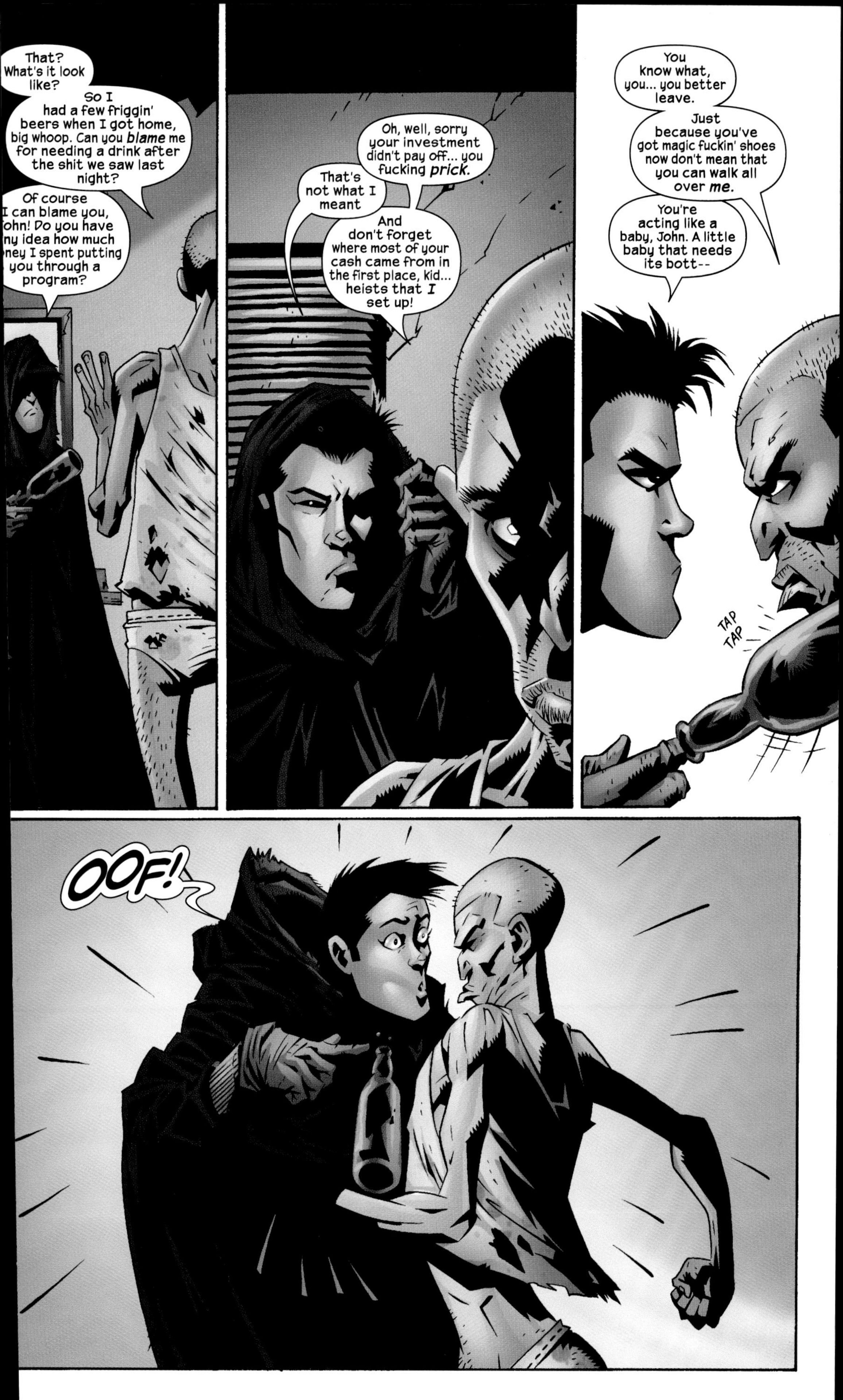

That? What's it look like?
So I had a few friggin' beers when I got home, big whoop. Can you *blame* me for needing a drink after the shit we saw last night?
Of course I can blame you, John! Do you have ny idea how much ney I spent putting you through a program?
That's not what I meant
Oh, well, sorry your investment didn't pay off... you fucking *prick.*
And don't forget where most of your cash came from in the first place, kid... heists that *I* set up!
You know what, you... you better leave.
Just because you've got magic fuckin' shoes now don't mean that you can walk all over *me.*
You're acting like a baby, John. A little baby that needs its bott--
TAP TAP
OOF!

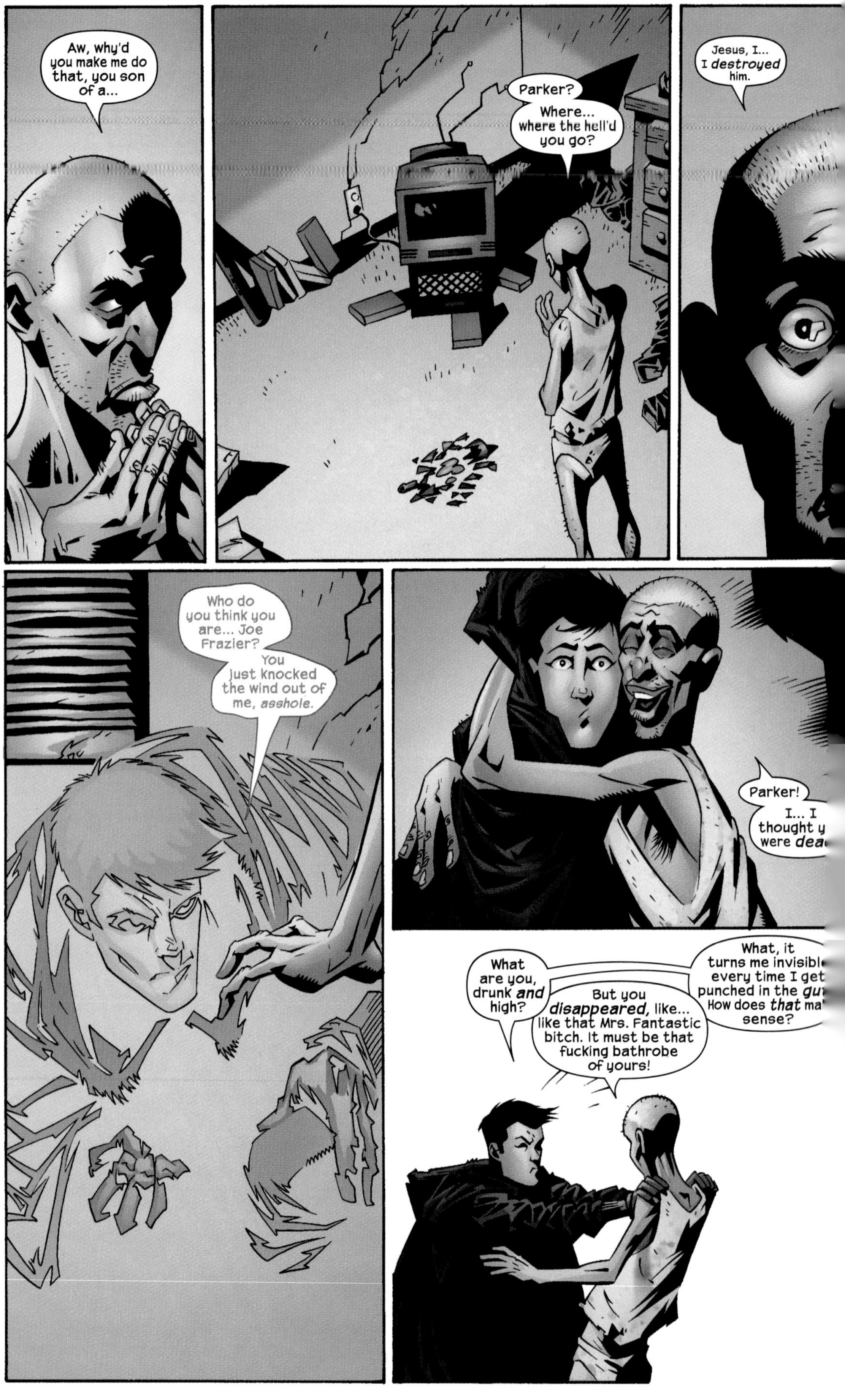
Aw, why'd you make me do that, you son of a...
Parker?
Where... where the hell'd you go?
Jesus, I... I *destroyed* him.
Who do you think you are... Joe Frazier?
You just knocked the wind out of me, *asshole.*
Parker!
I... I thought y were *dea*
What are you, drunk *and* high?
But you *disappeared,* like... like that Mrs. Fantastic bitch. It must be that fucking bathrobe of yours!
What, it turns me invisibl every time I get punched in the *gu* How does *that* ma sense?

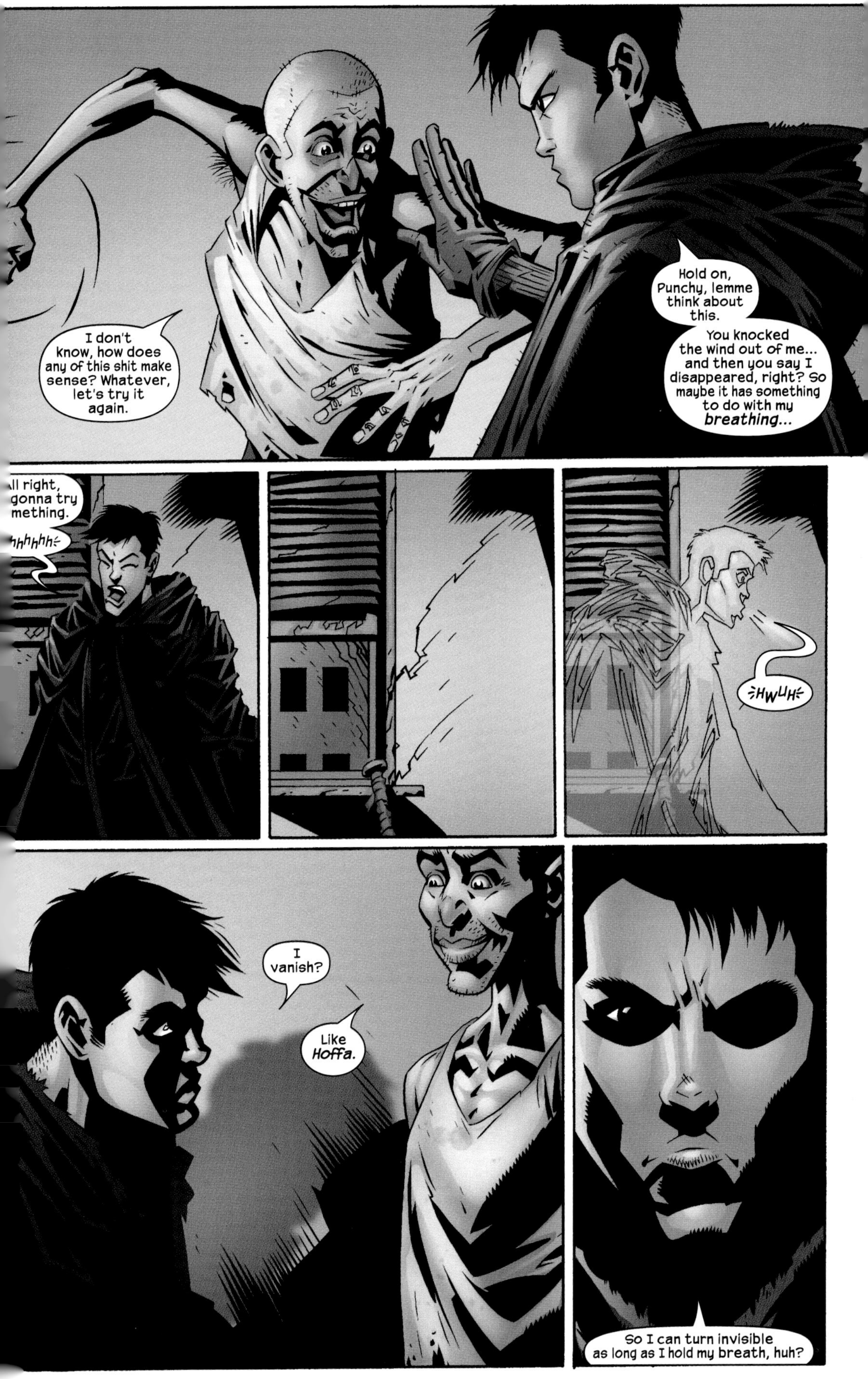

I don't know, how does any of this shit make sense? Whatever, let's try it again.
Hold on, Punchy, lemme think about this.
You knocked the wind out of me... and then you say I disappeared, right? So maybe it has something to do with my *breathing*...
ll right, gonna try mething.
hhhhhh
HWUH
I vanish?
Like *Hoffa*.
So I can turn invisible as long as I hold my breath, huh?

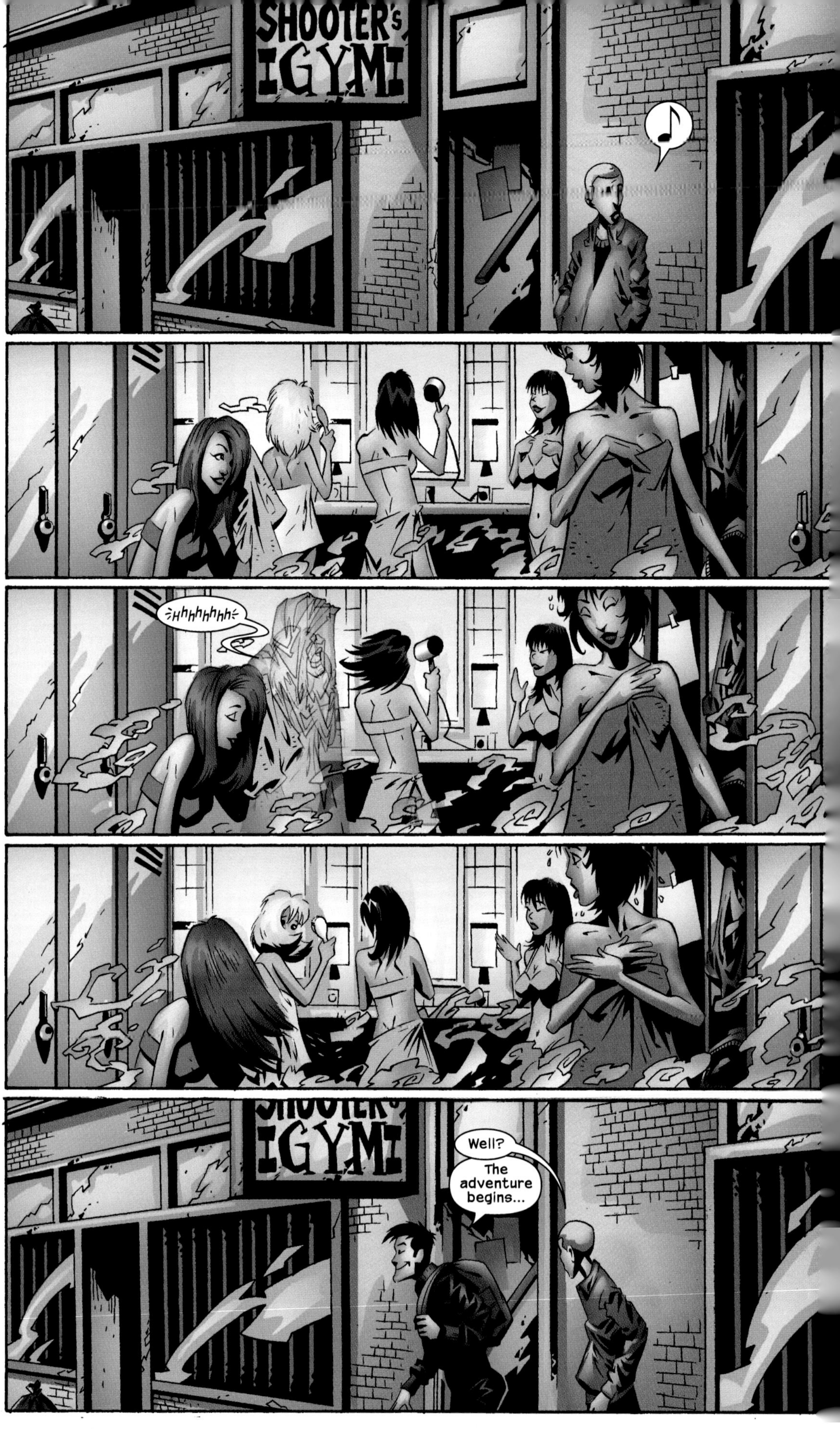
SHOOTER's
GYM
♪
Hhhhhhhh
SHOOTER's
GYM
Well?
The adventure begins...

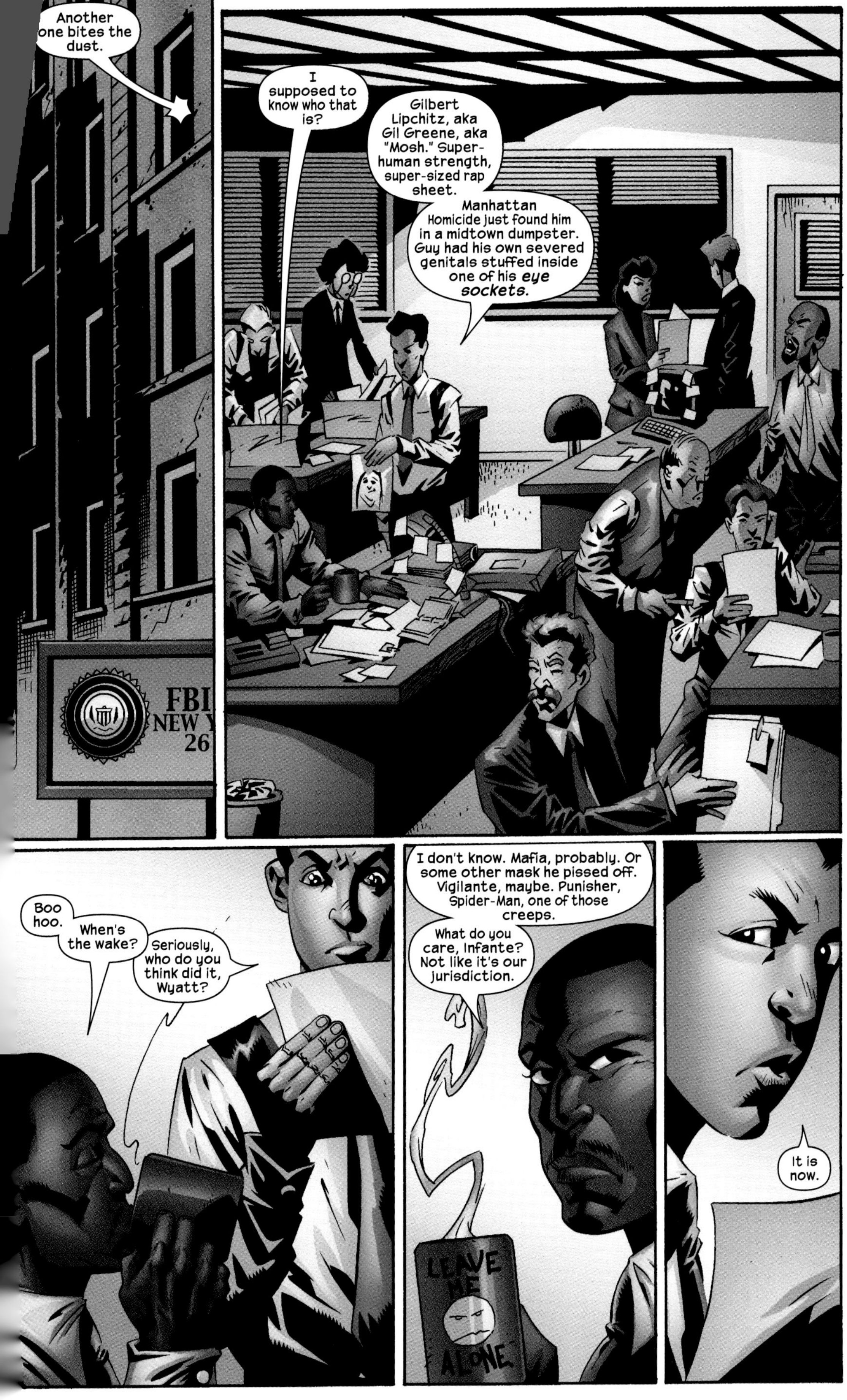
Another one bites the dust.
FBI NEW Y 26
I supposed to know who that is?
Gilbert Lipchitz, aka Gil Greene, aka "Mosh." Super-human strength, super-sized rap sheet.
Manhattan Homicide just found him in a midtown dumpster. Guy had his own severed genitals stuffed inside one of his eye sockets.
Boo hoo.
When's the wake?
Seriously, who do you think did it, Wyatt?
I don't know. Mafia, probably. Or some other mask he pissed off. Vigilante, maybe. Punisher, Spider-Man, one of those creeps.
What do you care, Infante? Not like it's our jurisdiction.
LEAVE ME ALONE
It is now.

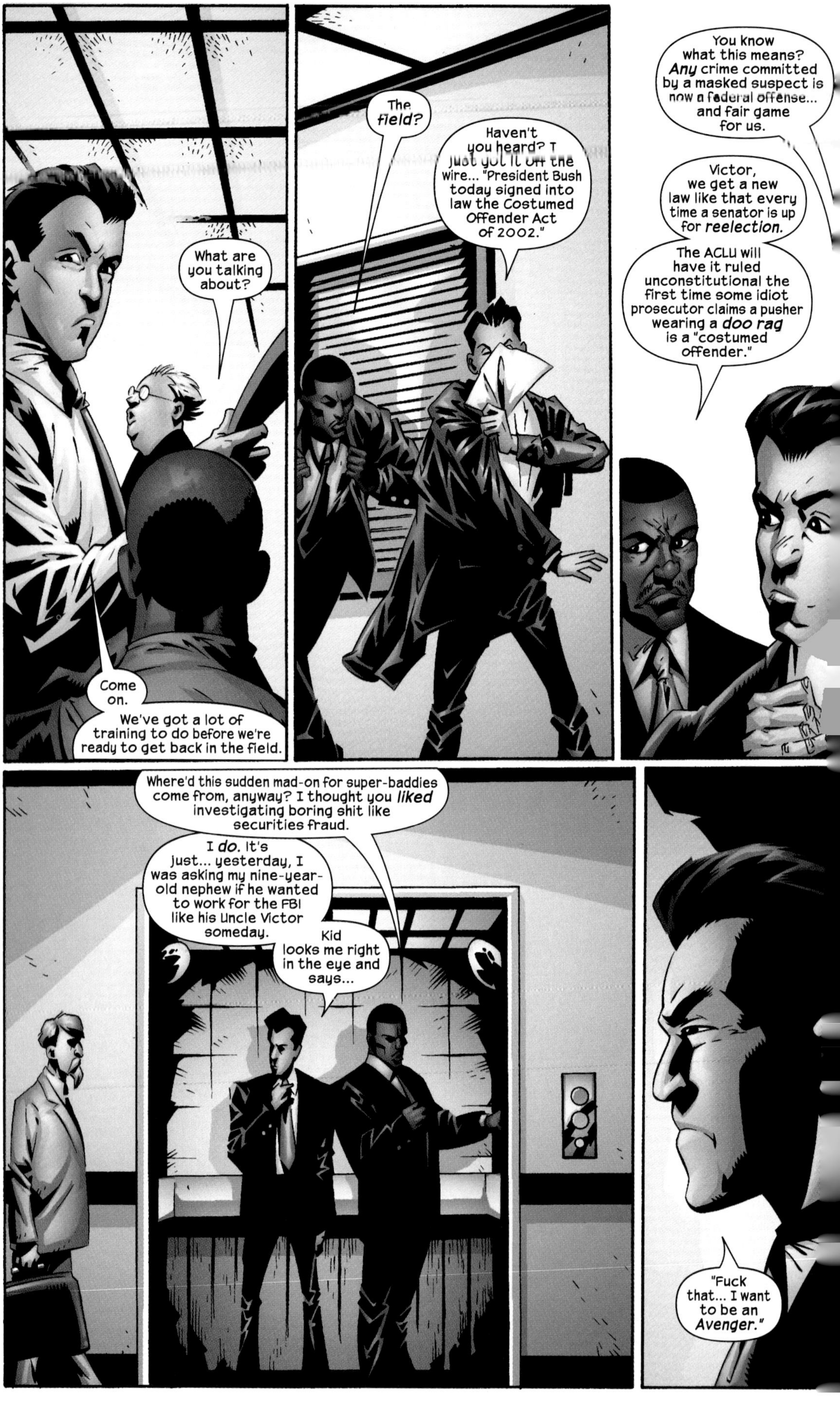

What are you talking about?
Come on.
We've got a lot of training to do before we're ready to get back in the field.
The *field?*
Haven't you heard? I just got it off the wire... "President Bush today signed into law the Costumed Offender Act of 2002."
You know what this means? *Any* crime committed by a masked suspect is now a federal offense... and fair game for us.
Victor, we get a new law like that every time a senator is up for *reelection.*
The ACLU will have it ruled unconstitutional the first time some idiot prosecutor claims a pusher wearing a *doo rag* is a "costumed offender."
Where'd this sudden mad-on for super-baddies come from, anyway? I thought you *liked* investigating boring shit like securities fraud.
I *do.* It's just... yesterday, I was asking my nine-year-old nephew if he wanted to work for the FBI like his Uncle Victor someday.
Kid looks me right in the eye and says...
"Fuck that... I want to be an *Avenger.*"

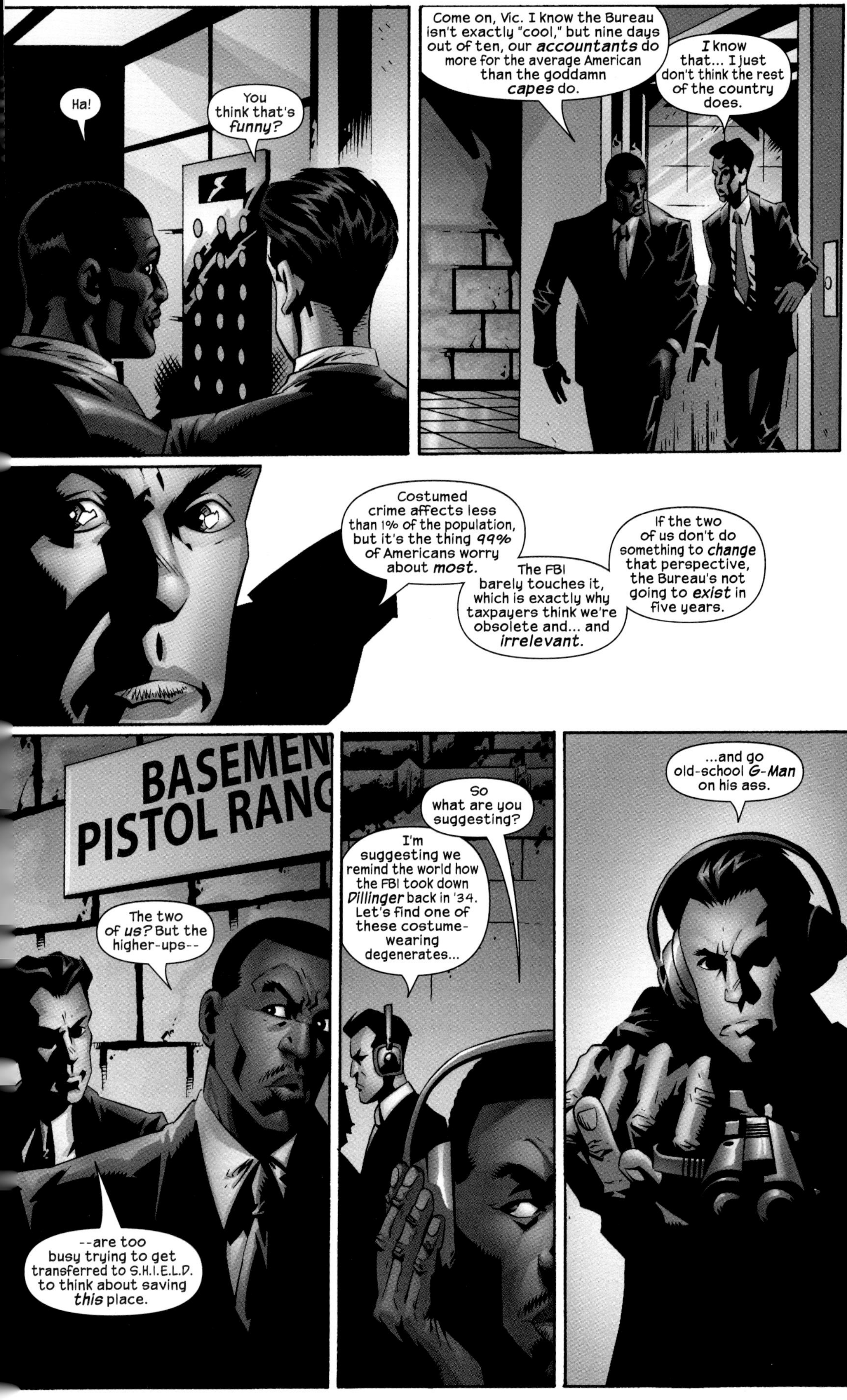

Ha!
You think that's *funny?*
Come on, Vic. I know the Bureau isn't exactly "cool," but nine days out of ten, our *accountants* do more for the average American than the goddamn *capes* do.
*I* know that... I just don't think the rest of the country does.
Costumed crime affects less than 1% of the population, but it's the thing *99%* of Americans worry about *most.*
The FBI barely touches it, which is exactly why taxpayers think we're obsolete and... and *irrelevant.*
If the two of us don't do something to *change* that perspective, the Bureau's not going to *exist* in five years.
BASEMEN
PISTOL RANG
The two of *us?* But the higher-ups--
--are too busy trying to get transferred to S.H.I.E.L.D. to think about saving *this* place.
So what are you suggesting?
I'm suggesting we remind the world how the FBI took down *Dillinger* back in '34. Let's find one of these costume-wearing degenerates...
...and go old-school *G-Man* on his ass.

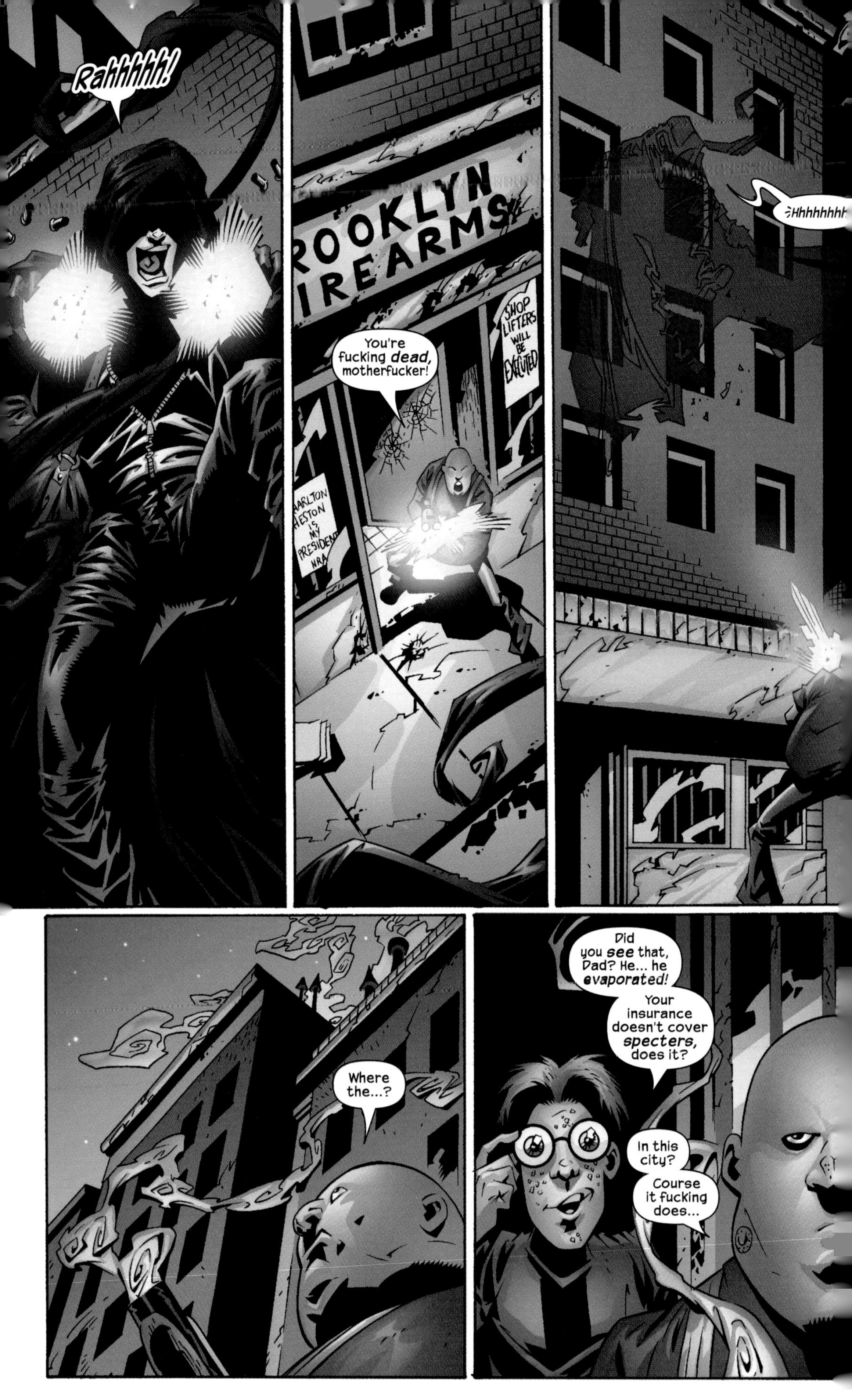
Rahhhhh!
ROOKLYN
IREARMS
SHOP LIFTERS WILL BE EXECUTED
You're fucking *dead,* motherfucker!
ARLTON HESTON IS MY PRESIDENT NRA
Hhhhhhhh
Where the...?
Did you *see* that, Dad? He... he *evaporated!*
Your insurance doesn't cover *specters,* does it?
In this city?
Course it fucking does...

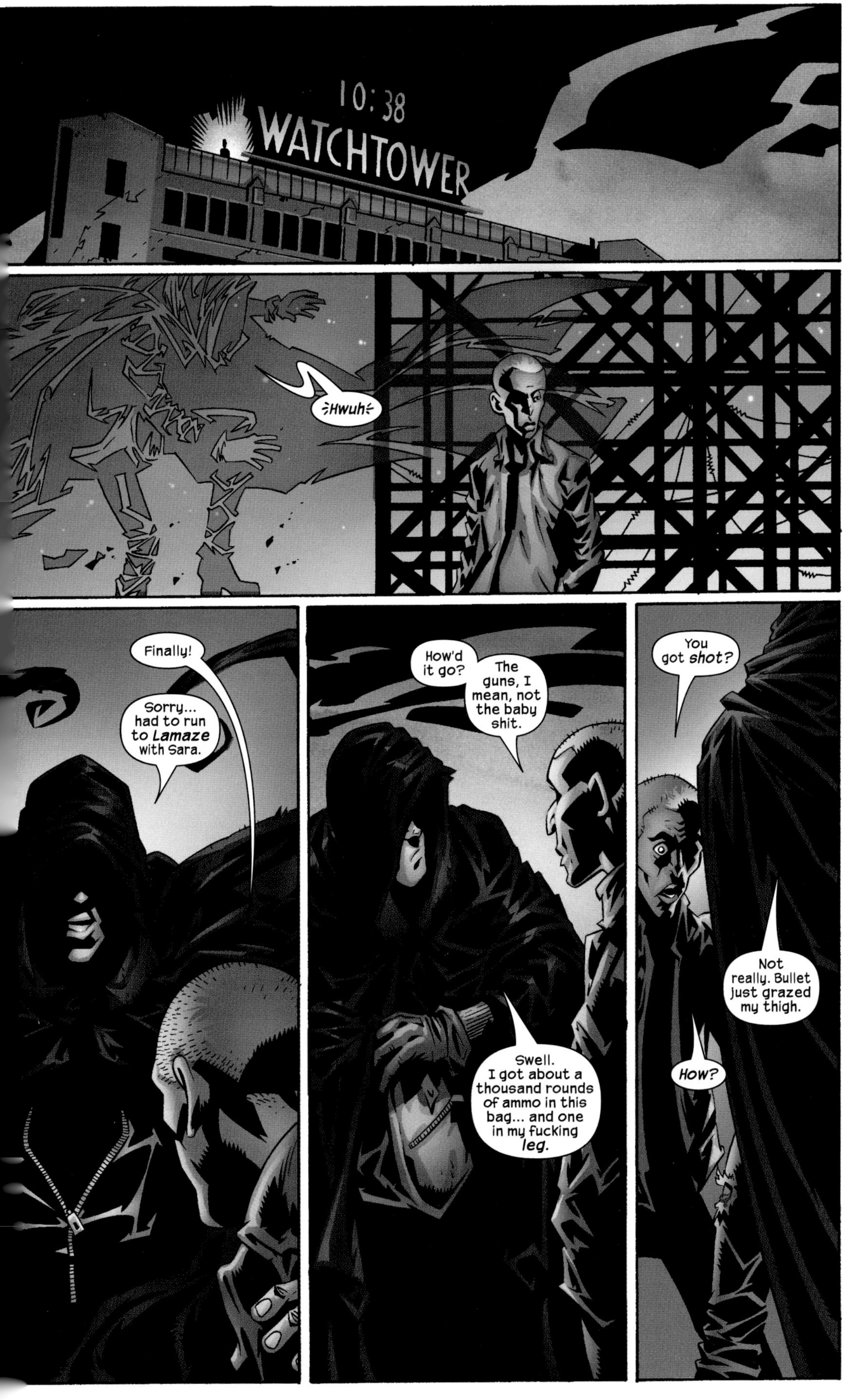
10:38
WATCHTOWER
Hwuh
Finally!
Sorry... had to run to *Lamaze* with Sara.
How'd it go?
The guns, I mean, not the baby shit.
Swell. I got about a thousand rounds of ammo in this bag... and one in my fucking *leg*.
You got *shot*?
Not really. Bullet just grazed my thigh.
*How?*

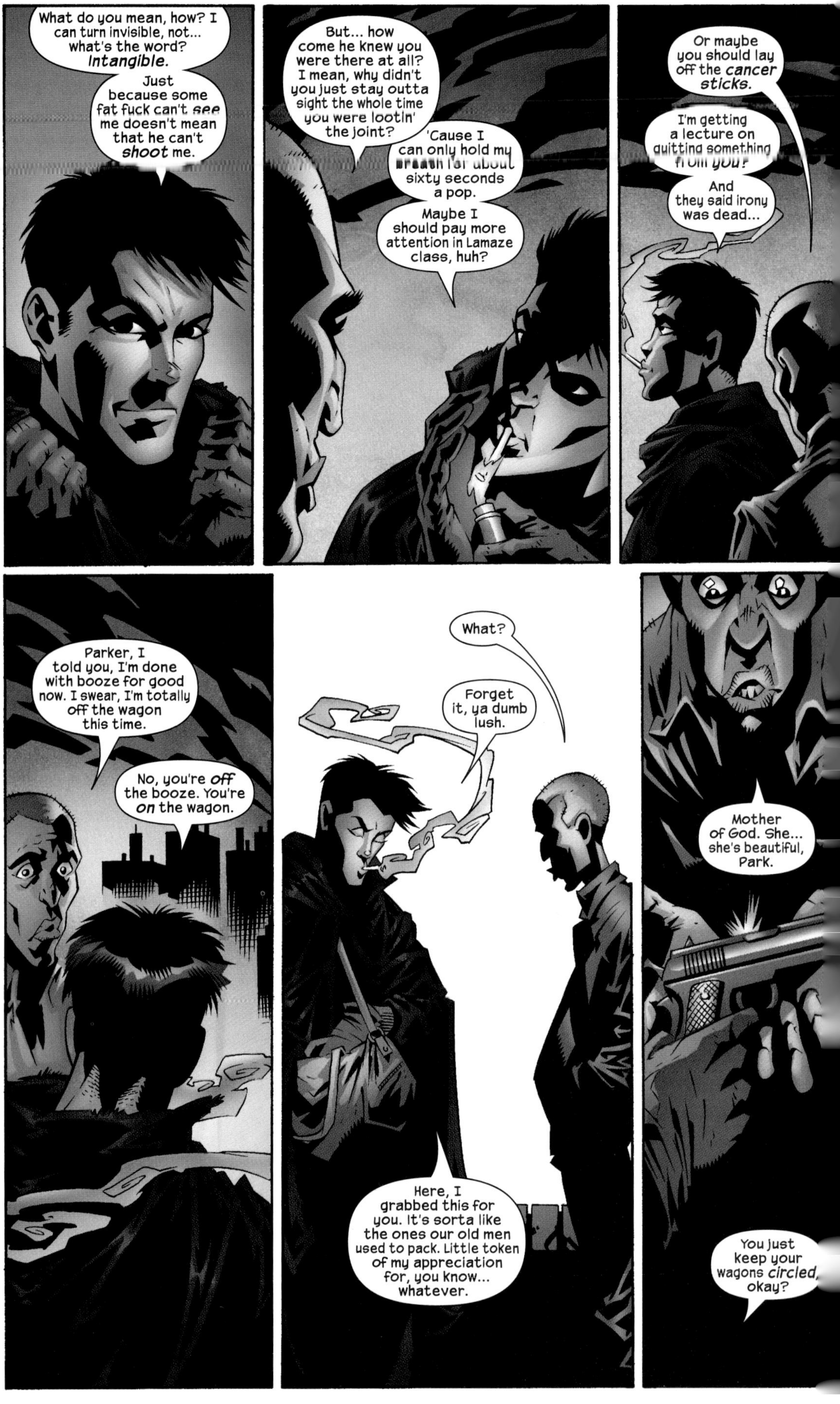
What do you mean, how? I can turn invisible, not... what's the word? *Intangible*.
Just because some fat fuck can't *see* me doesn't mean that he can't *shoot* me.
But... how come he knew you were there at all? I mean, why didn't you just stay outta sight the whole time you were lootin' the joint?
'Cause I can only hold my breath for about sixty seconds a pop.
Maybe I should pay more attention in Lamaze class, huh?
Or maybe you should lay off the *cancer sticks*.
I'm getting a lecture on quitting something from *you?*
And they said irony was dead...
Parker, I told you, I'm done with booze for good now. I swear, I'm totally off the wagon this time.
No, you're *off* the booze. You're *on* the wagon.
What?
Forget it, ya dumb lush.
Here, I grabbed this for you. It's sorta like the ones our old men used to pack. Little token of my appreciation for, you know... whatever.
Mother of God. She... she's beautiful, Park.
You just keep your wagons *circled*, okay?

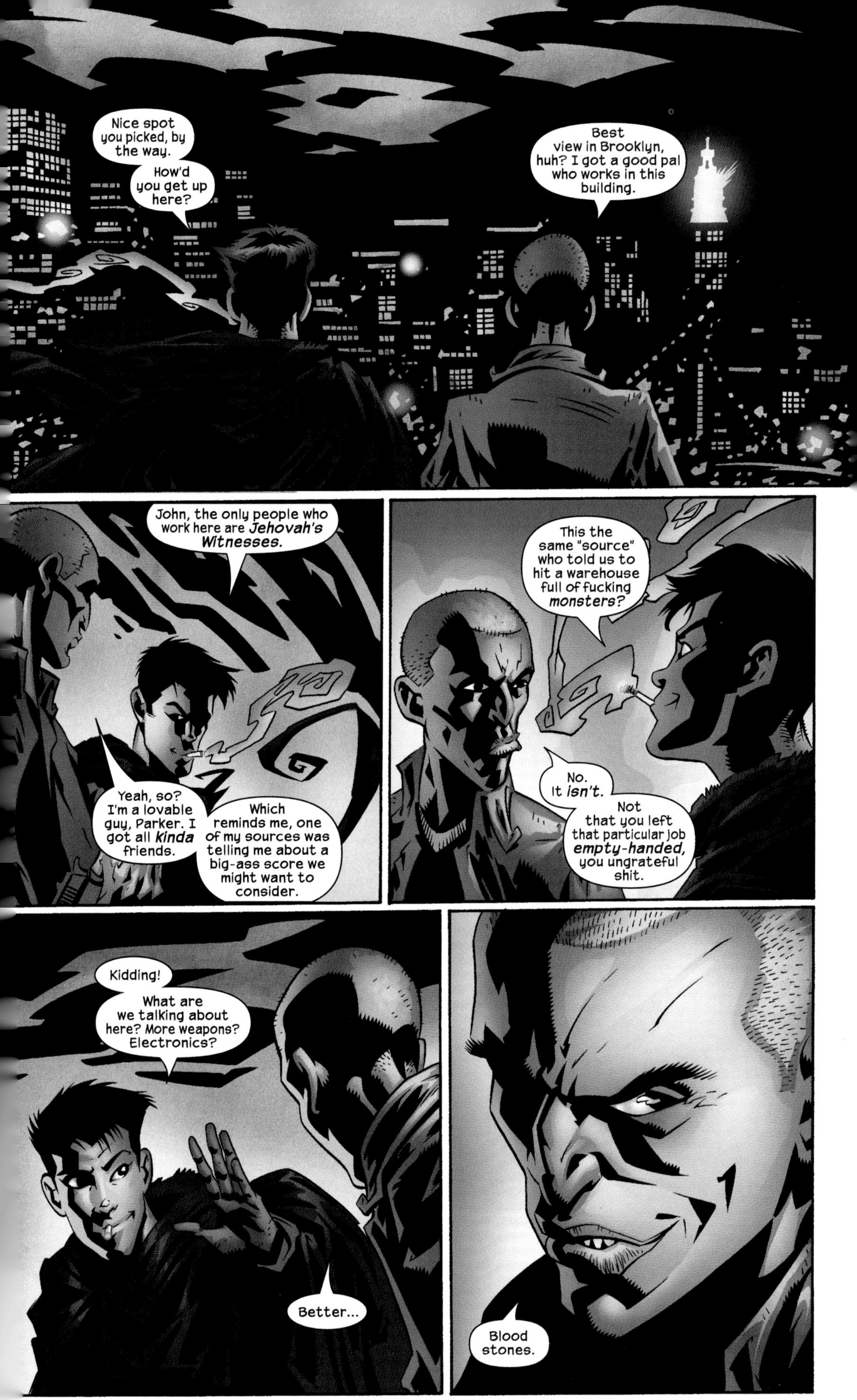
Nice spot you picked, by the way.
How'd you get up here?
Best view in Brooklyn, huh? I got a good pal who works in this building.
John, the only people who work here are *Jehovah's Witnesses.*
Yeah, so? I'm a lovable guy, Parker. I got all *kinda* friends.
Which reminds me, one of my sources was telling me about a big-ass score we might want to consider.
This the same "source" who told us to hit a warehouse full of fucking *monsters?*
No. It *isn't.*
Not that you left that particular job *empty-handed,* you ungrateful shit.
Kidding!
What are we talking about here? More weapons? Electronics?
Better...
Blood stones.

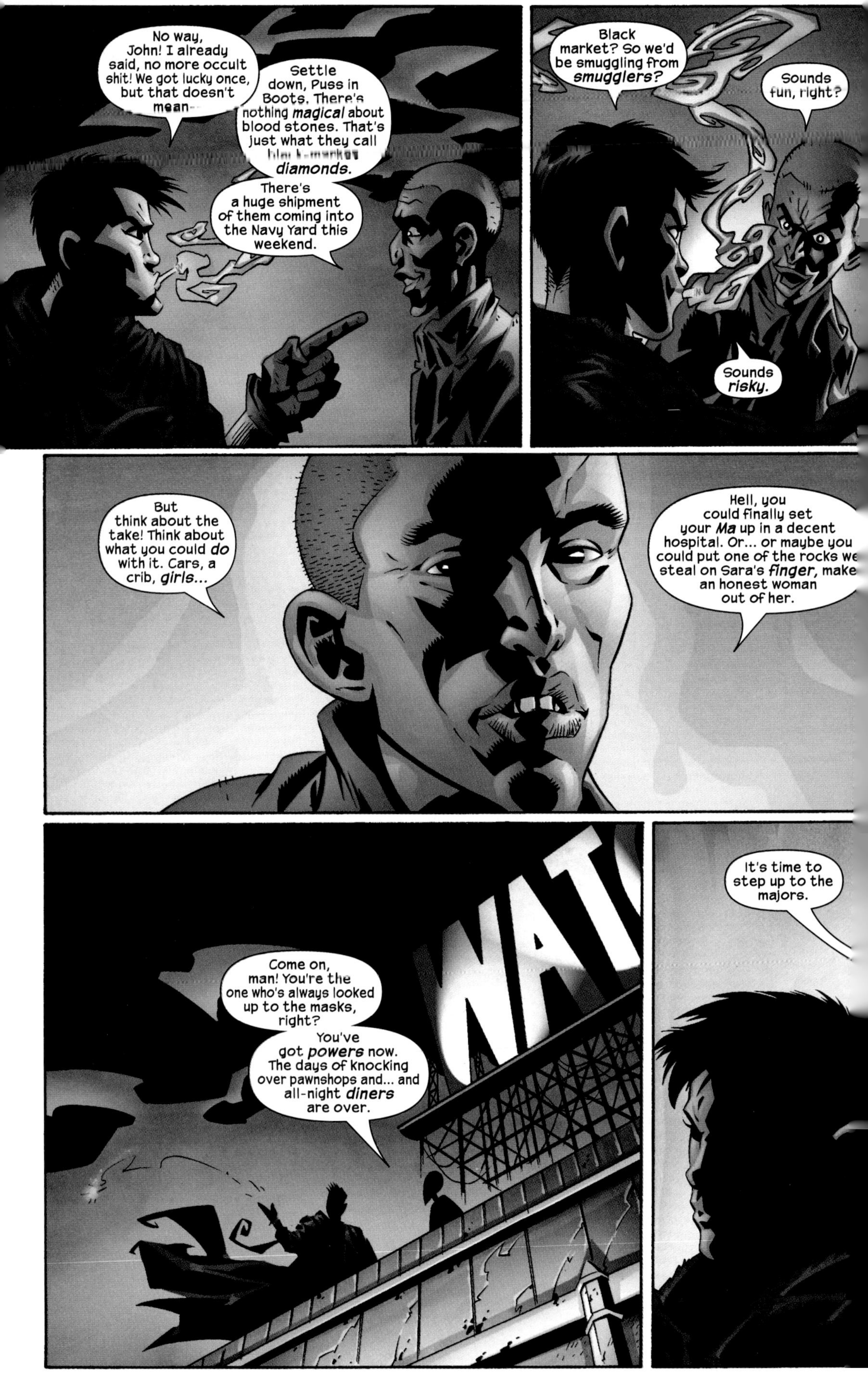
No way, John! I already said, no more occult shit! We got lucky once, but that doesn't mean--
Settle down, Puss in Boots. There's nothing *magical* about blood stones. That's just what they call *diamonds.*
There's a huge shipment of them coming into the Navy Yard this weekend.
Black market? So we'd be smuggling from *smugglers?*
Sounds fun, right?
Sounds *risky.*
But think about the take! Think about what you could *do* with it. Cars, a crib, *girls...*
Hell, you could finally set your *Ma* up in a decent hospital. Or... or maybe you could put one of the rocks we steal on Sara's *finger,* make an honest woman out of her.
Come on, man! You're the one who's always looked up to the masks, right?
You've got *powers* now. The days of knocking over pawnshops and... and all-night *diners* are over.
It's time to step up to the majors.

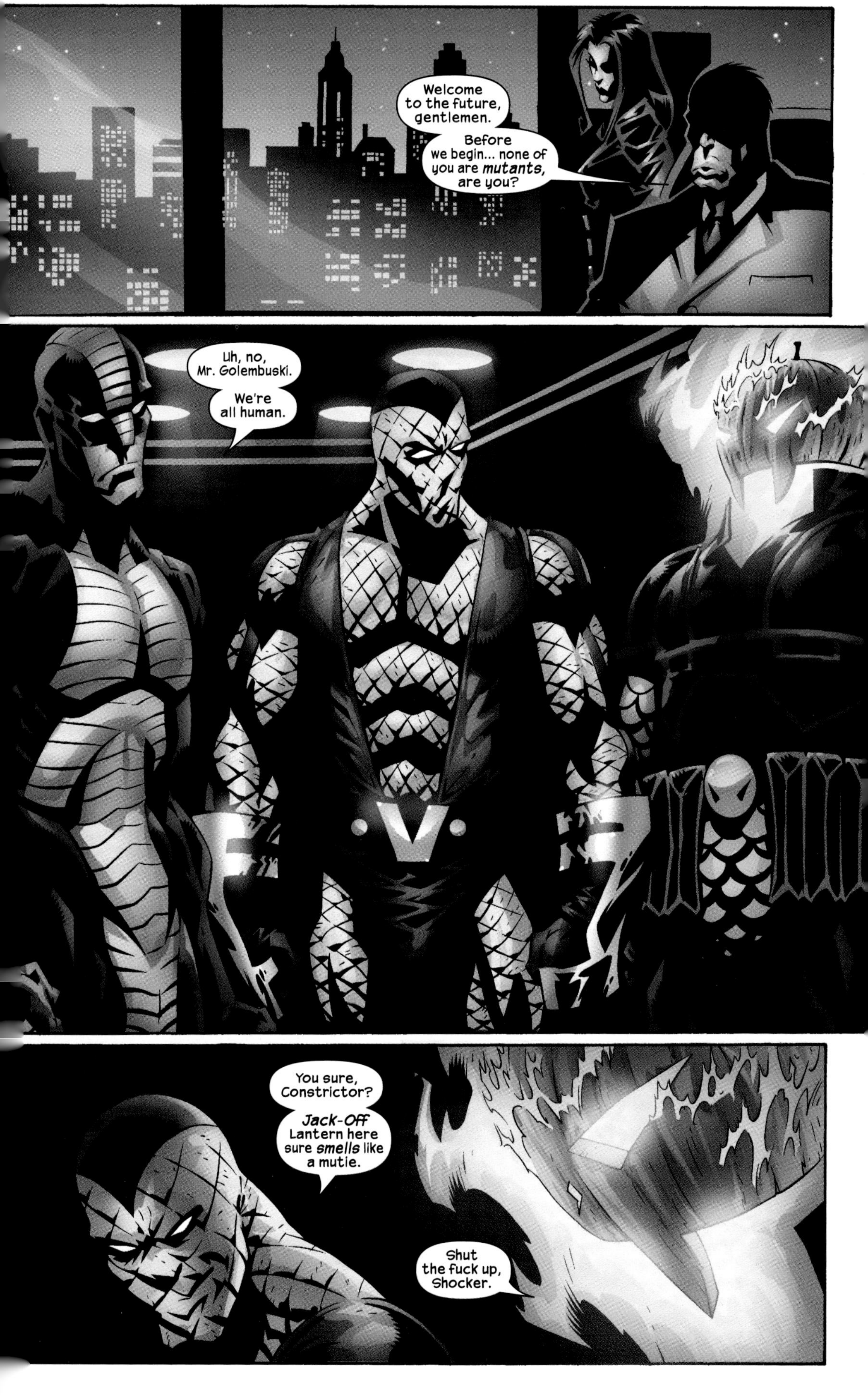

Welcome to the future, gentlemen.
Before we begin... none of you are *mutants,* are you?
Uh, no, Mr. Golembuski.
We're all human.
You sure, Constrictor?
*Jack-Off* Lantern here sure *smells* like a mutie.
Shut the fuck up, Shocker.

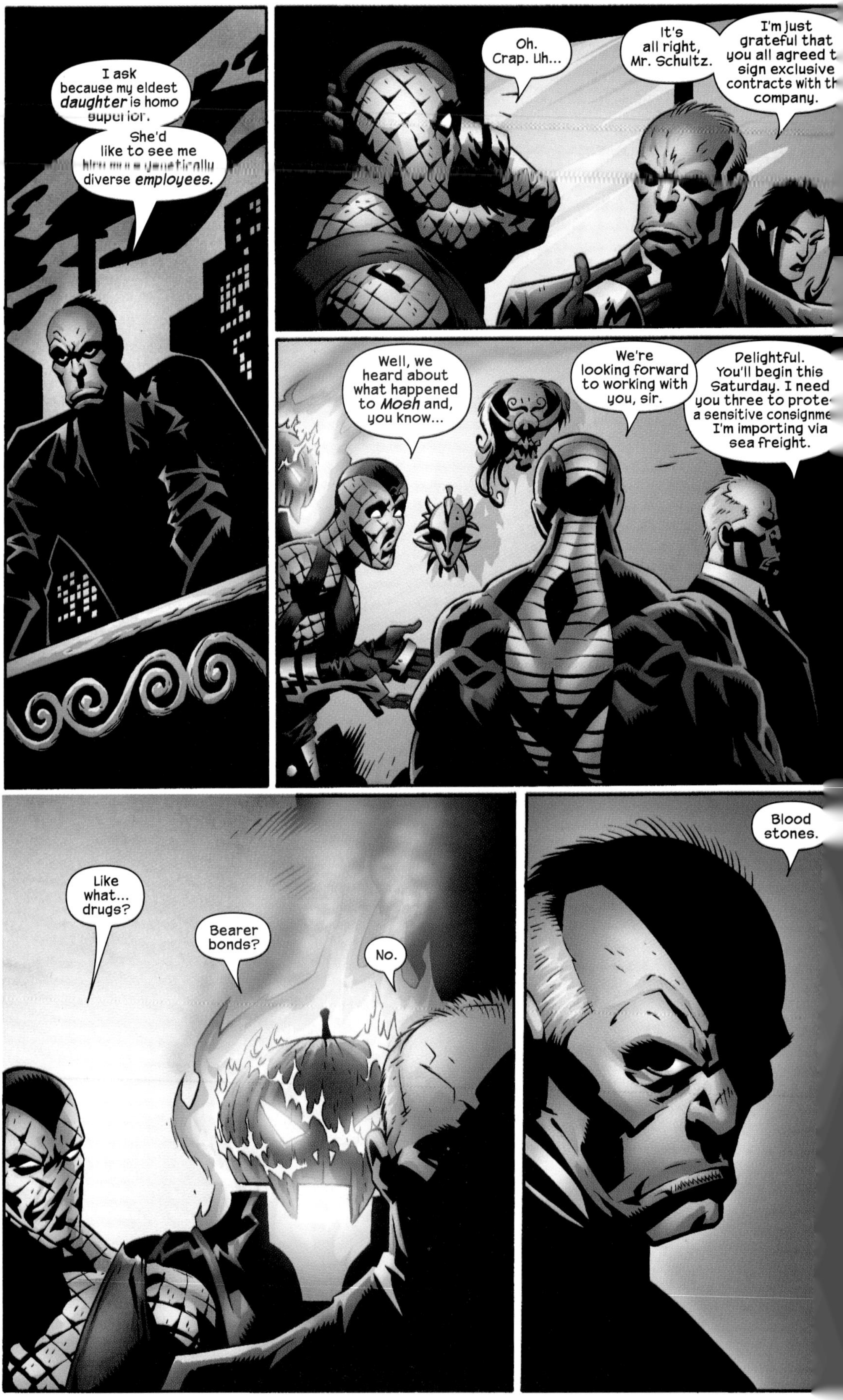
I ask because my eldest *daughter* is homo superior.
She'd like to see me hire more genetically diverse *employees.*
Oh. Crap. Uh...
It's all right, Mr. Schultz.
I'm just grateful that you all agreed t sign exclusive contracts with th company.
Well, we heard about what happened to *Mosh* and, you know...
We're looking forward to working with you, sir.
Delightful. You'll begin this Saturday. I need you three to prote a sensitive consignme I'm importing via sea freight.
Like what... drugs?
Bearer bonds?
No.
Blood stones.

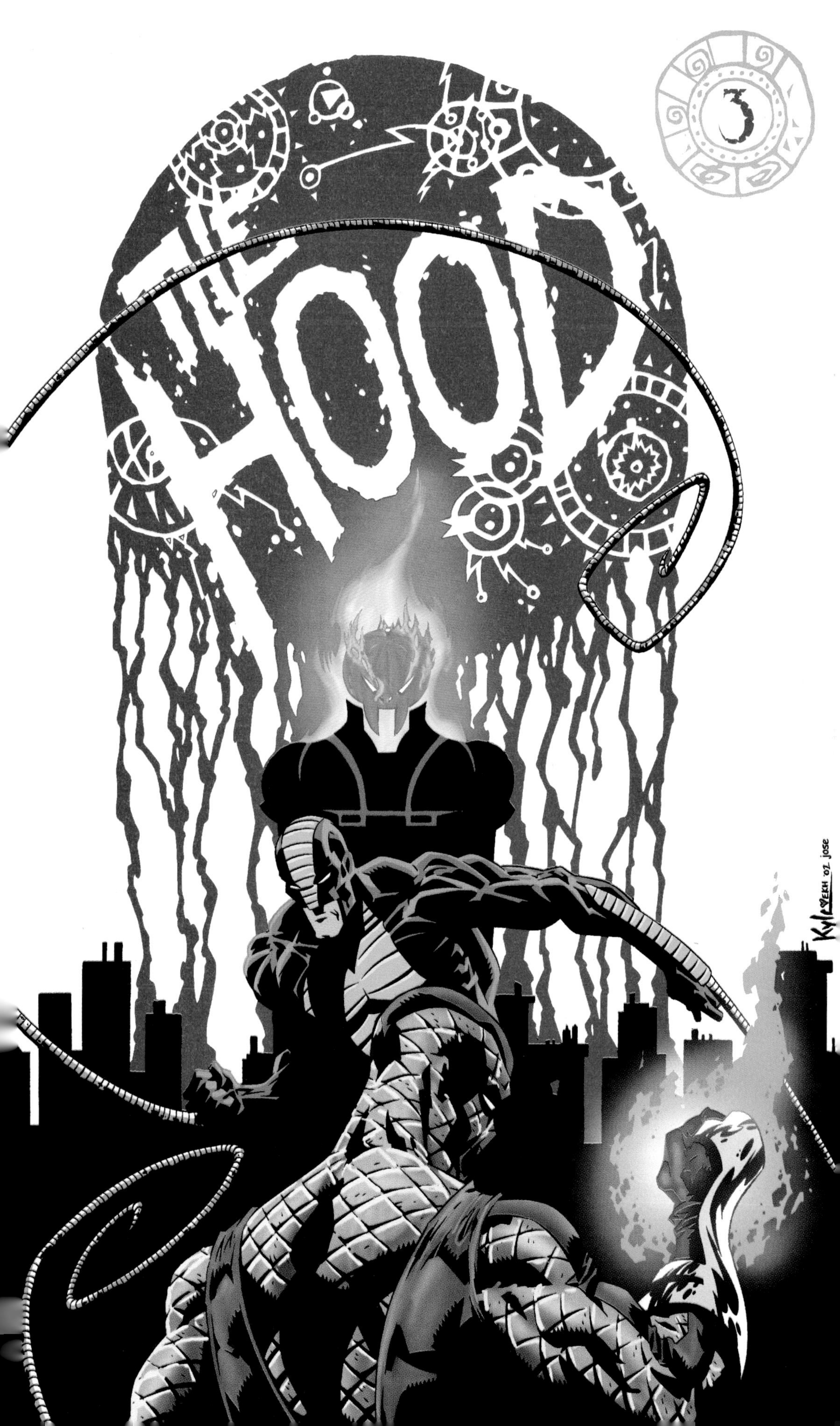
THE HOOD
3

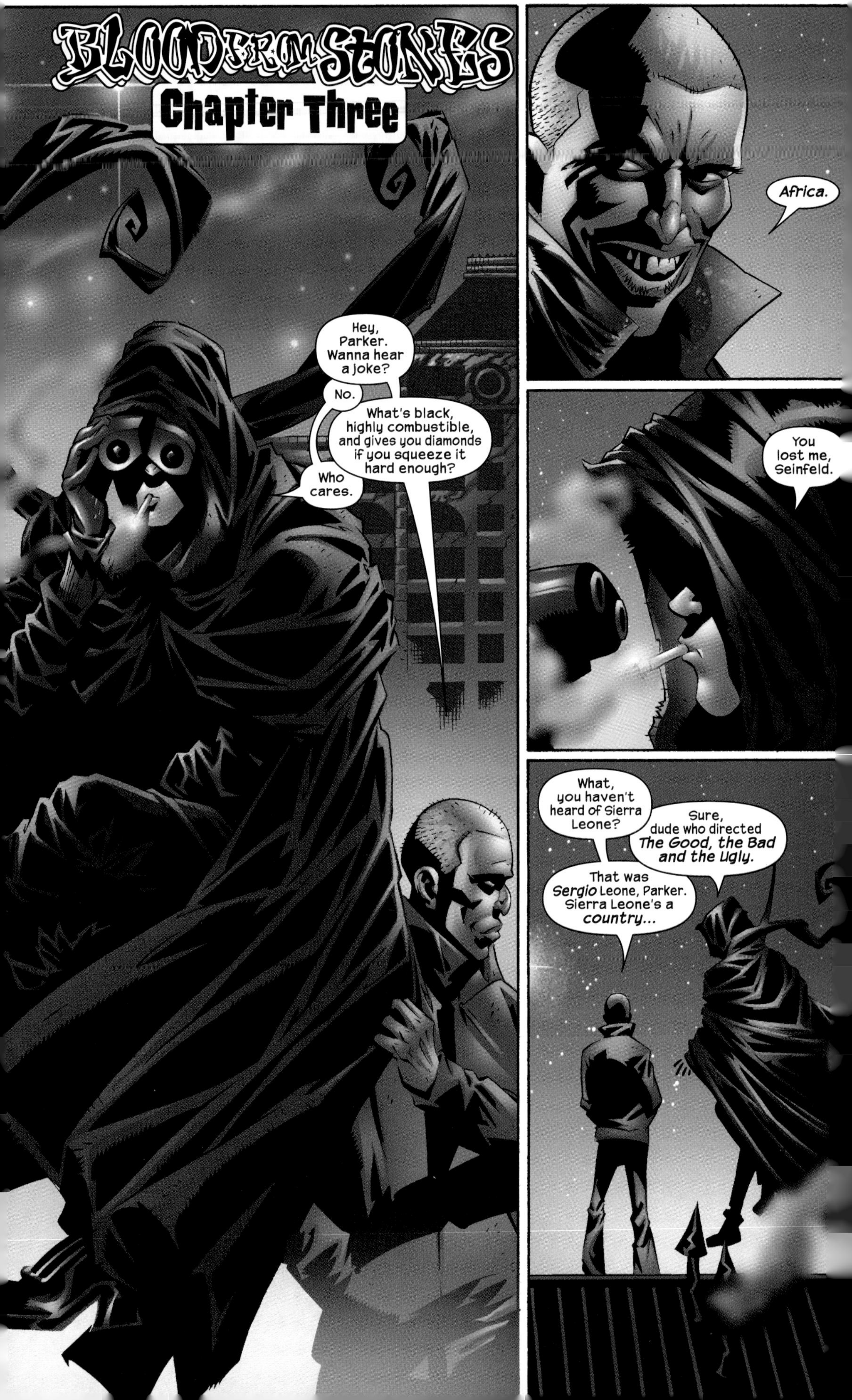
BLOOD FROM STONES
Chapter Three
Hey, Parker. Wanna hear a joke?
No.
What's black, highly combustible, and gives you diamonds if you squeeze it hard enough?
Who cares.
Africa.
You lost me, Seinfeld.
What, you haven't heard of Sierra Leone?
Sure, dude who directed The Good, the Bad and the Ugly.
That was Sergio Leone, Parker. Sierra Leone's a country...

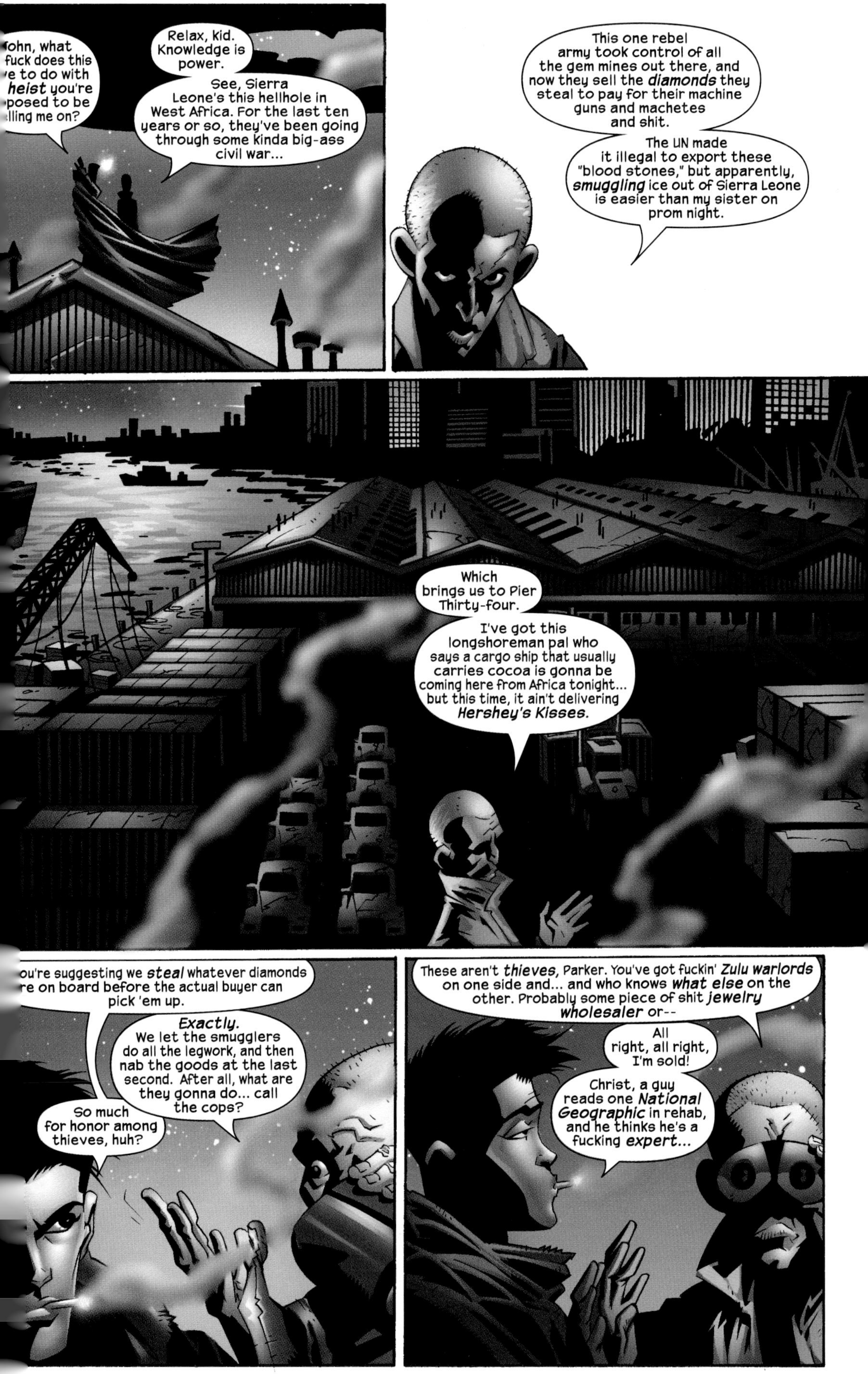
ohn, what fuck does this e to do with heist you're posed to be lling me on?
Relax, kid. Knowledge is power.
See, Sierra Leone's this hellhole in West Africa. For the last ten years or so, they've been going through some kinda big-ass civil war...
This one rebel army took control of all the gem mines out there, and now they sell the *diamonds* they steal to pay for their machine guns and machetes and shit.
The UN made it illegal to export these "blood stones," but apparently, *smuggling* ice out of Sierra Leone is easier than my sister on prom night.
Which brings us to Pier Thirty-four.
I've got this longshoreman pal who says a cargo ship that usually carries cocoa is gonna be coming here from Africa tonight... but this time, it ain't delivering *Hershey's Kisses*.
ou're suggesting we *steal* whatever diamonds re on board before the actual buyer can pick 'em up.
*Exactly.* We let the smugglers do all the legwork, and then nab the goods at the last second. After all, what are they gonna do... call the cops?
So much for honor among thieves, huh?
These aren't *thieves*, Parker. You've got fuckin' *Zulu warlords* on one side and... and who knows *what else* on the other. Probably some piece of shit *jewelry wholesaler* or--
All right, all right, I'm sold!
Christ, a guy reads one *National Geographic* in rehab, and he thinks he's a fucking *expert*...

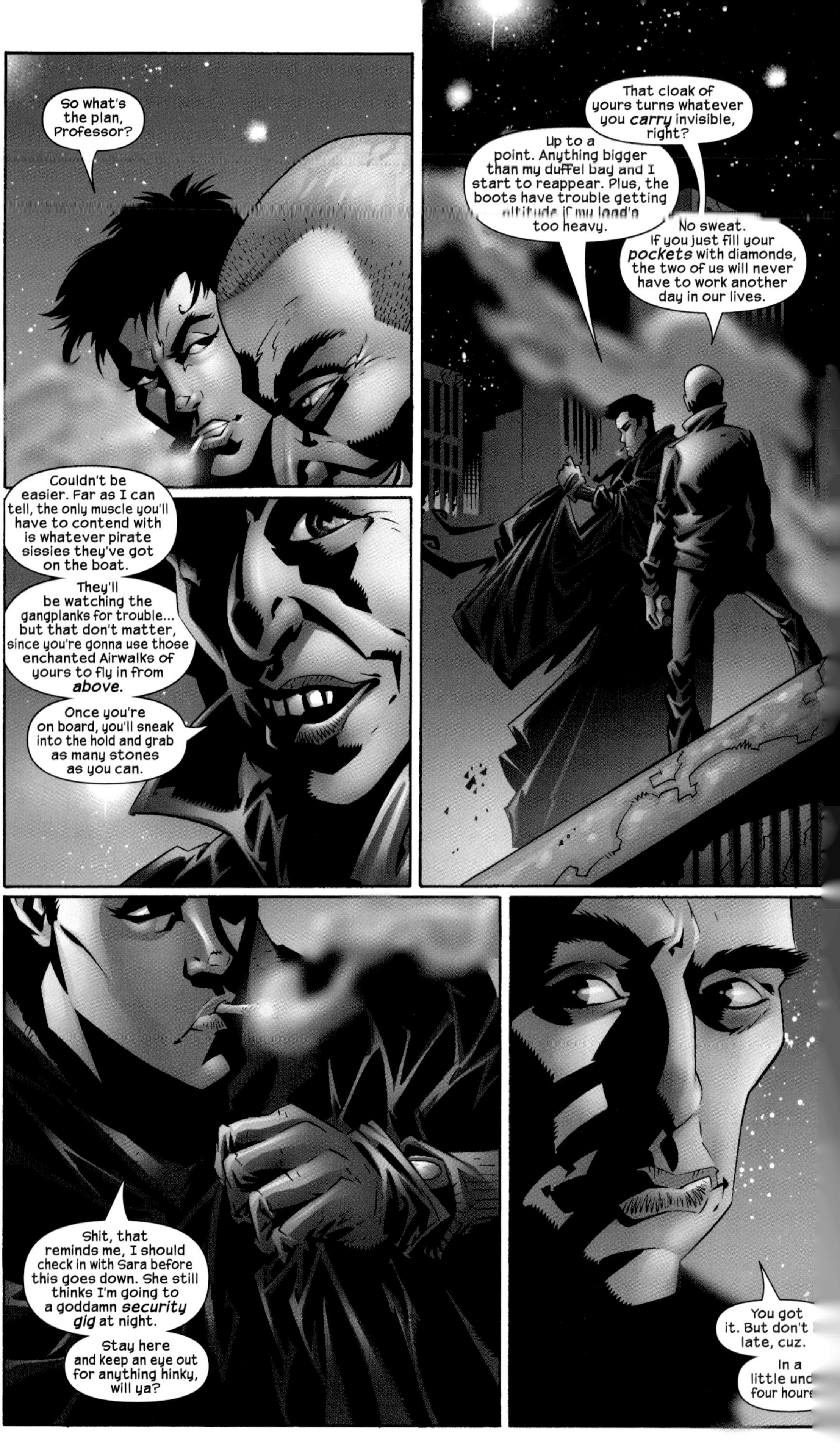
So what's the plan, Professor?
Couldn't be easier. Far as I can tell, the only muscle you'll have to contend with is whatever pirate sissies they've got on the boat.
They'll be watching the gangplanks for trouble... but that don't matter, since you're gonna use those enchanted Airwalks of yours to fly in from *above*.
Once you're on board, you'll sneak into the hold and grab as many stones as you can.
That cloak of yours turns whatever you *carry* invisible, right?
Up to a point. Anything bigger than my duffel bag and I start to reappear. Plus, the boots have trouble getting altitude if my load's too heavy.
No sweat. If you just fill your *pockets* with diamonds, the two of us will never have to work another day in our lives.
Shit, that reminds me, I should check in with Sara before this goes down. She still thinks I'm going to a goddamn *security gig* at night.
Stay here and keep an eye out for anything hinky, will ya?
You got it. But don't late, cuz.
In a little und four hours

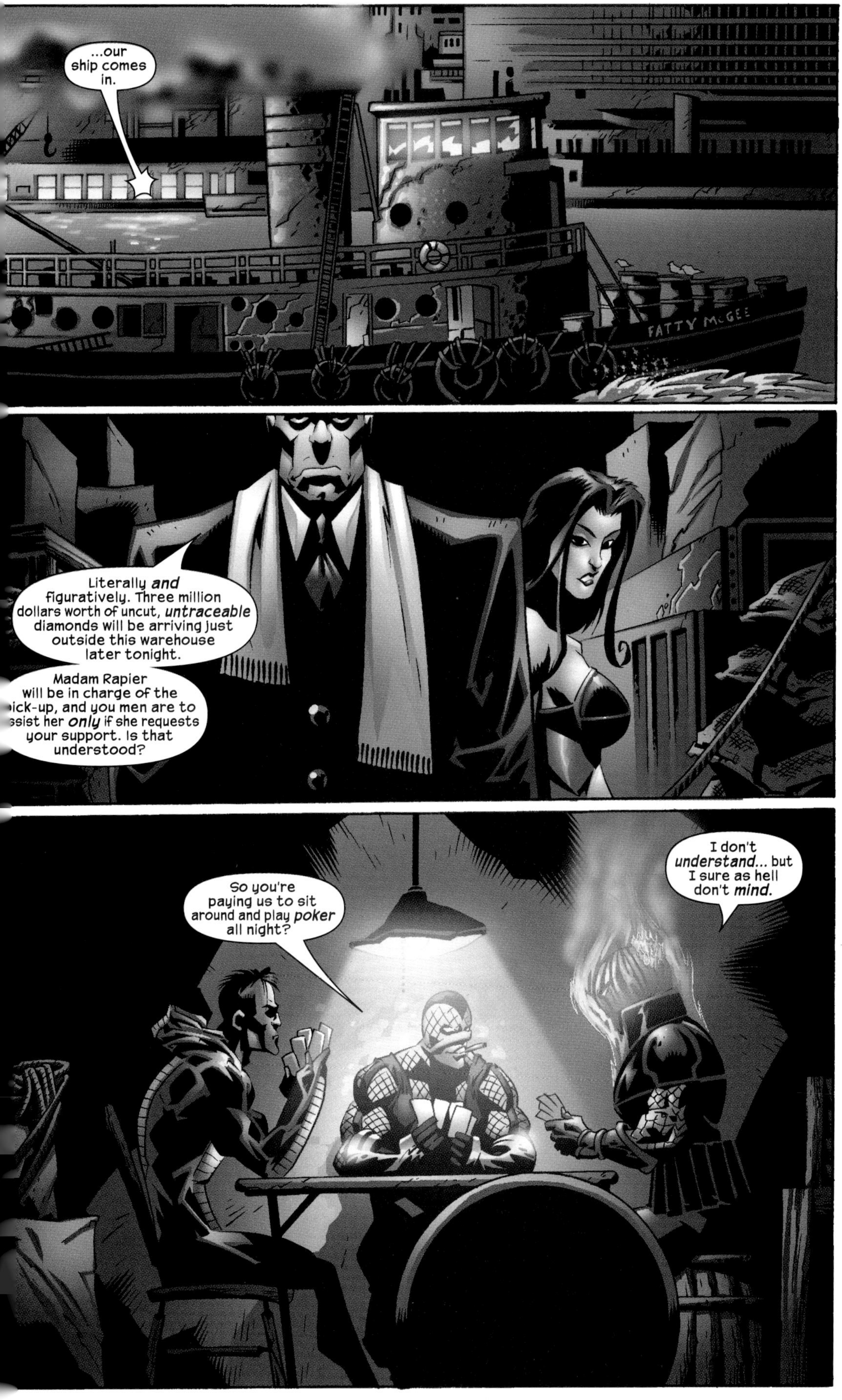
...our ship comes in.
FATTY McGEE
Literally *and* figuratively. Three million dollars worth of uncut, *untraceable* diamonds will be arriving just outside this warehouse later tonight.
Madam Rapier will be in charge of the pick-up, and you men are to assist her *only* if she requests your support. Is that understood?
So you're paying us to sit around and play *poker* all night?
I don't *understand*... but I sure as hell don't *mind*.

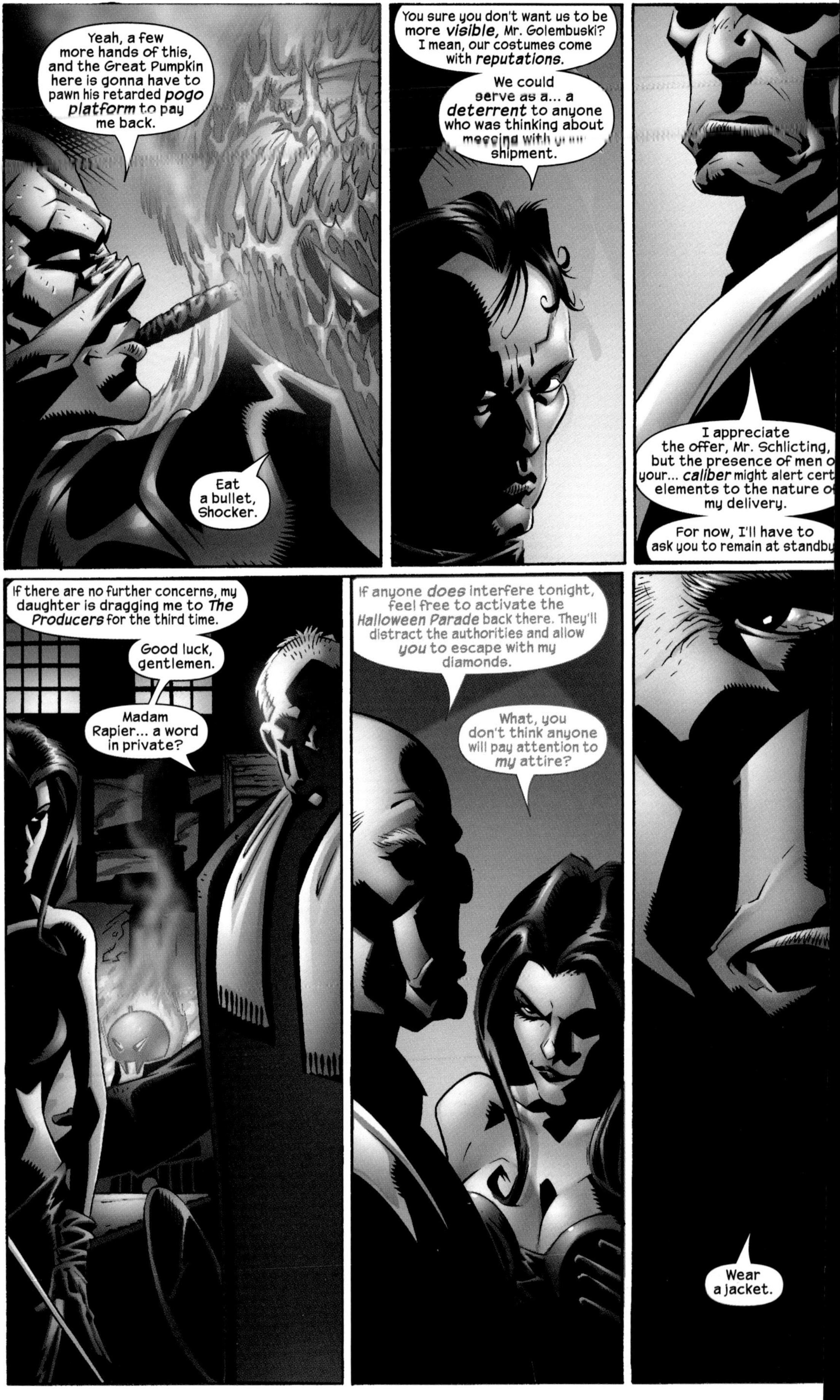
Yeah, a few more hands of this, and the Great Pumpkin here is gonna have to pawn his retarded *pogo platform* to pay me back.
Eat a bullet, Shocker.
You sure you don't want us to be more *visible*, Mr. Golembuski? I mean, our costumes come with *reputations*.
We could serve as a... a *deterrent* to anyone who was thinking about messing with
shipment.
I appreciate the offer, Mr. Schlicting, but the presence of men o your... *caliber* might alert cert elements to the nature o my delivery.
For now, I'll have to ask you to remain at standb
If there are no further concerns, my daughter is dragging me to *The Producers* for the third time.
Good luck, gentlemen.
Madam Rapier... a word in private?
If anyone *does* interfere tonight, feel free to activate the *Halloween Parade* back there. They'll distract the authorities and allow *you* to escape with my diamonds.
What, you don't think anyone will pay attention to *my* attire?
Wear a jacket.

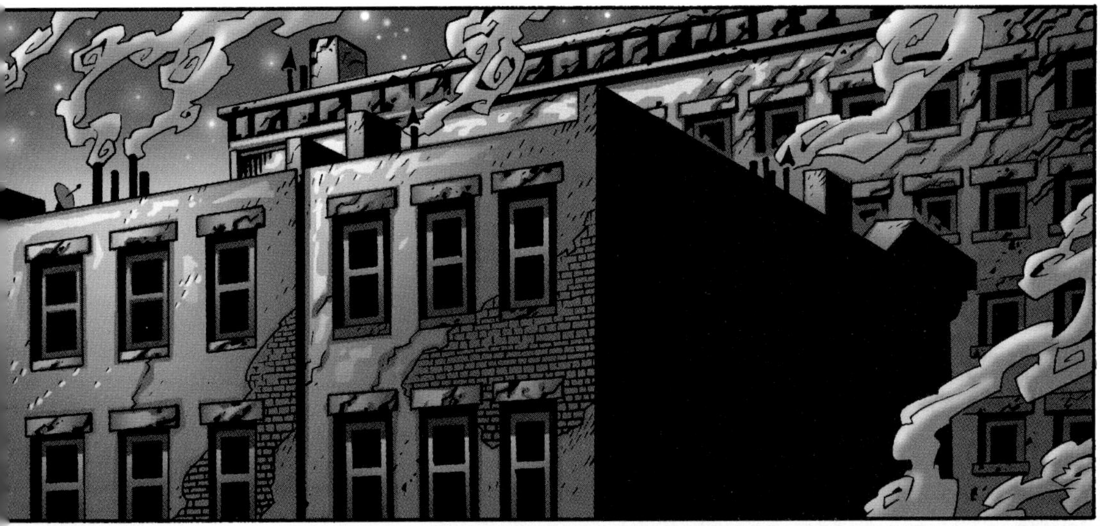

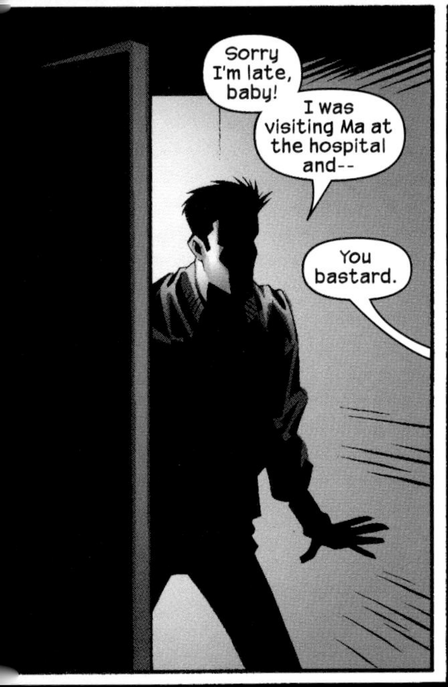

Sorry I'm late, baby!
I was visiting Ma at the hospital and--
You bastard.


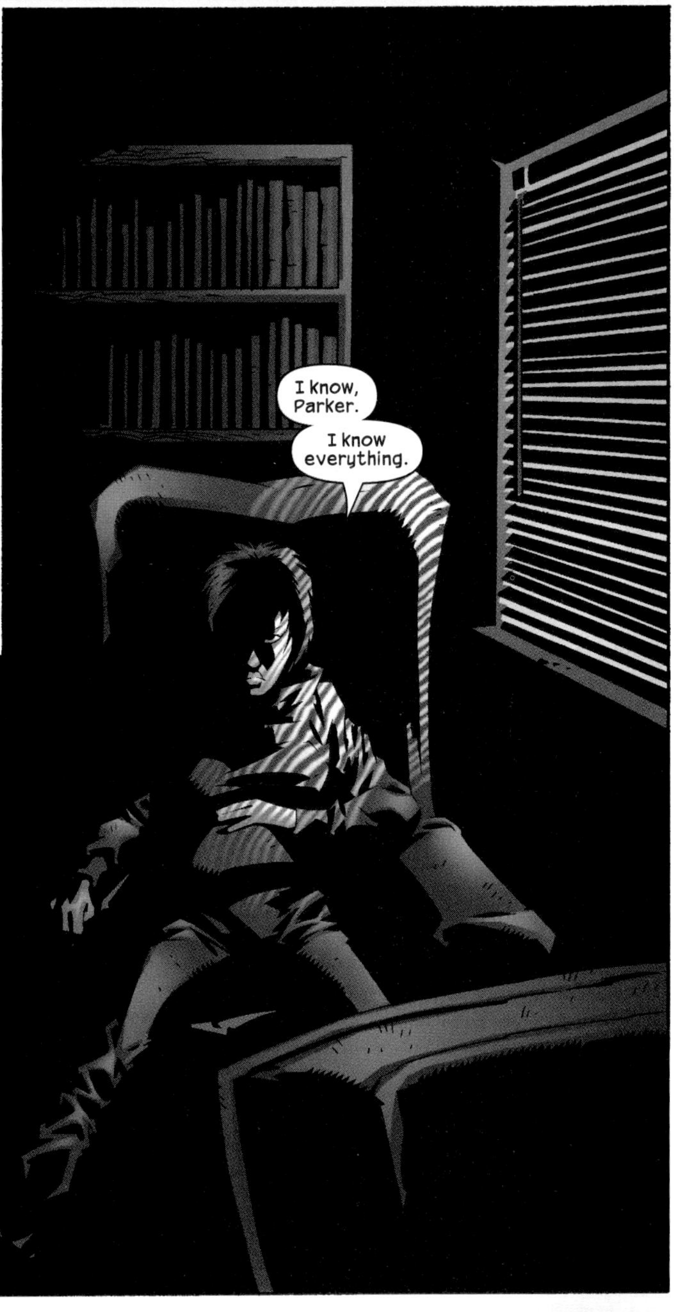

I know, Parker.
I know everything.

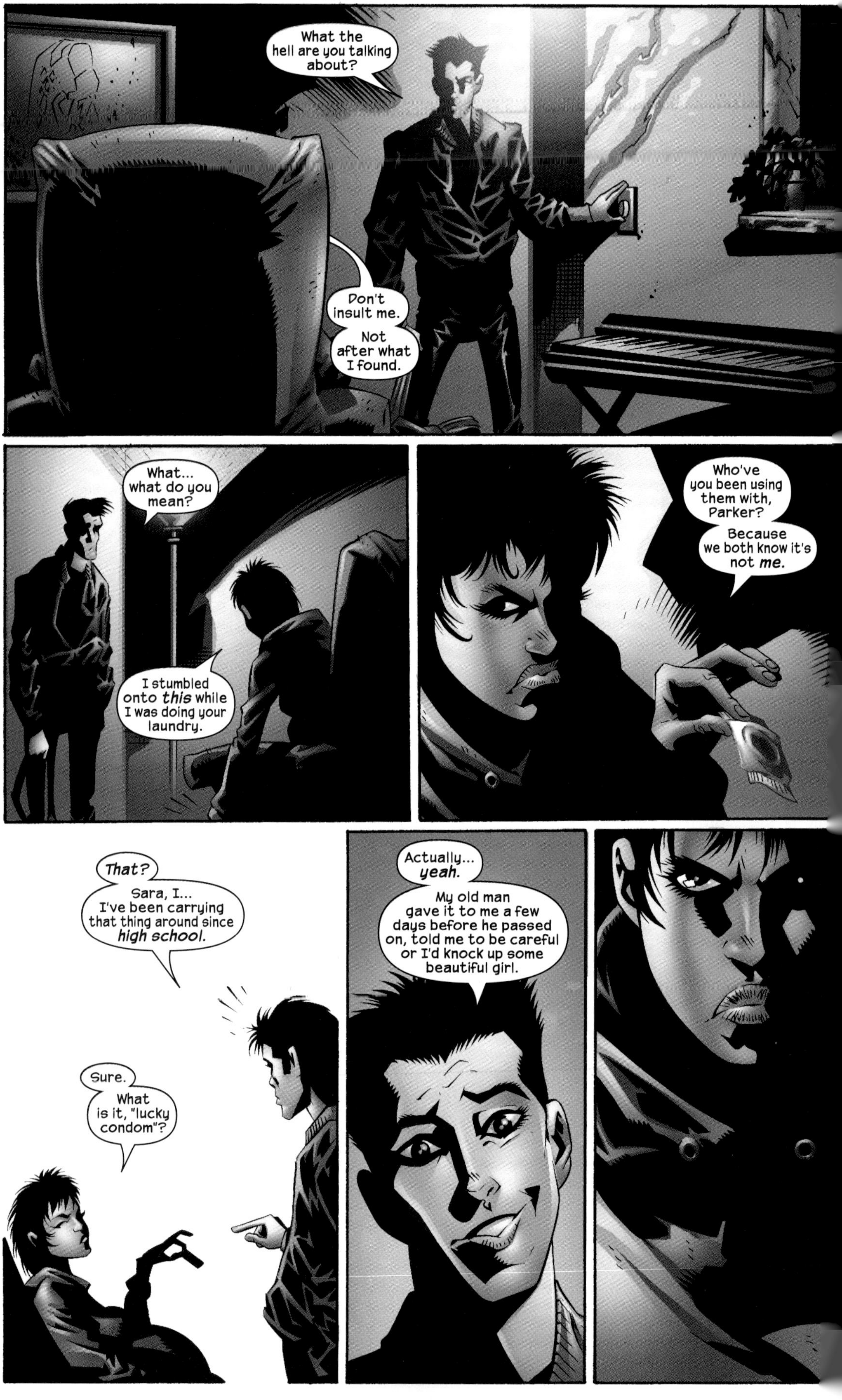

What the hell are you talking about?
Don't insult me.
Not after what I found.
What... what do you mean?
I stumbled onto *this* while I was doing your laundry.
Who've you been using them with, Parker?
Because we both know it's not *me*.
*That?*
Sara, I... I've been carrying that thing around since *high school*.
Sure.
What is it, "lucky condom"?
Actually... *yeah*.
My old man gave it to me a few days before he passed on, told me to be careful or I'd knock up some beautiful girl.

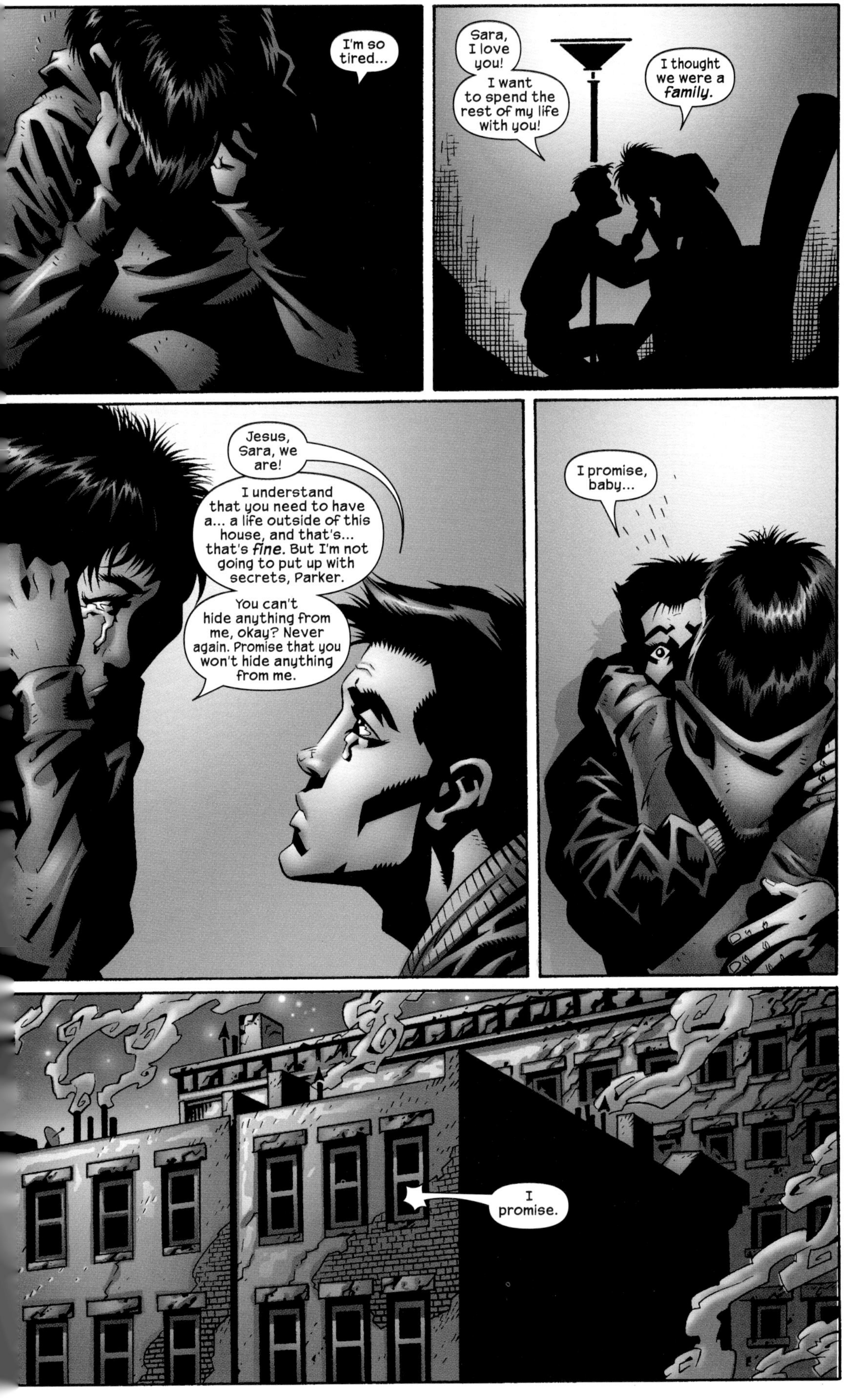
I'm so tired...
Sara, I love you!
I want to spend the rest of my life with you!
I thought we were a *family.*
Jesus, Sara, we are!
I understand that you need to have a... a life outside of this house, and that's... that's *fine.* But I'm not going to put up with secrets, Parker.
You can't hide anything from me, okay? Never again. Promise that you won't hide anything from me.
I promise, baby...
I promise.

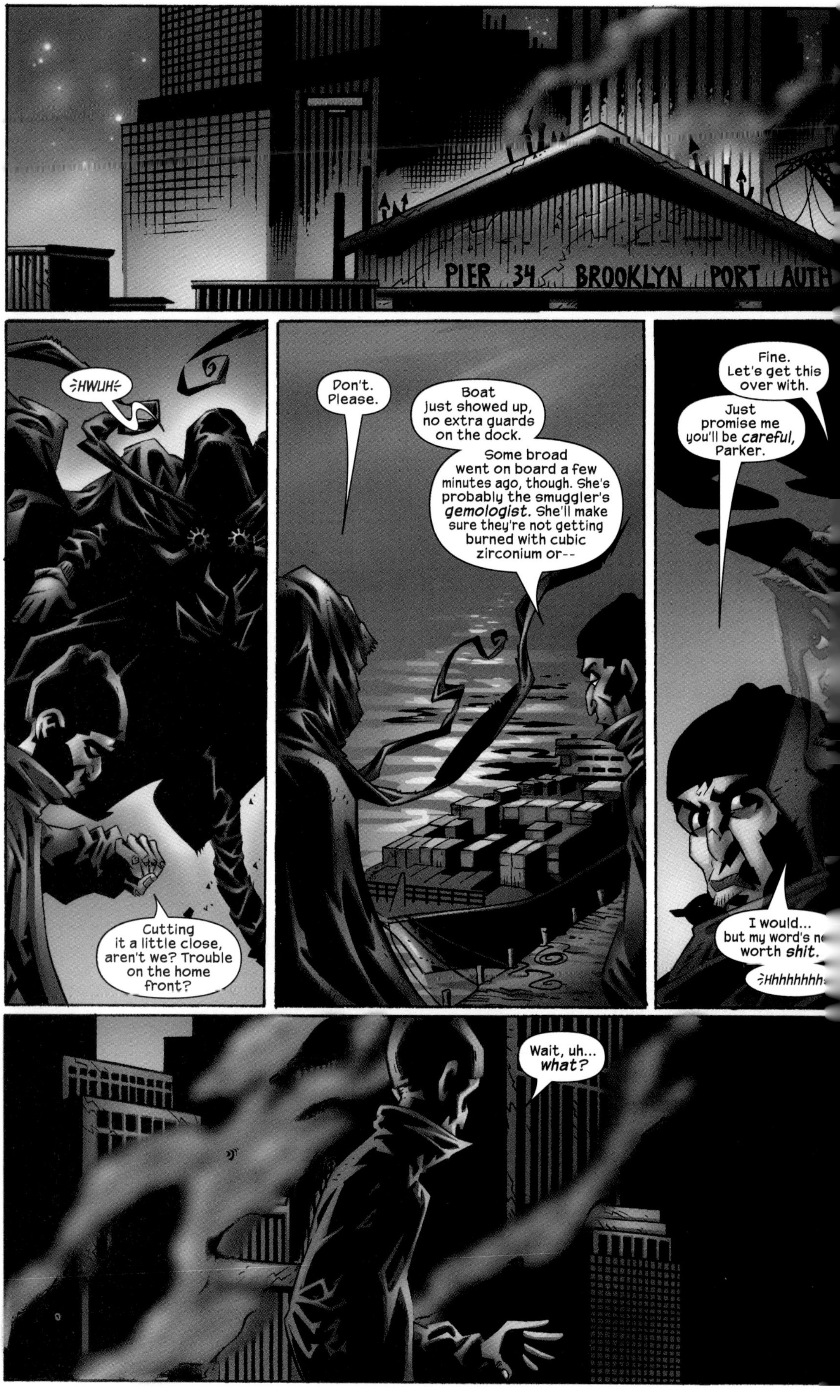
PIER 34 BROOKLYN PORT AUTH
HWUH
Cutting it a little close, aren't we? Trouble on the home front?
Don't. Please.
Boat just showed up, no extra guards on the dock.
Some broad went on board a few minutes ago, though. She's probably the smuggler's *gemologist.* She'll make sure they're not getting burned with cubic zirconium or--
Fine. Let's get this over with.
Just promise me you'll be *careful,* Parker.
I would... but my word's n worth *shit.*
Hhhhhhhh
Wait, uh... *what?*

That's all of it?

Yes, ma'am. Ninety-four carats in two unmarked pouches, as agreed.

Please, I owe your employer my *life*, and I would be honored to personally escort his jewels to their final destination.

Thank you, Captain, but I'm pretty sure I can handle it from here.

Just let me--

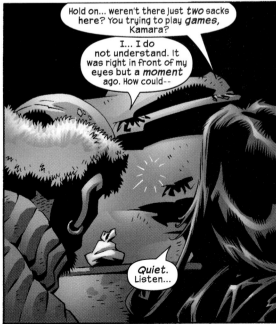

Hold on... weren't there just *two* sacks here? You trying to play *games*, Kamara?

I... I do not understand. It was right in front of my eyes but a *moment* ago. How could--

*Quiet.* Listen...

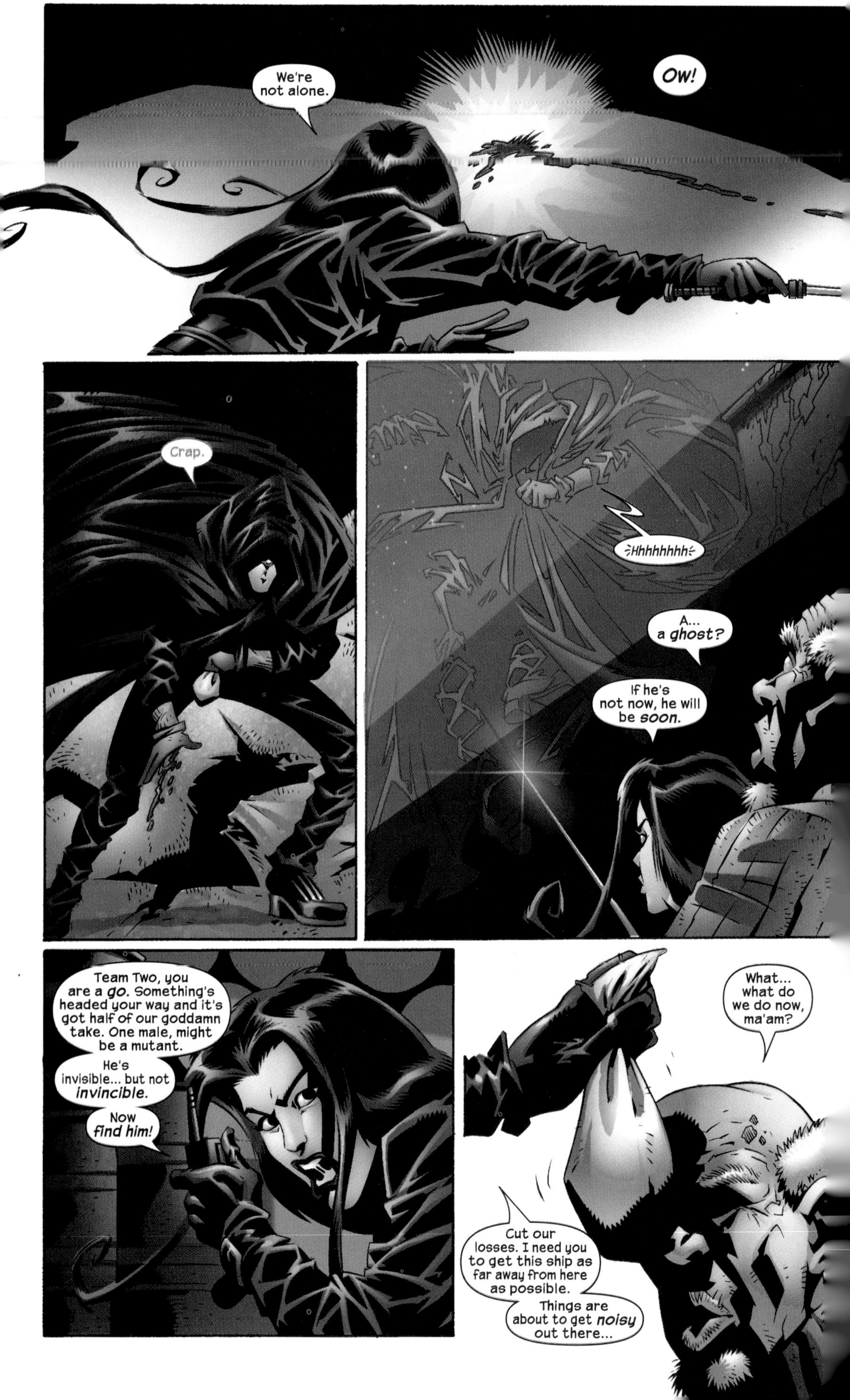
We're not alone.
Ow!
Crap.
Hhhhhhhh
A... a ghost?
If he's not now, he will be soon.
Team Two, you are a go. Something's headed your way and it's got half of our goddamn take. One male, might be a mutant.
He's invisible... but not invincible.
Now find him!
What... what do we do now, ma'am?
Cut our losses. I need you to get this ship as far away from here as possible.
Things are about to get noisy out there...

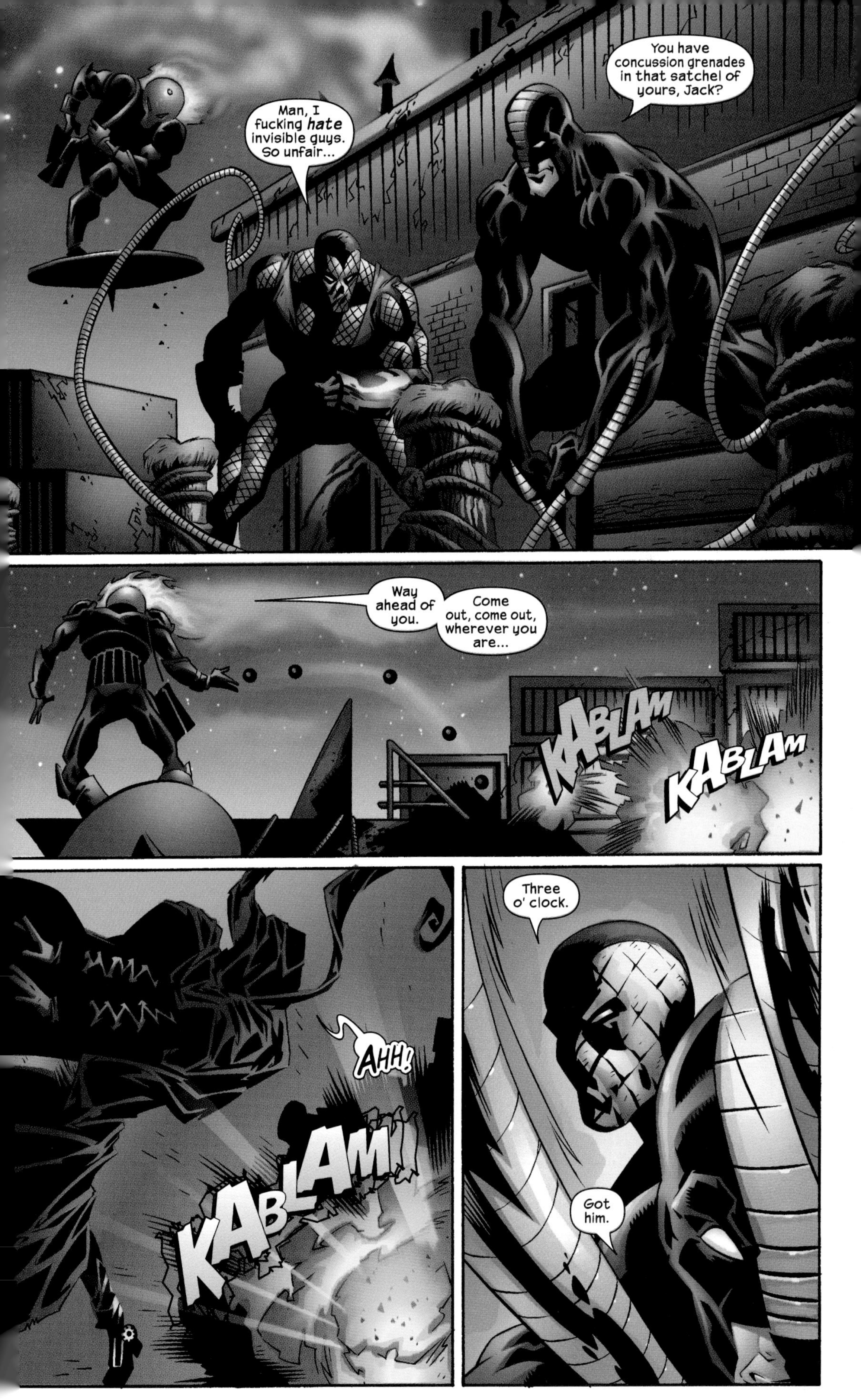

Man, I fucking *hate* invisible guys. So unfair...
You have concussion grenades in that satchel of yours, Jack?
Way ahead of you.
Come out, come out, wherever you are...
KABLAM
KABLAM
AHH!
KABLAM!
Three o' clock.
Got him.

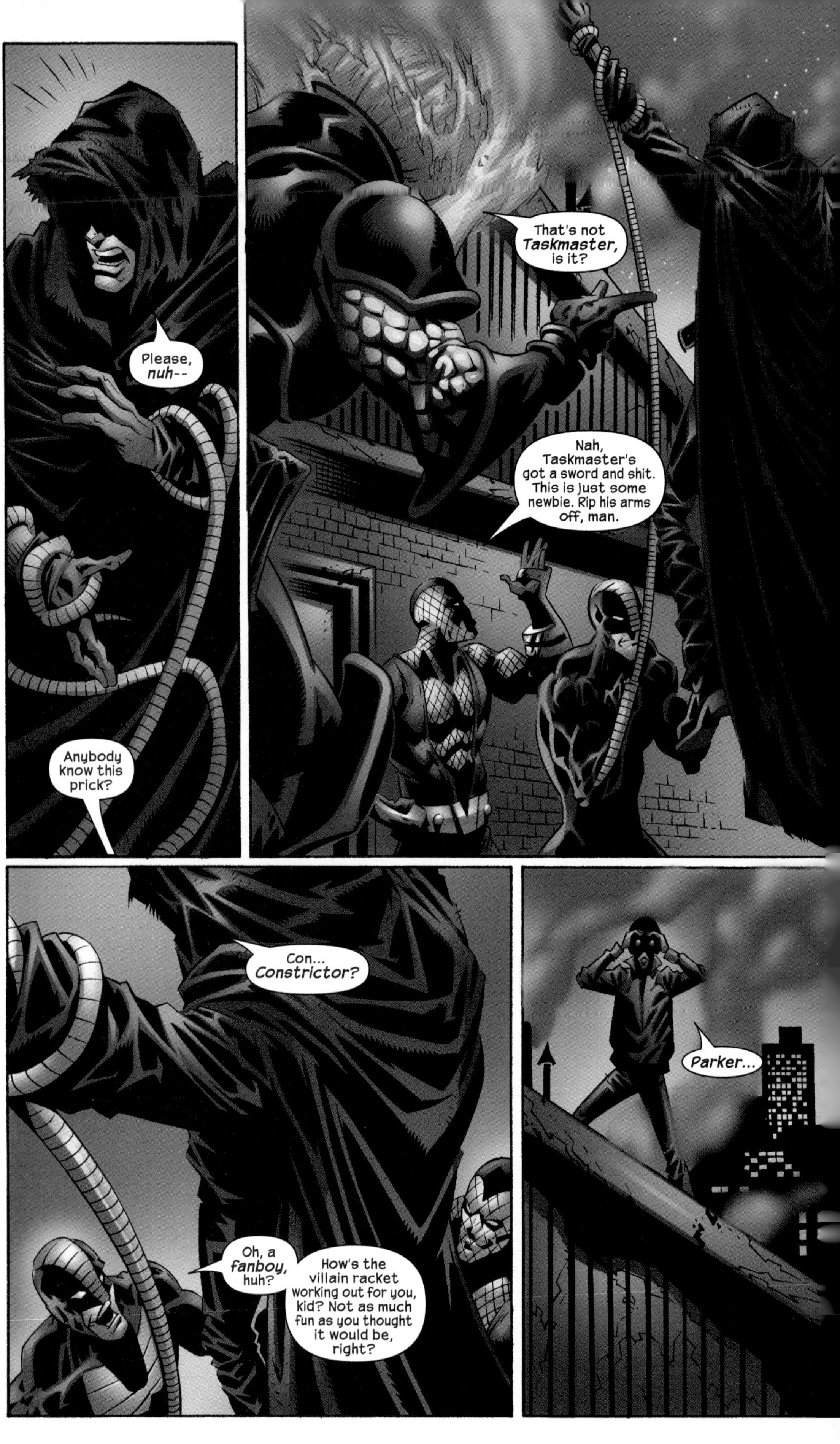
Please, *nuh*--
Anybody know this prick?
That's not *Taskmaster,* is it?
Nah, Taskmaster's got a sword and shit. This is just some newbie. Rip his arms off, man.
Con... *Constrictor?*
Oh, a *fanboy,* huh?
How's the villain racket working out for you, kid? Not as much fun as you thought it would be, right?
*Parker...*

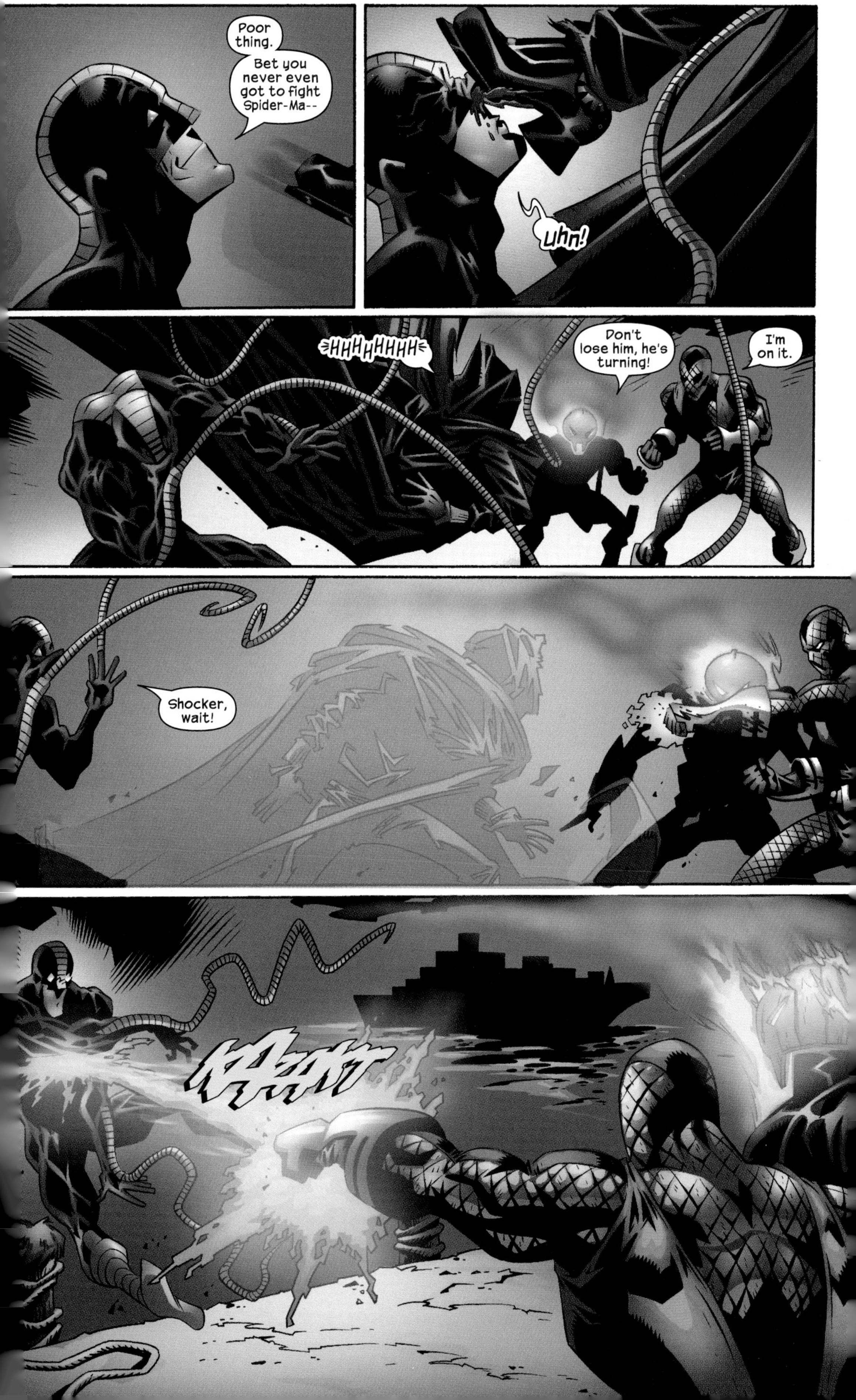
Poor thing.
Bet you never even got to fight Spider-Ma--
Uhn!
HHHHHHHHH
Don't lose him, he's turning!
I'm on it.
Shocker, wait!
KRAKKT

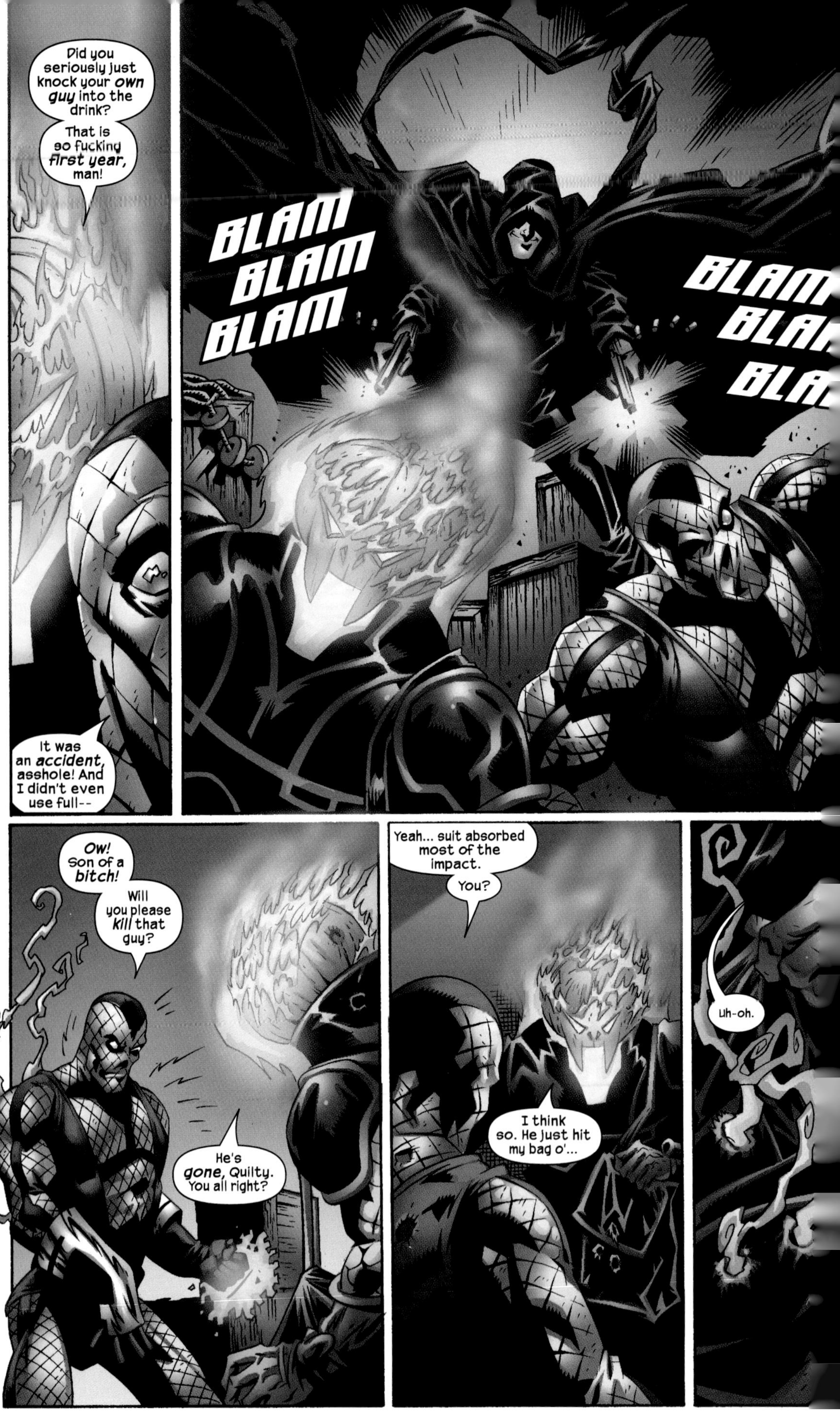
Did you seriously just knock your *own guy* into the drink?
That is so fucking *first year,* man!
It was an *accident,* asshole! And I didn't even use full--
BLAM BLAM BLAM
BLAM BLA BLA
*Ow!* Son of a *bitch!*
Will you please *kill* that guy?
He's *gone,* Quilty. You all right?
Yeah... suit absorbed most of the impact.
You?
I think so. He just hit my bag o'...
Uh-oh.

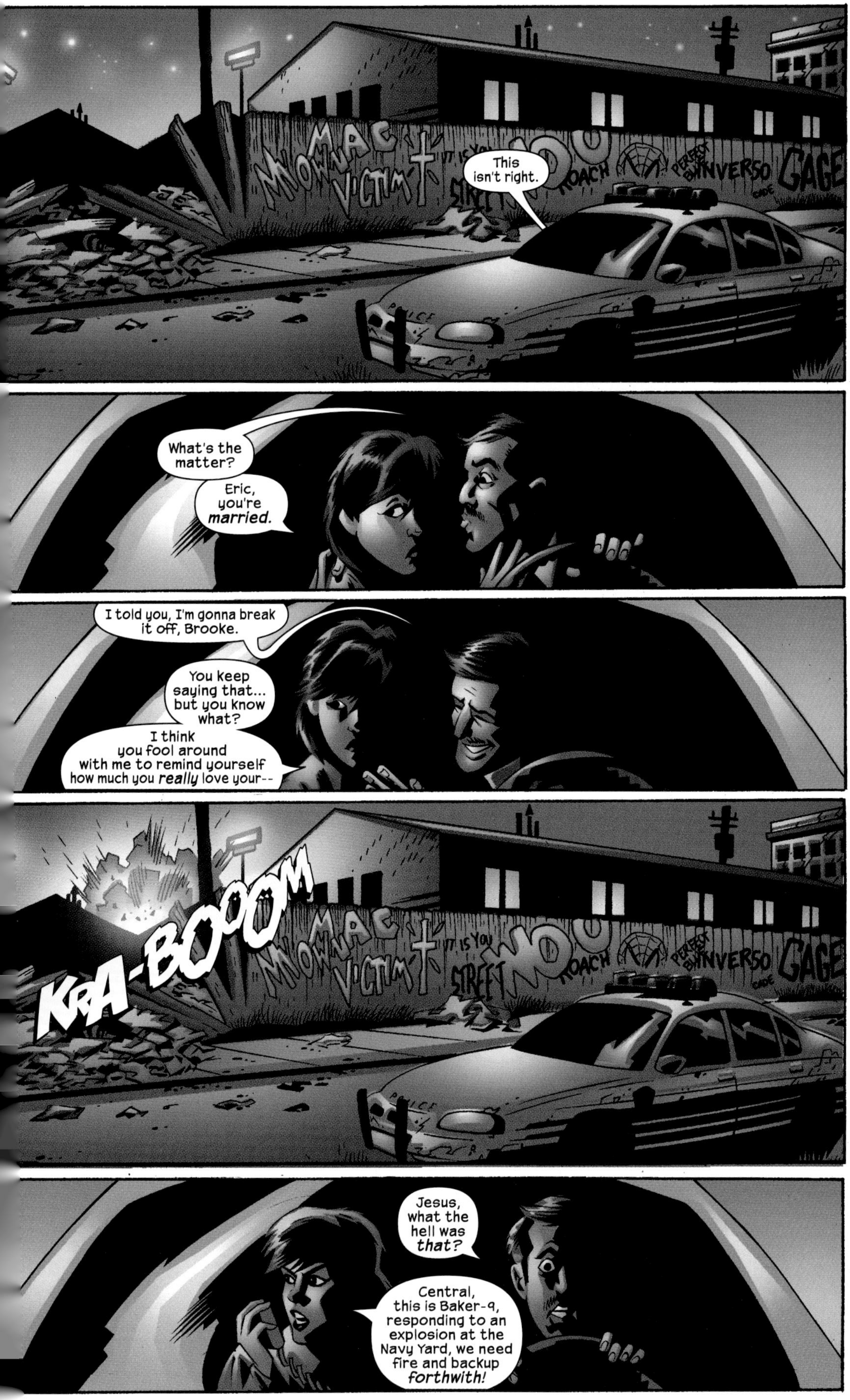

This isn't right.
What's the matter?
Eric, you're *married.*
I told you, I'm gonna break it off, Brooke.
You keep saying that... but you know what?
I think you fool around with me to remind yourself how much you *really* love your--
KRA-BOOOM
Jesus, what the hell was *that?*
Central, this is Baker-9, responding to an explosion at the Navy Yard, we need fire and backup *forthwith!*

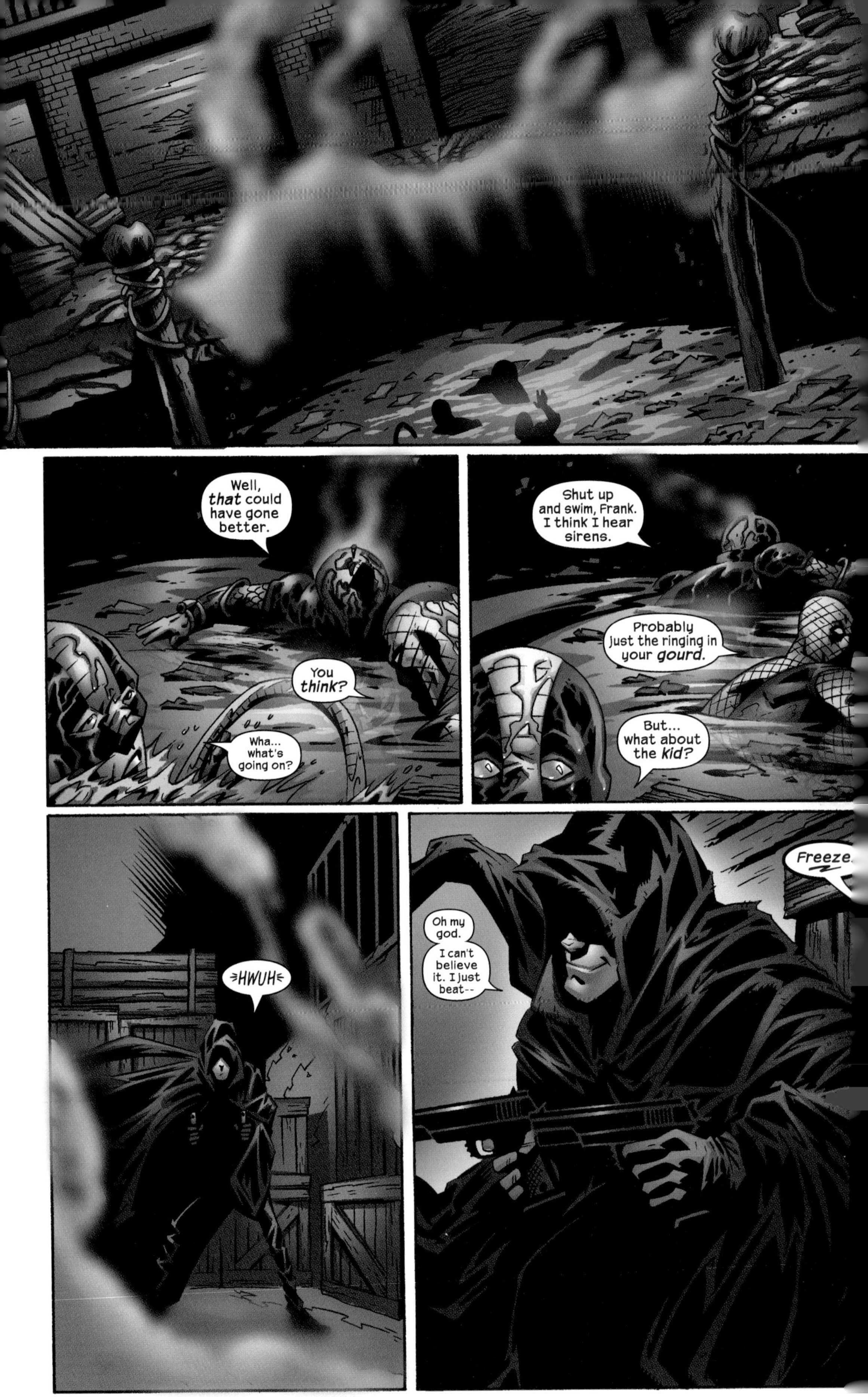
Well, that could have gone better.
You think?
Wha... what's going on?
Shut up and swim, Frank. I think I hear sirens.
Probably just the ringing in your gourd.
But... what about the kid?
HWUH
Freeze.
Oh my god.
I can't believe it. I just beat--

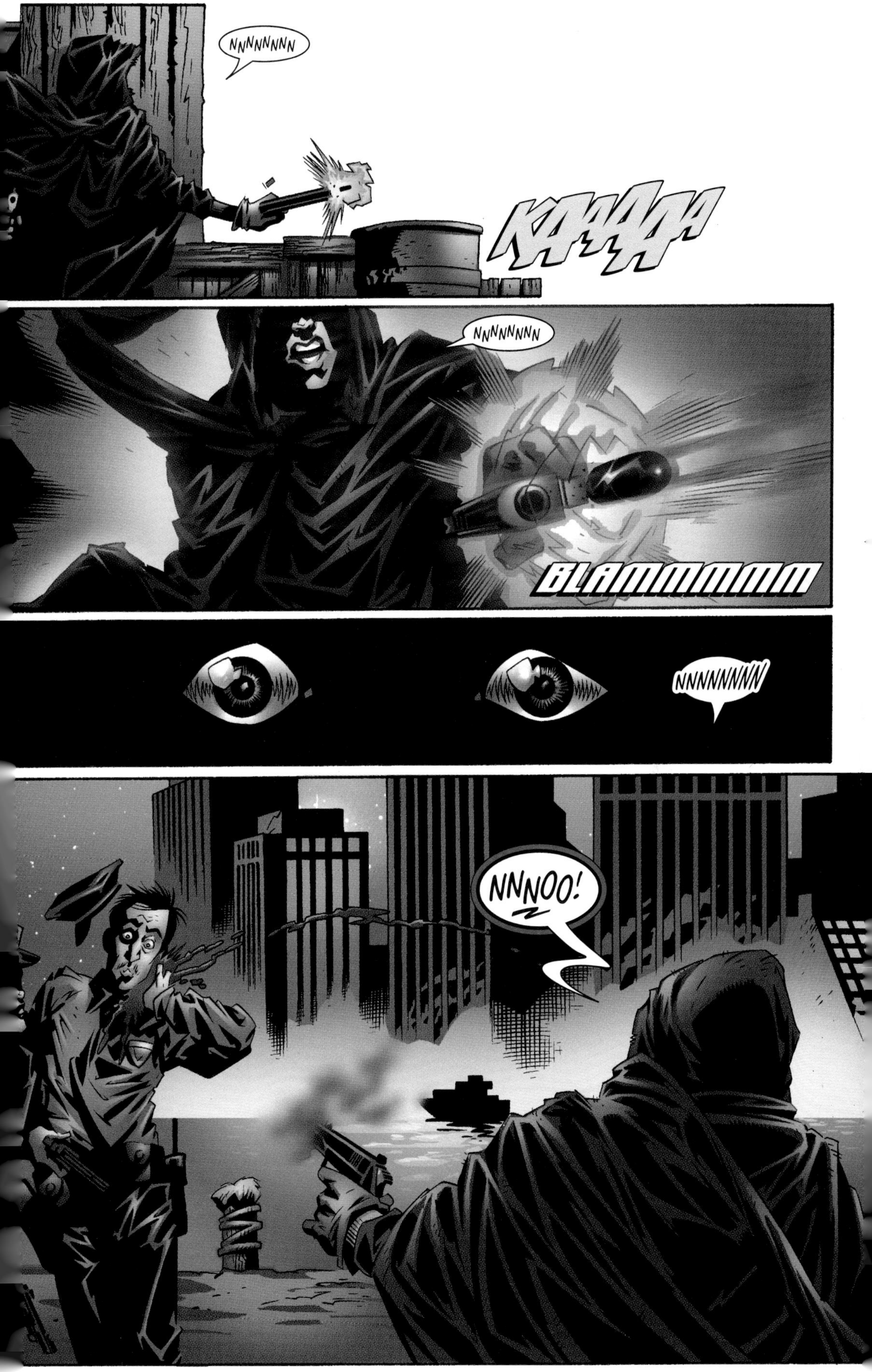
NNNNNNN
KAAAAA
NNNNNNN
BLAMMMMMM
NNNNNNN
NNNOO!

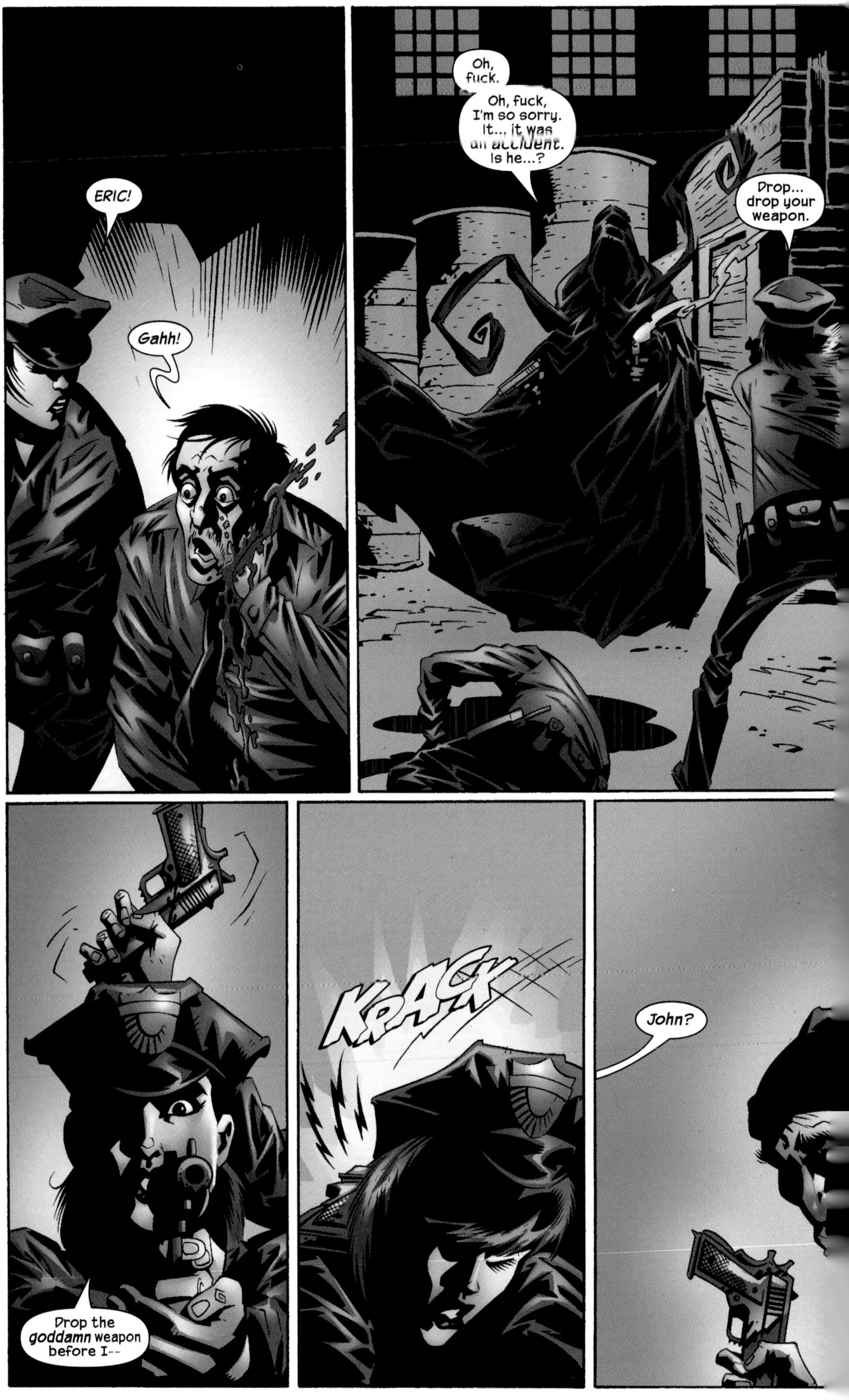
ERIC!
Gahh!
Oh, fuck.
Oh, fuck, I'm so sorry. It... it was an accident. Is he...?
Drop... drop your weapon.
Drop the goddamn weapon before I--
KRACK
John?

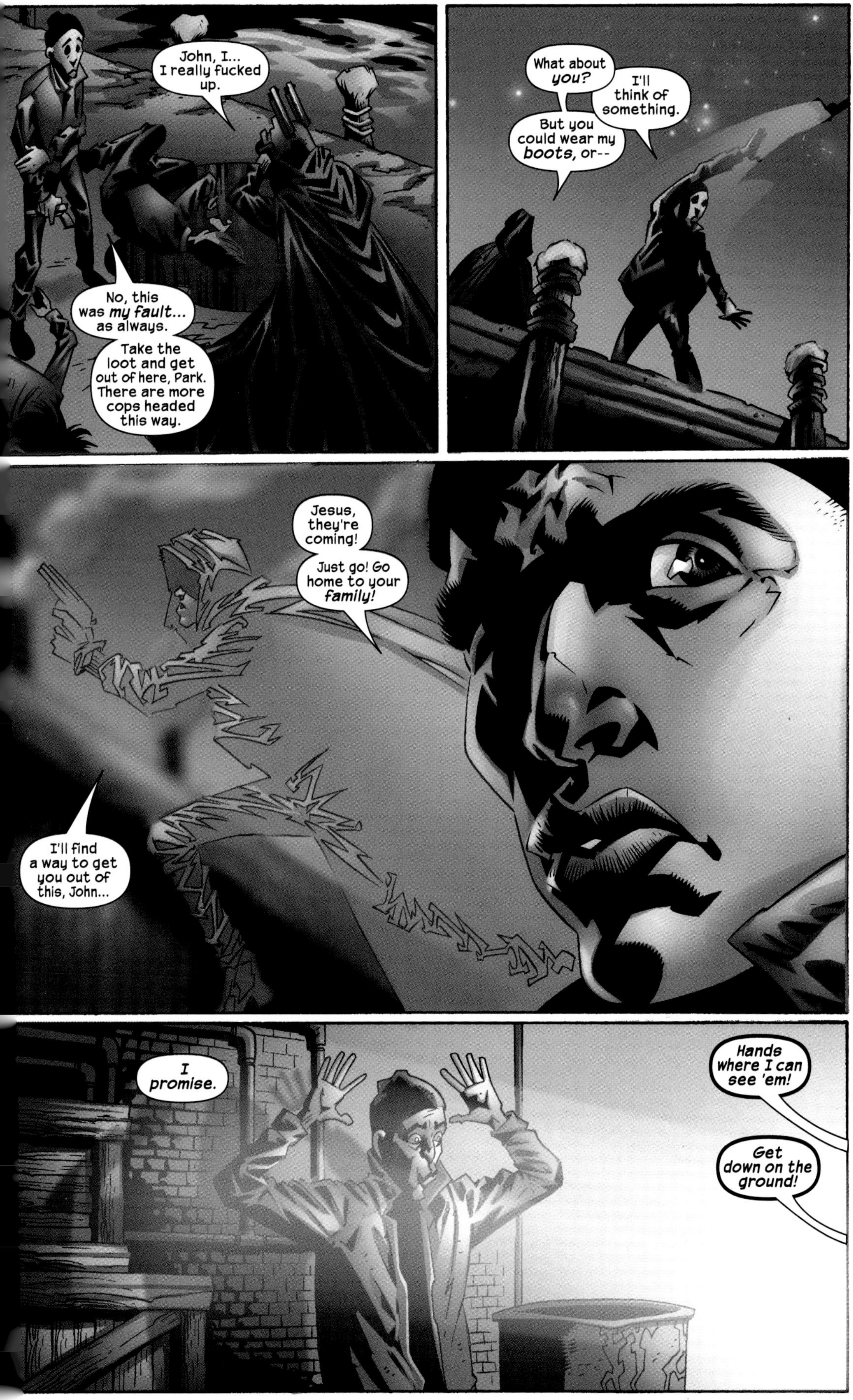
John, I... I really fucked up.
No, this was my fault... as always.
Take the loot and get out of here, Park. There are more cops headed this way.
What about you?
But you could wear my boots, or--
I'll think of something.
Jesus, they're coming!
Just go! Go home to your family!
I'll find a way to get you out of this, John...
I promise.
Hands where I can see 'em!
Get down on the ground!

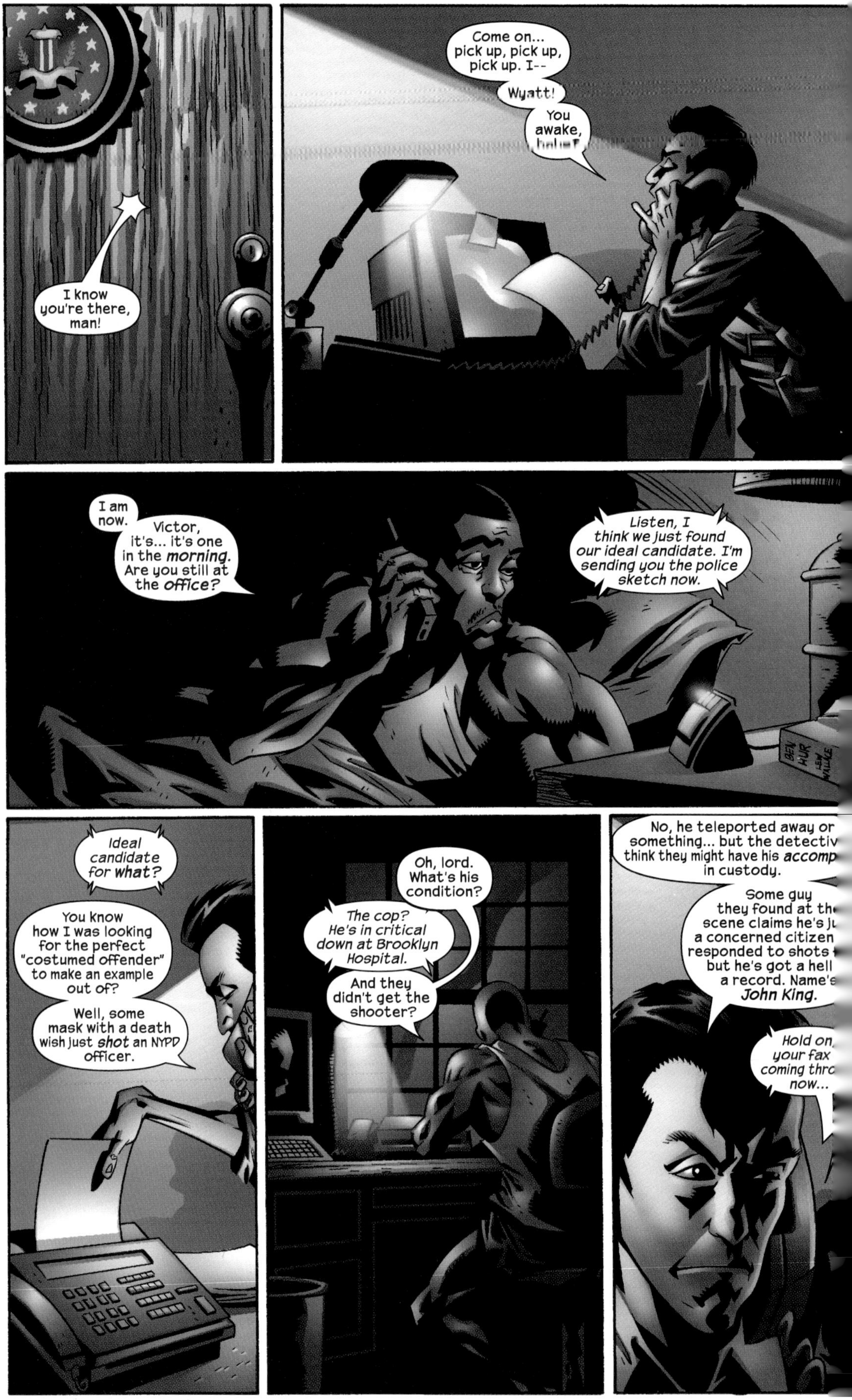

I know you're there, man!
Come on... pick up, pick up, pick up. I--
Wyatt!
You awake,
I am now.
Victor, it's... it's one in the *morning*. Are you still at the *office*?
Listen, I think we just found our ideal candidate. I'm sending you the police sketch now.
Ideal candidate for *what*?
You know how I was looking for the perfect "costumed offender" to make an example out of?
Well, some mask with a death wish just *shot* an NYPD officer.
Oh, lord. What's his condition?
The cop? He's in critical down at Brooklyn Hospital.
And they didn't get the shooter?
No, he teleported away or something... but the detectiv think they might have his accomp in custody.
Some guy they found at th scene claims he's j a concerned citizen responded to shots but he's got a hell a record. Name's *John King*.
Hold on your fax coming thr now...

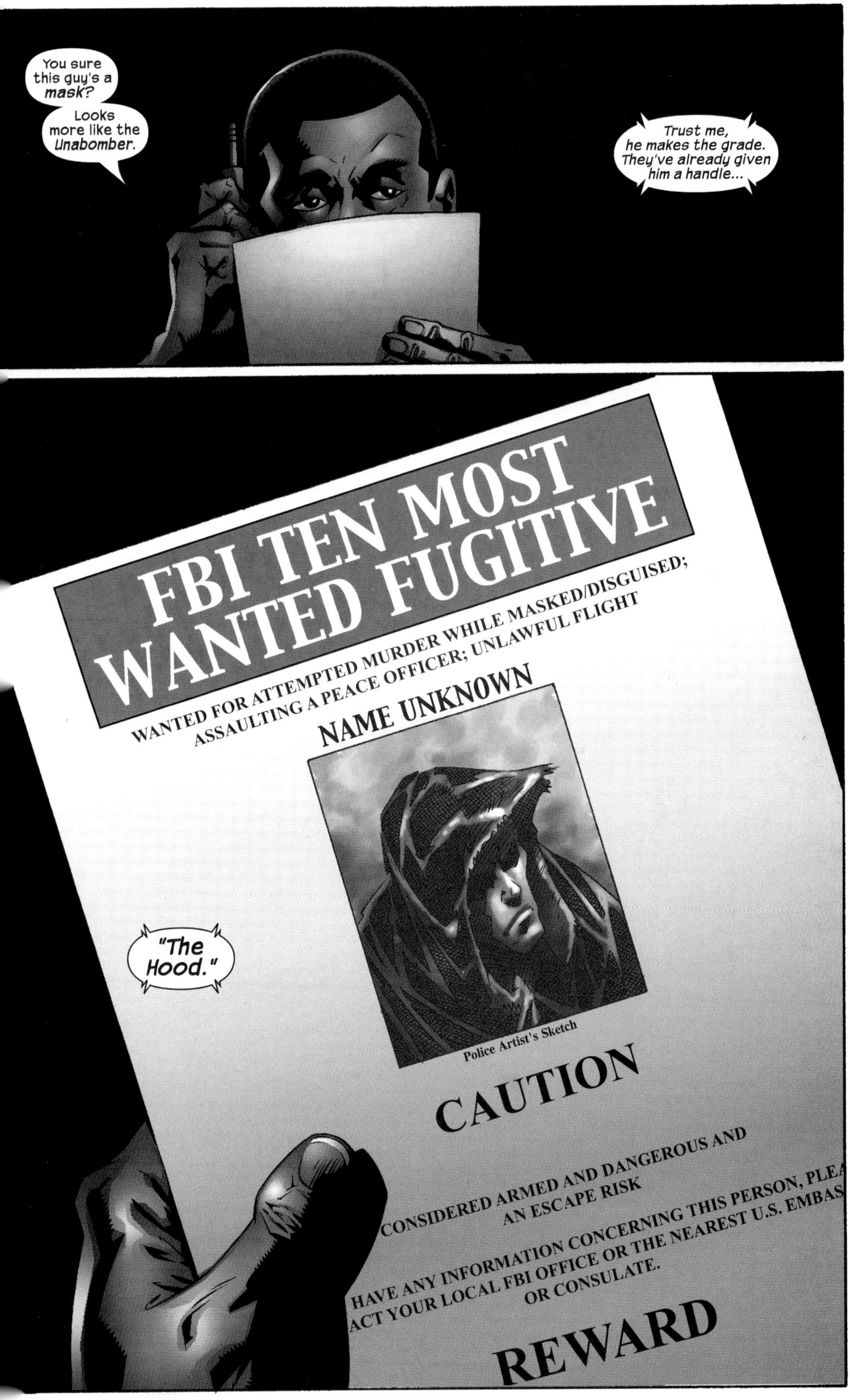
You sure this guy's a *mask*?
Looks more like the *Unabomber*.
Trust me, he makes the grade. They've already given him a handle...
FBI TEN MOST WANTED FUGITIVE
WANTED FOR ATTEMPTED MURDER WHILE MASKED/DISGUISED; ASSAULTING A PEACE OFFICER; UNLAWFUL FLIGHT
NAME UNKNOWN
Police Artist's Sketch
CAUTION
CONSIDERED ARMED AND DANGEROUS AND AN ESCAPE RISK
HAVE ANY INFORMATION CONCERNING THIS PERSON, PLEA
ACT YOUR LOCAL FBI OFFICE OR THE NEAREST U.S. EMBAS
OR CONSULATE.
REWARD
"The Hood."

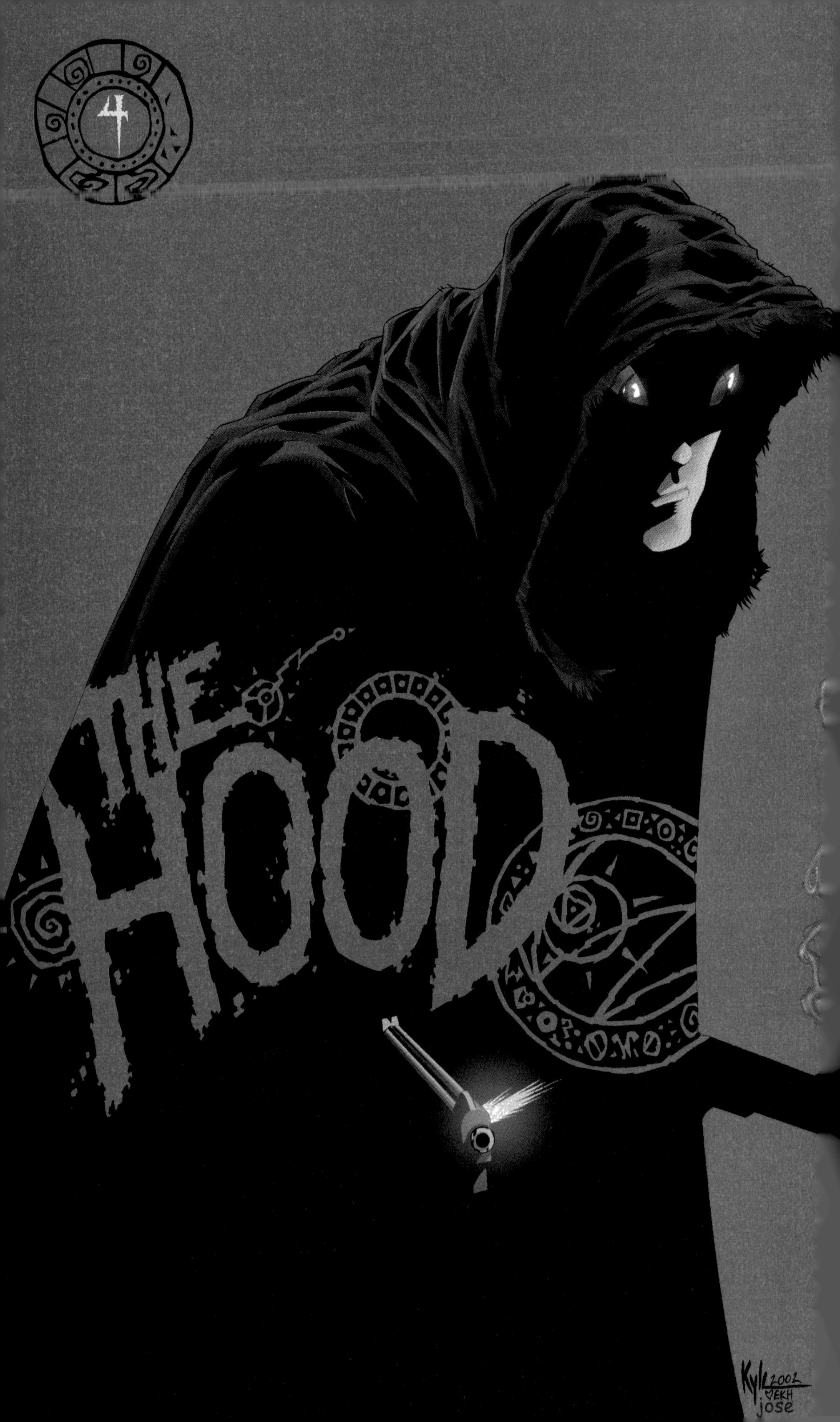
4
THE HOOD

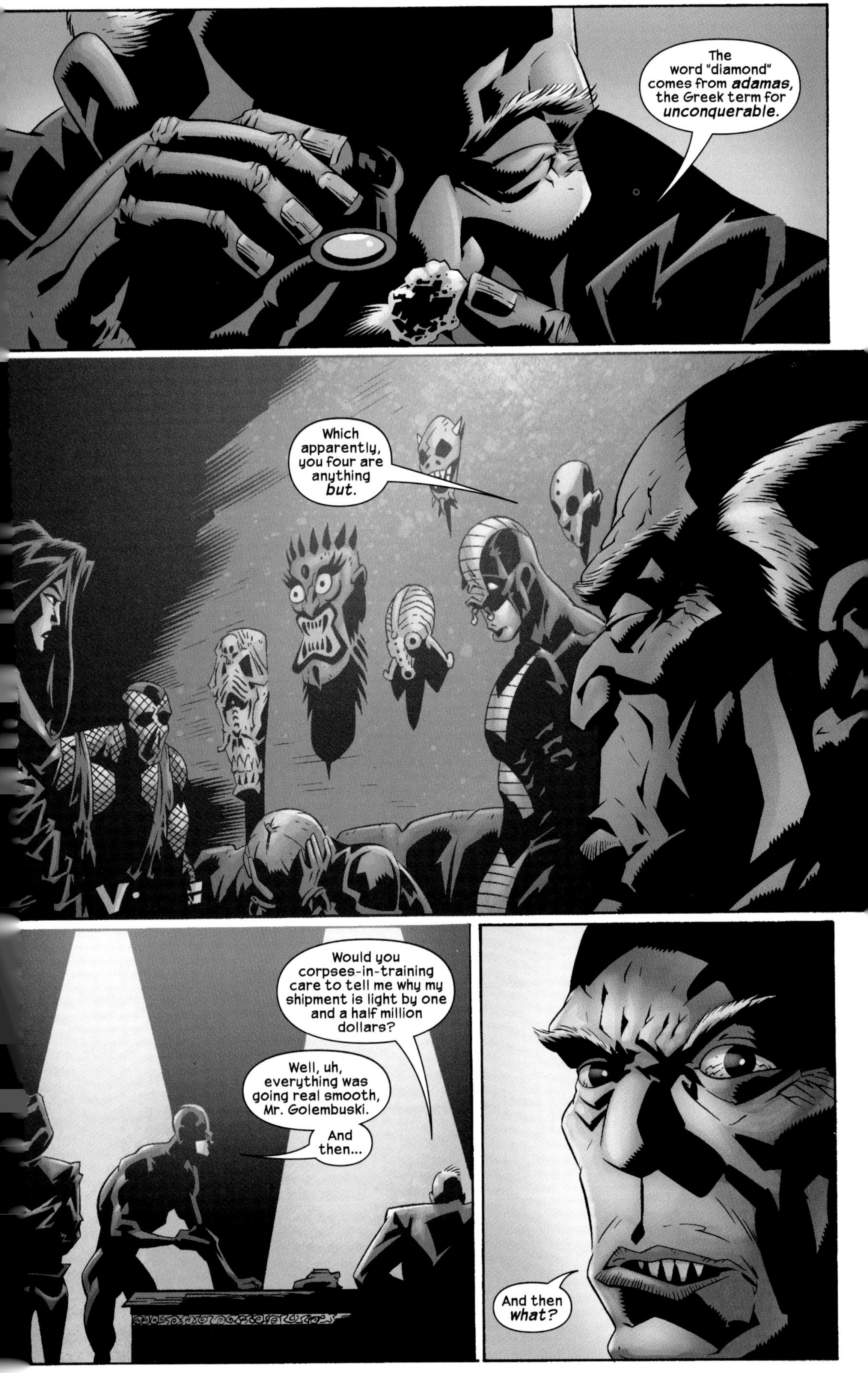
The word "diamond" comes from *adamas*, the Greek term for *unconquerable.*
Which apparently, you four are anything *but.*
Would you corpses-in-training care to tell me why my shipment is light by one and a half million dollars?
Well, uh, everything was going real smooth, Mr. Golembuski.
And then...
And then *what?*

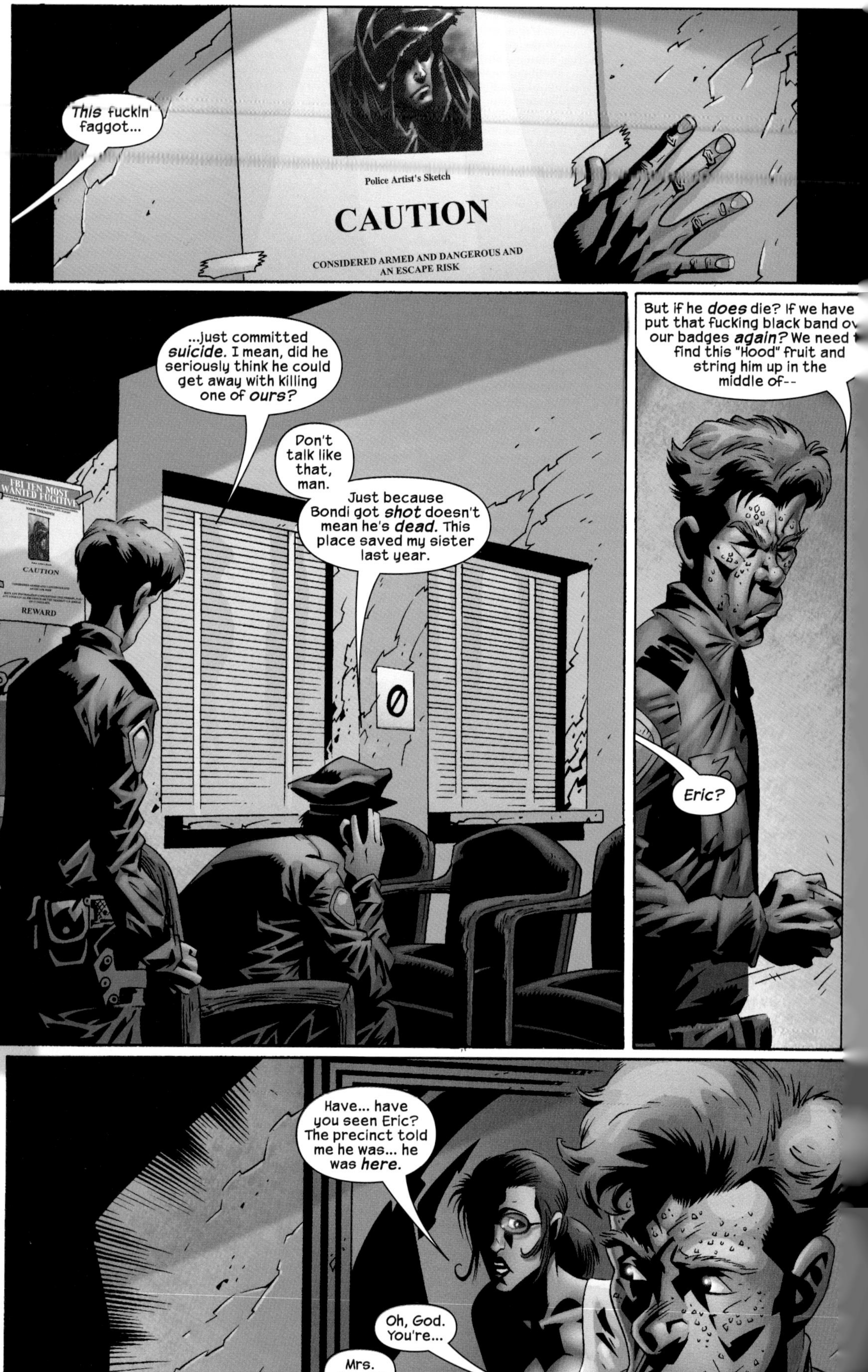
This fuckin' faggot...
Police Artist's Sketch
CAUTION
CONSIDERED ARMED AND DANGEROUS AND AN ESCAPE RISK
...just committed suicide. I mean, did he seriously think he could get away with killing one of ours?
FBI TEN MOST WANTED FUGITIVE
CAUTION
REWARD
Don't talk like that, man.
Just because Bondi got shot doesn't mean he's dead. This place saved my sister last year.
But if he does die? If we have put that fucking black band ov our badges again? We need t find this "Hood" fruit and string him up in the middle of--
Eric?
Have... have you seen Eric? The precinct told me he was... he was here.
Oh, God. You're...
Mrs. Bondi?

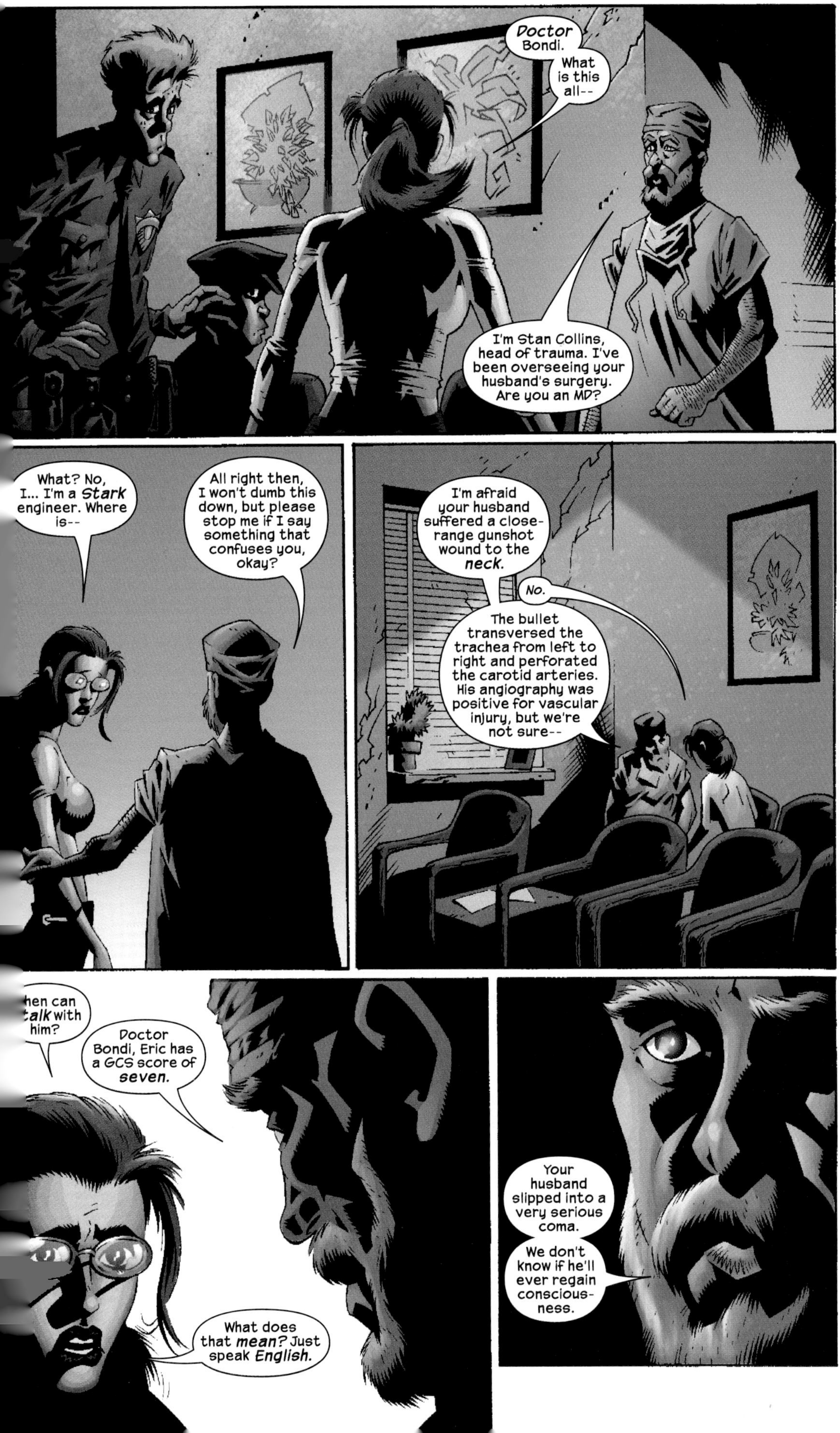
Doctor Bondi.
What is this all--
I'm Stan Collins, head of trauma. I've been overseeing your husband's surgery. Are you an MD?
What? No, I... I'm a Stark engineer. Where is--
All right then, I won't dumb this down, but please stop me if I say something that confuses you, okay?
I'm afraid your husband suffered a close-range gunshot wound to the neck.
No.
The bullet transversed the trachea from left to right and perforated the carotid arteries. His angiography was positive for vascular injury, but we're not sure--
hen can talk with him?
Doctor Bondi, Eric has a GCS score of seven.
What does that mean? Just speak English.
Your husband slipped into a very serious coma.
We don't know if he'll ever regain conscious-ness.

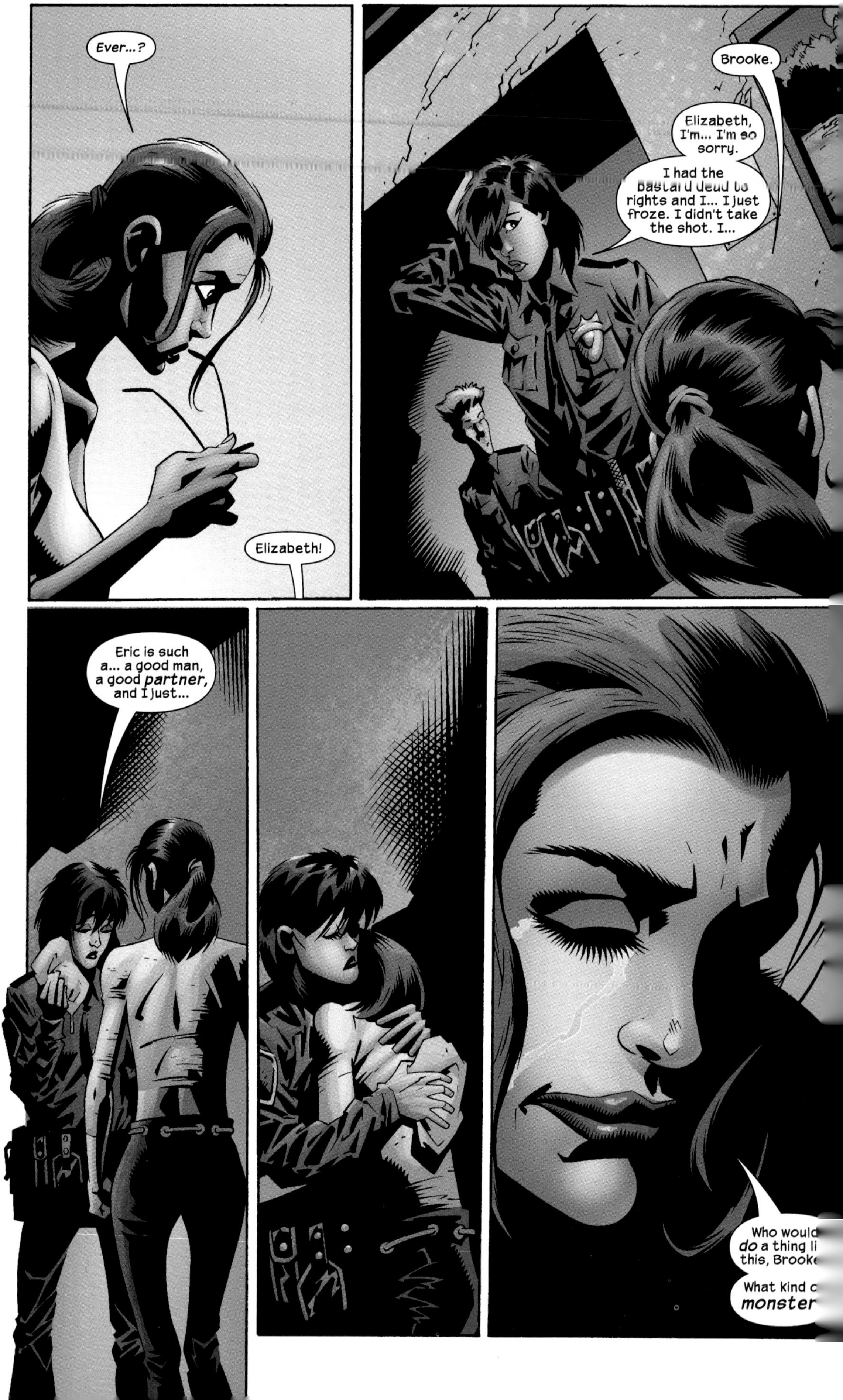
Ever...?
Elizabeth!
Brooke.
Elizabeth, I'm... I'm so sorry.
I had the bastard dead to rights and I... I just froze. I didn't take the shot. I...
Eric is such a... a good man, a good *partner*, and I just...
Who would *do* a thing li this, Brooke
What kind c *monster*

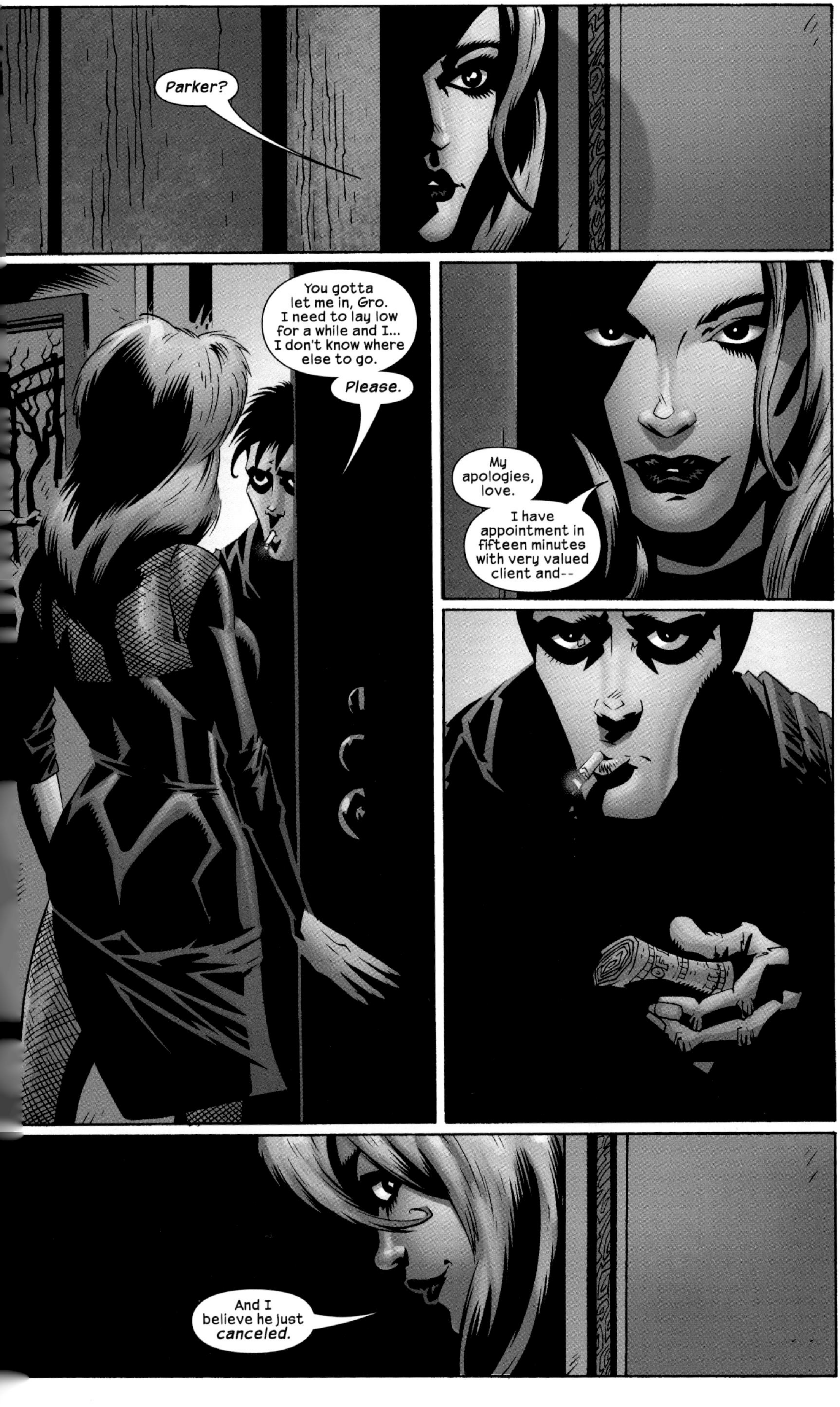

Parker?
You gotta let me in, Gro. I need to lay low for a while and I... I don't know where else to go.
Please.
My apologies, love.
I have appointment in fifteen minutes with very valued client and--
And I believe he just canceled.

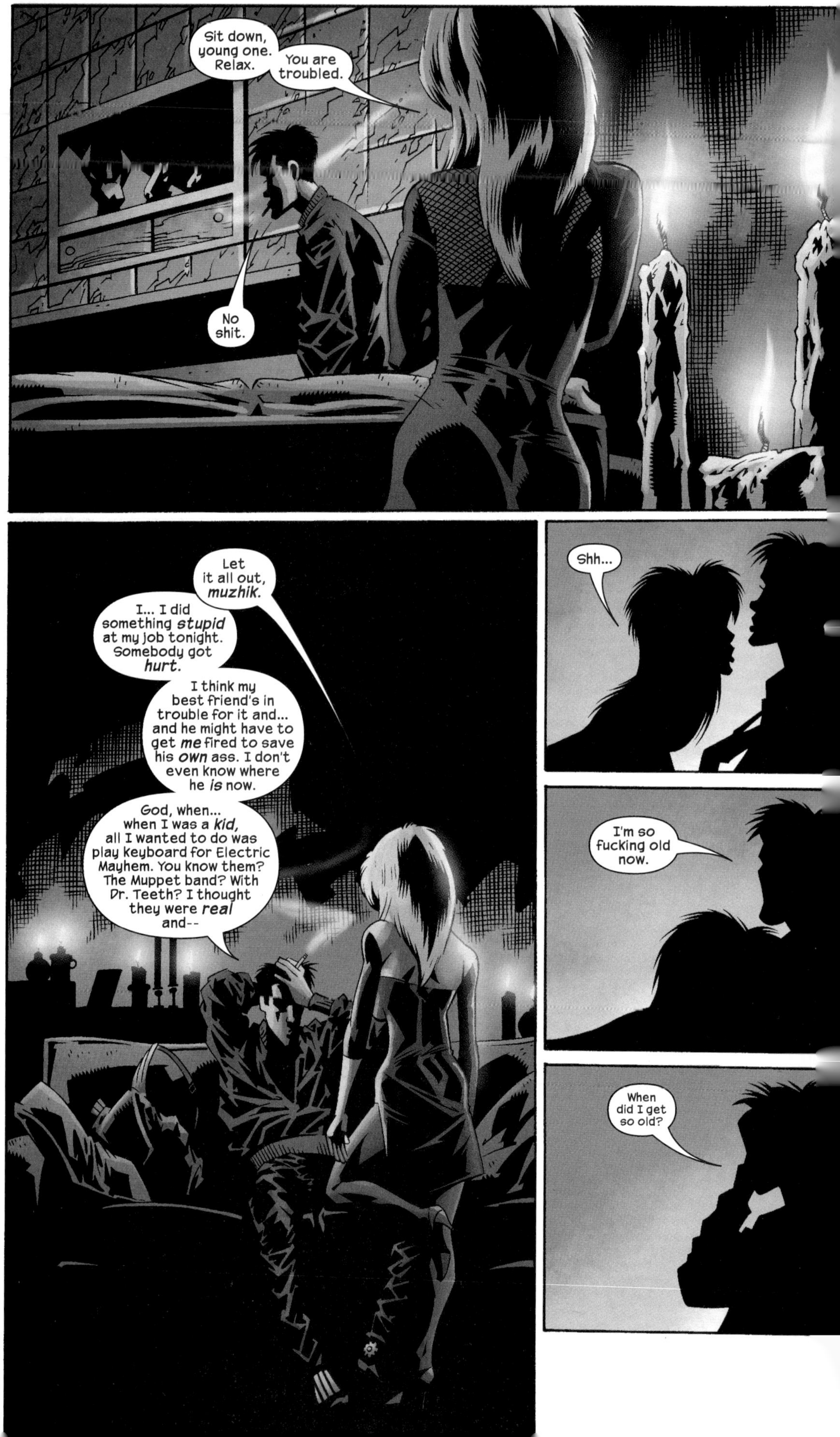
Sit down, young one. Relax.
You are troubled.
No shit.
Let it all out, *muzhik.*
I... I did something *stupid* at my job tonight. Somebody got *hurt*.
I think my best friend's in trouble for it and... and he might have to get *me* fired to save his *own* ass. I don't even know where he *is* now.
God, when... when I was a *kid*, all I wanted to do was play keyboard for Electric Mayhem. You know them? The Muppet band? With Dr. Teeth? I thought they were *real* and--
Shh...
I'm so fucking old now.
When did I get so old?

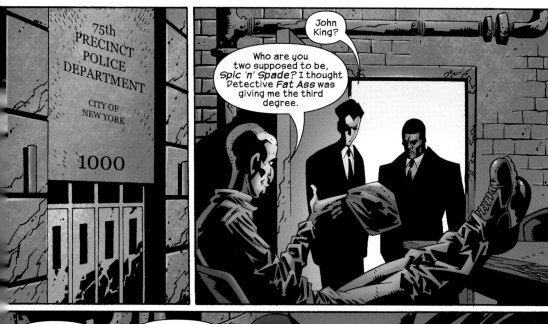

75th
PRECINCT
POLICE
DEPARTMENT

CITY OF
NEW YORK

1000

John King?

Who are you two supposed to be, *Spic 'n' Spade?* I thought Detective *Fat Ass* was giving me the third degree.

Hey, you guys ever wondered if there's a *second degree?* I'm in a bit of a hurry, so maybe you could just gimme the *first de--*

We're not here to interrogate you, Mr. King.

My name is Special Agent Victor Infante. This is my partner, Wyatt Sobel.

BI?

But... but I'm just a *witness.* What the hell do the feds want with *me?*

To *charge* you...

...with the murder of Officer Eric Bondi.

**What?**

Yeah, doesn't sound like that cop you shot is gonna make it.

You have the right to remain silent...

Wait! I didn't shoot *anybody!* For the ten-thousandth time, I saw some nut-case wearing a *hood* do it.

How do we know *you're* not that nutcase?

What do you mean, how do you know? I wasn't wearing the fucking *costume!*

Maybe you ditched it.

That's *bullshit.*

Then what wer you doing at the crime scene?

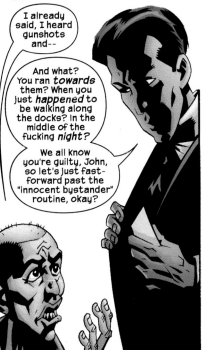

I already said, I heard gunshots and--

And what? You ran *towards* them? When you just *happened* to be walking along the docks? In the middle of the fucking *night?*

We all know you're guilty, John, so let's just fast-forward past the "innocent bystander" routine, okay?

You've got priors for larceny, assault and battery, possession, forging *prescriptions*...

We need a conviction here, pal, and if we say *you* shot that cop, there's not a jury on *God's* green earth that will argue with us.

*Unless...*

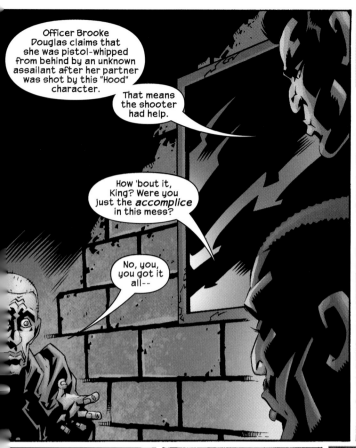

Officer Brooke Douglas claims that she was pistol-whipped from behind by an unknown assailant after her partner was shot by this "Hood" character.

That means the shooter had help.

How 'bout it, King? Were you just the *accomplice* in this mess?

No, you, you got it all--

Because either you were a lowly after-the-fact *accessory*... or you committed first-degree *murder.*

You get five to ten in Ryker's with one, 50 cc's of *potassium chloride* in your arm with the other.

on't lie to you, John... you're getting out of this without ing a little time. But if you nt to save your *life,* you'll write down the name of your *friend.*

Give it some thought while we go find you a nice *public defender...*

SLAM

I am *fucked.*

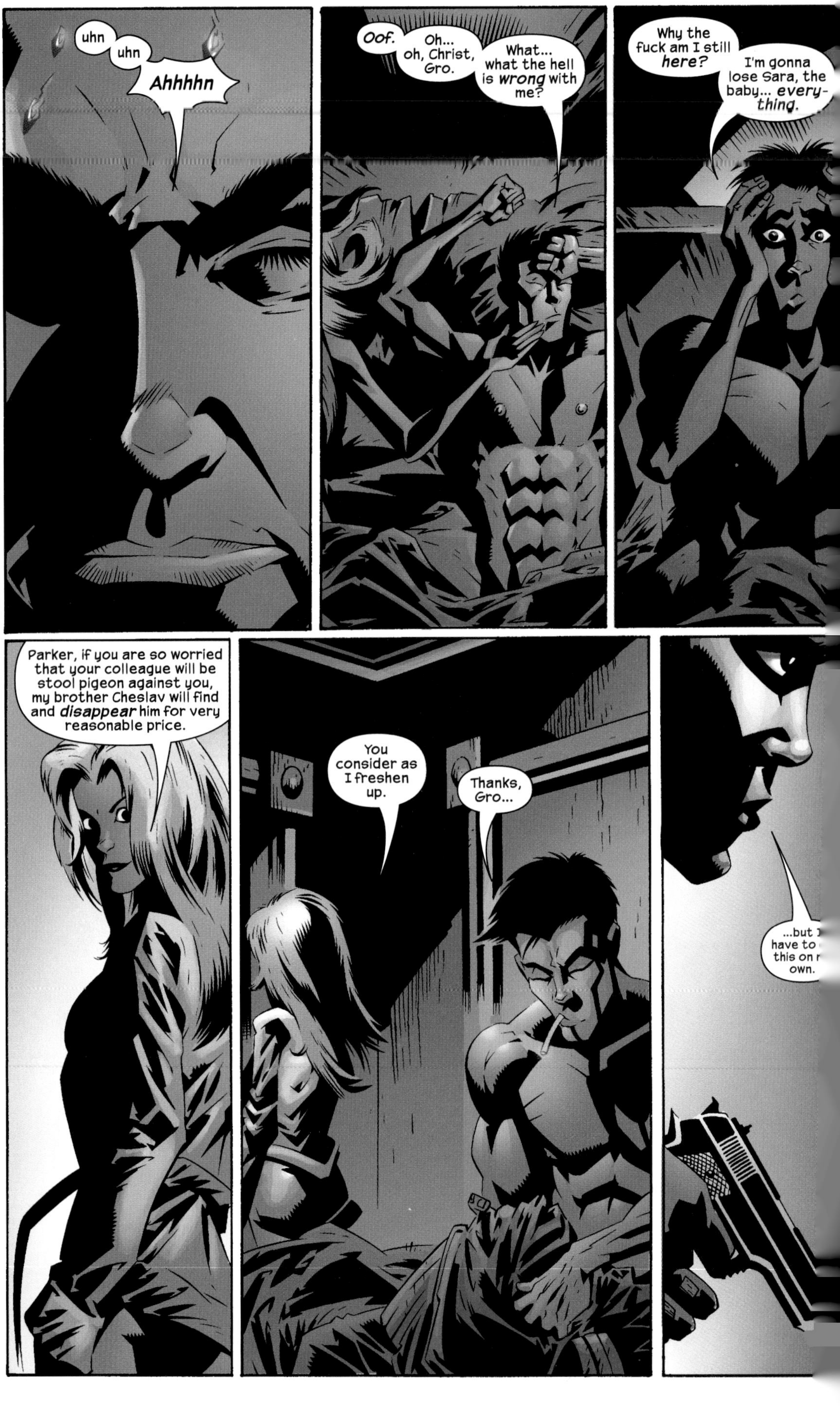
uhn
uhn
Ahhhhn
Oof.
Oh... oh, Christ, Gro.
What... what the hell is *wrong* with me?
Why the fuck am I still *here*?
I'm gonna lose Sara, the baby... *every-thing*.
Parker, if you are so worried that your colleague will be stool pigeon against you, my brother Cheslav will find and *disappear* him for very reasonable price.
You consider as I freshen up.
Thanks, Gro...
...but have to this on own.

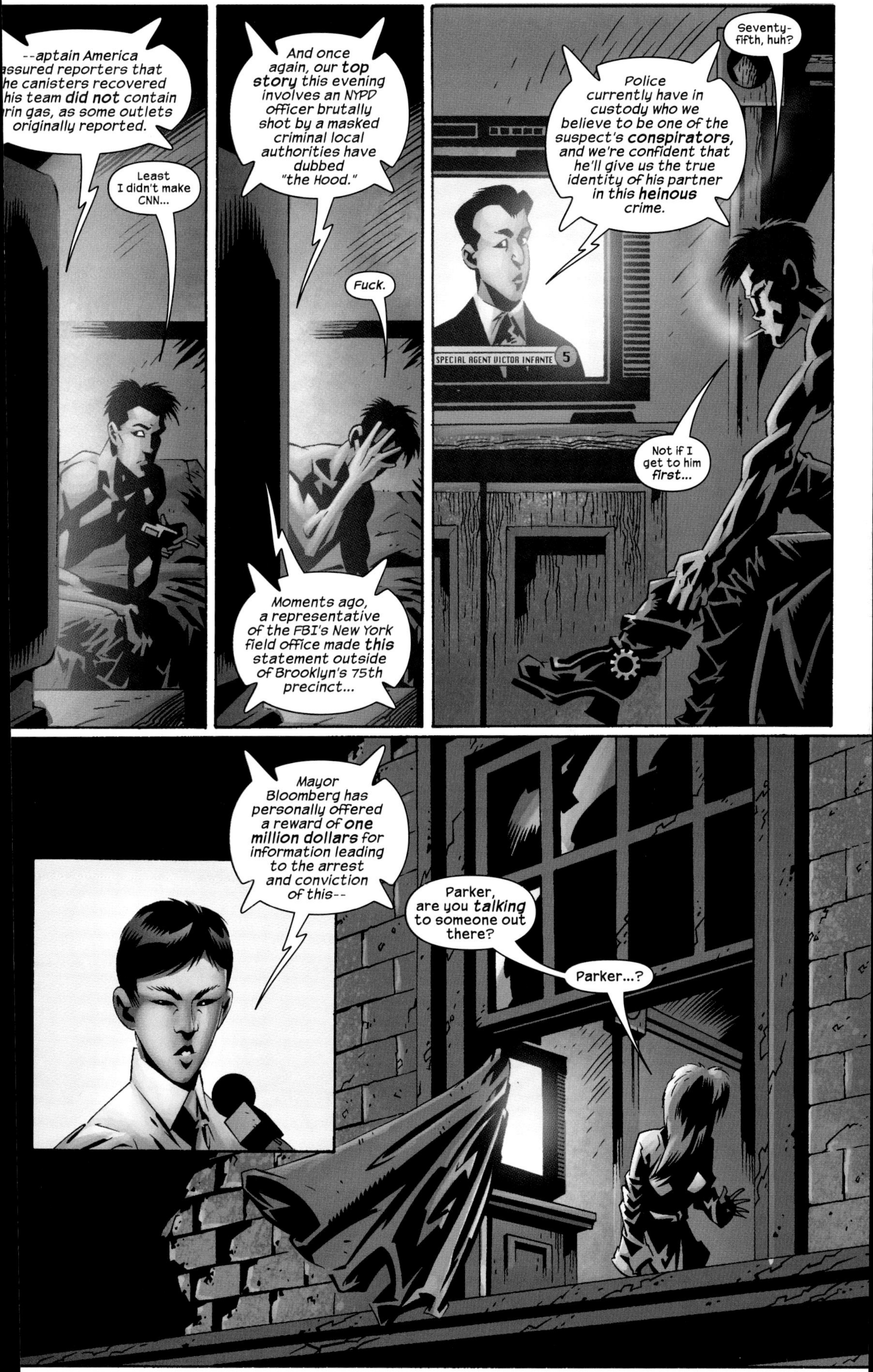
--aptain America assured reporters that he canisters recovered his team **did not** contain rin gas, as some outlets originally reported.
Least I didn't make CNN...
And once again, our **top story** this evening involves an NYPD officer brutally shot by a masked criminal local authorities have dubbed "the Hood."
Fuck.
Moments ago, a representative of the FBI's New York field office made **this** statement outside of Brooklyn's 75th precinct...
Police currently have in custody who we believe to be one of the suspect's **conspirators,** and we're confident that he'll give us the true identity of his partner in this **heinous** crime.
SPECIAL AGENT VICTOR INFANTE 5
Seventy-fifth, huh?
Not if I get to him *first...*
Mayor Bloomberg has personally offered a reward of **one million dollars** for information leading to the arrest and conviction of this--
Parker, are you *talking* to someone out there?
Parker...?

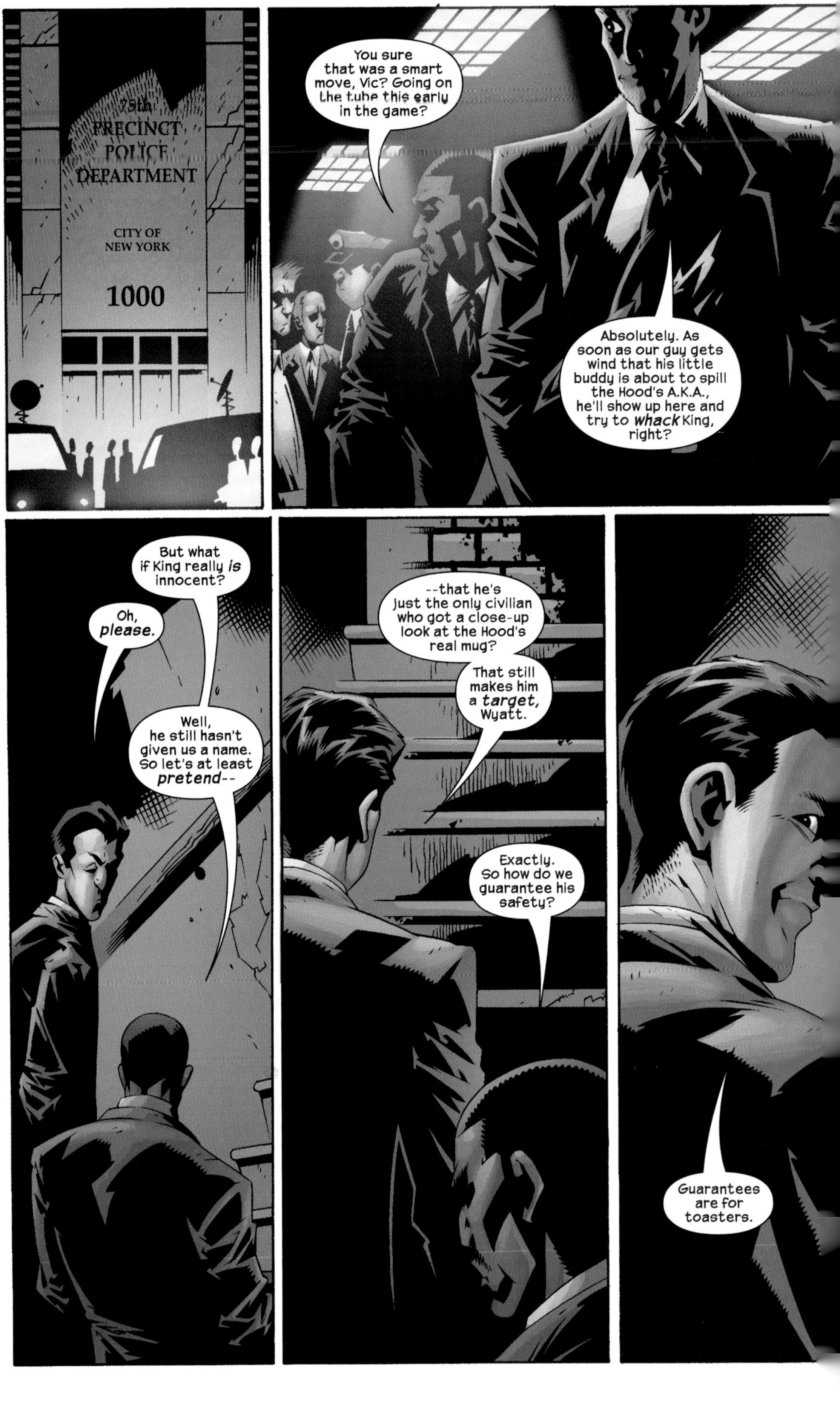
75th
PRECINCT
POLICE
DEPARTMENT
CITY OF
NEW YORK
1000
You sure that was a smart move, Vic? Going on the tube this early in the game?
Absolutely. As soon as our guy gets wind that his little buddy is about to spill the Hood's A.K.A., he'll show up here and try to *whack* King, right?
But what if King really *is* innocent?
Oh, *please*.
Well, he still hasn't given us a name. So let's at least *pretend*--
--that he's just the only civilian who got a close-up look at the Hood's real mug?
That still makes him a *target*, Wyatt.
Exactly. So how do we guarantee his safety?
Guarantees are for toasters.

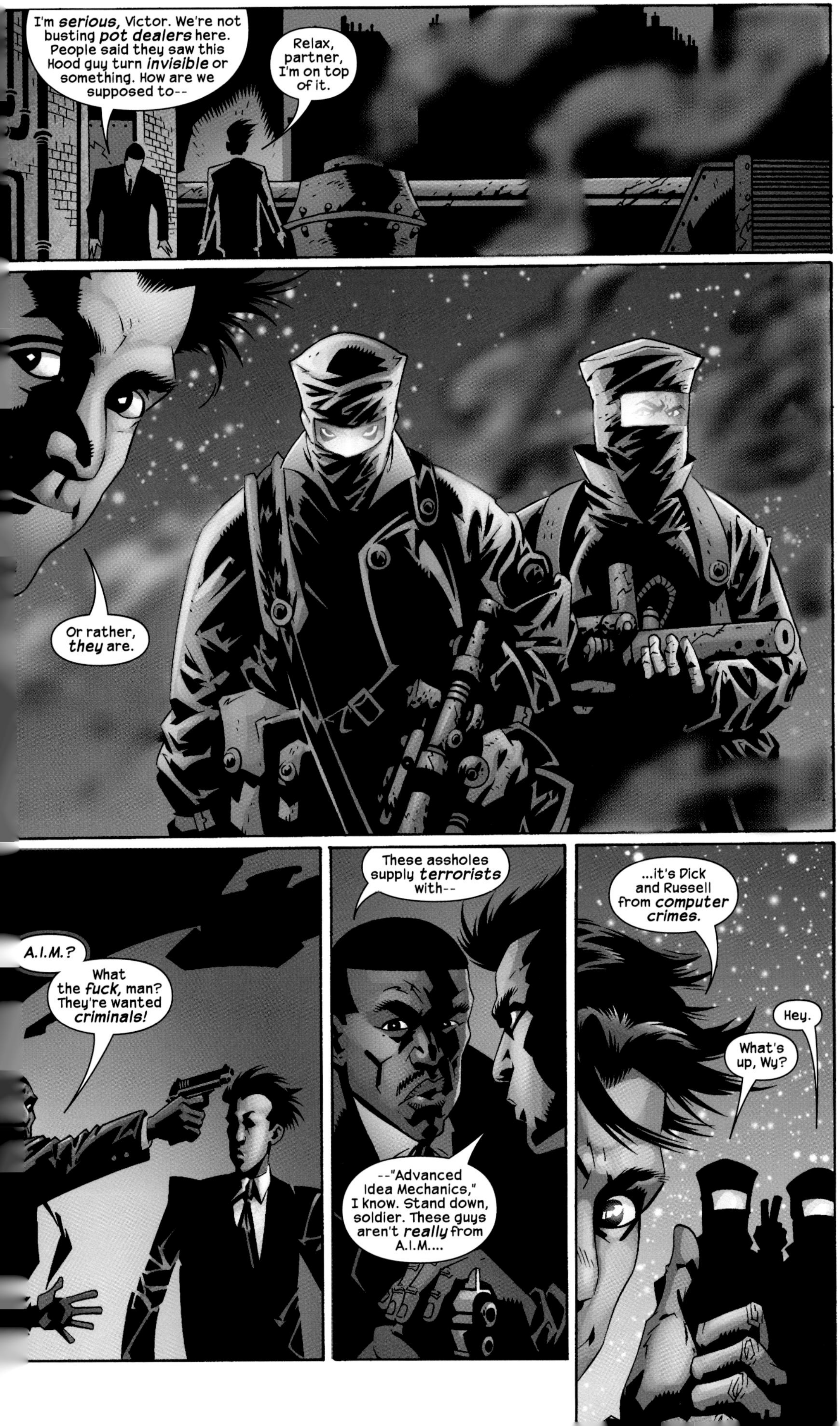
I'm serious, Victor. We're not busting pot dealers here. People said they saw this Hood guy turn invisible or something. How are we supposed to--
Relax, partner, I'm on top of it.
Or rather, they are.
A.I.M.?
What the fuck, man? They're wanted criminals!
These assholes supply terrorists with--
--"Advanced Idea Mechanics," I know. Stand down, soldier. These guys aren't really from A.I.M....
...it's Dick and Russell from computer crimes.
Hey.
What's up, Wy?

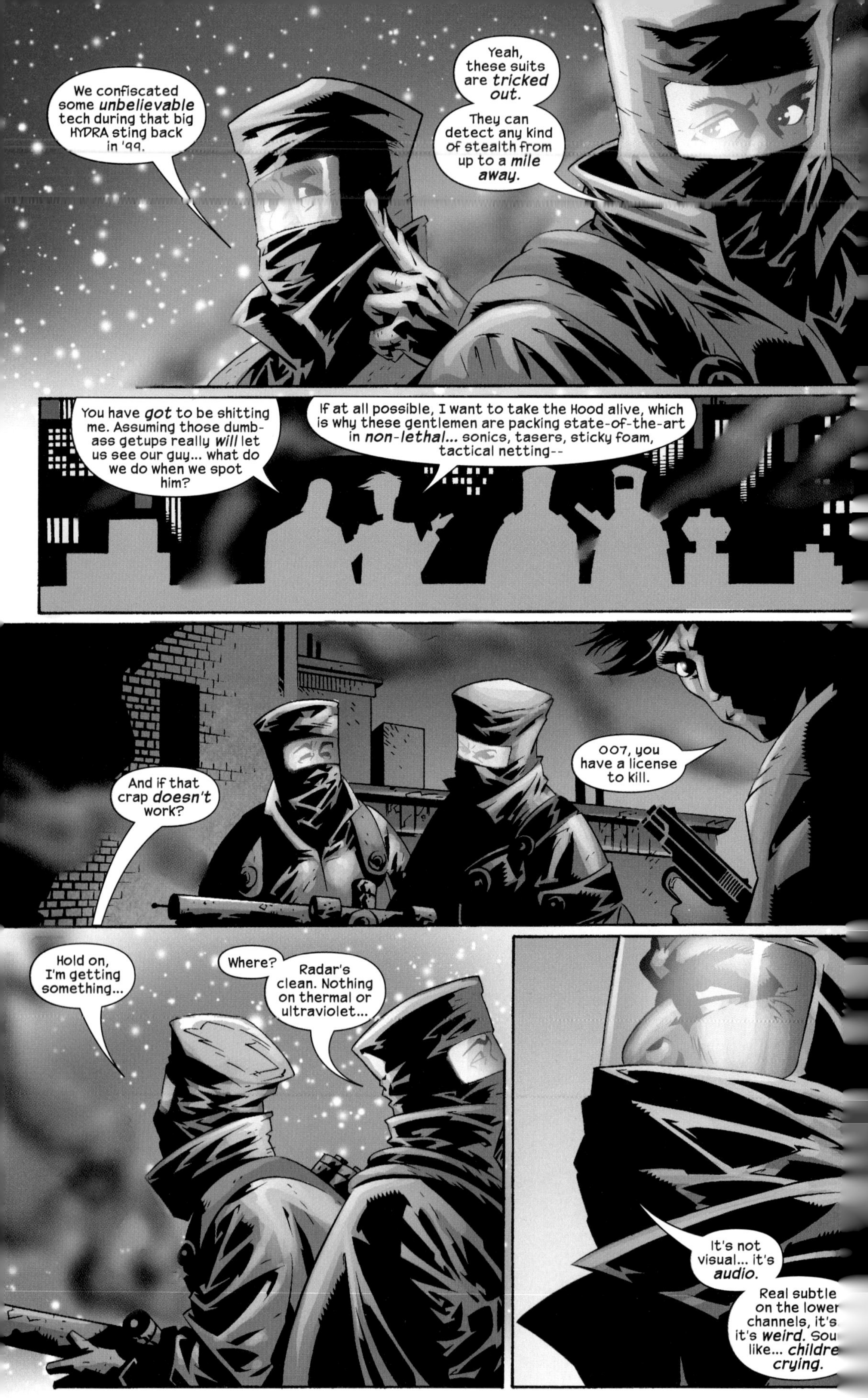
We confiscated some *unbelievable* tech during that big HYDRA sting back in '99.
Yeah, these suits are *tricked out.*
They can detect any kind of stealth from up to a *mile away.*
You have *got* to be shitting me. Assuming those dumb-ass getups really *will* let us see our guy... what do we do when we spot him?
If at all possible, I want to take the Hood alive, which is why these gentlemen are packing state-of-the-art in *non-lethal...* sonics, tasers, sticky foam, tactical netting--
And if that crap *doesn't* work?
007, you have a license to kill.
Hold on, I'm getting something...
Where?
Radar's clean. Nothing on thermal or ultraviolet...
It's not visual... it's *audio.*
Real subtle on the lower channels, it's it's *weird.* Sou like... *childre crying.*

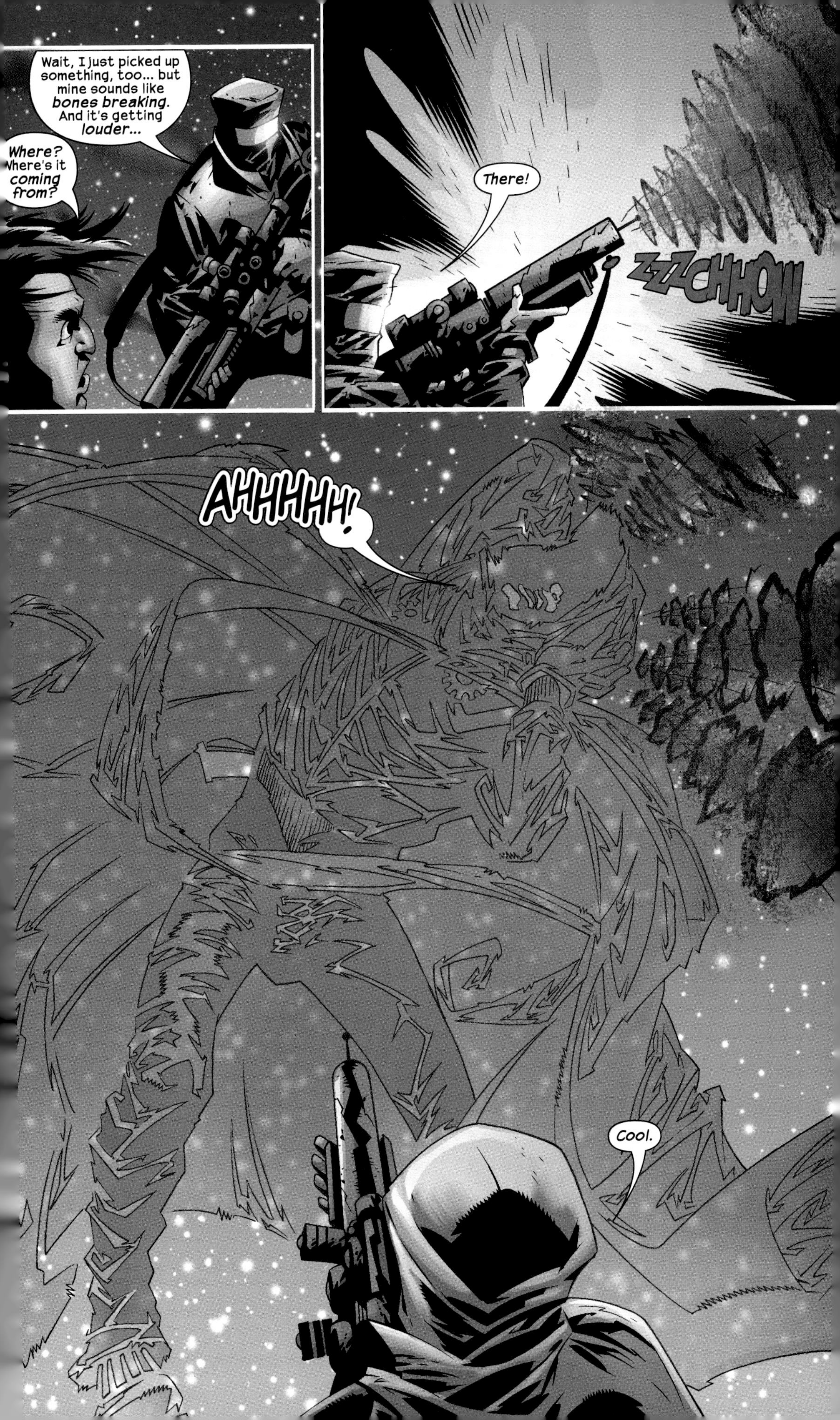
Wait, I just picked up something, too... but mine sounds like *bones breaking*. And it's getting *louder*...
Where? Where's it *coming from?*
There!
ZZZCHHOW
AHHHHH!
Cool.

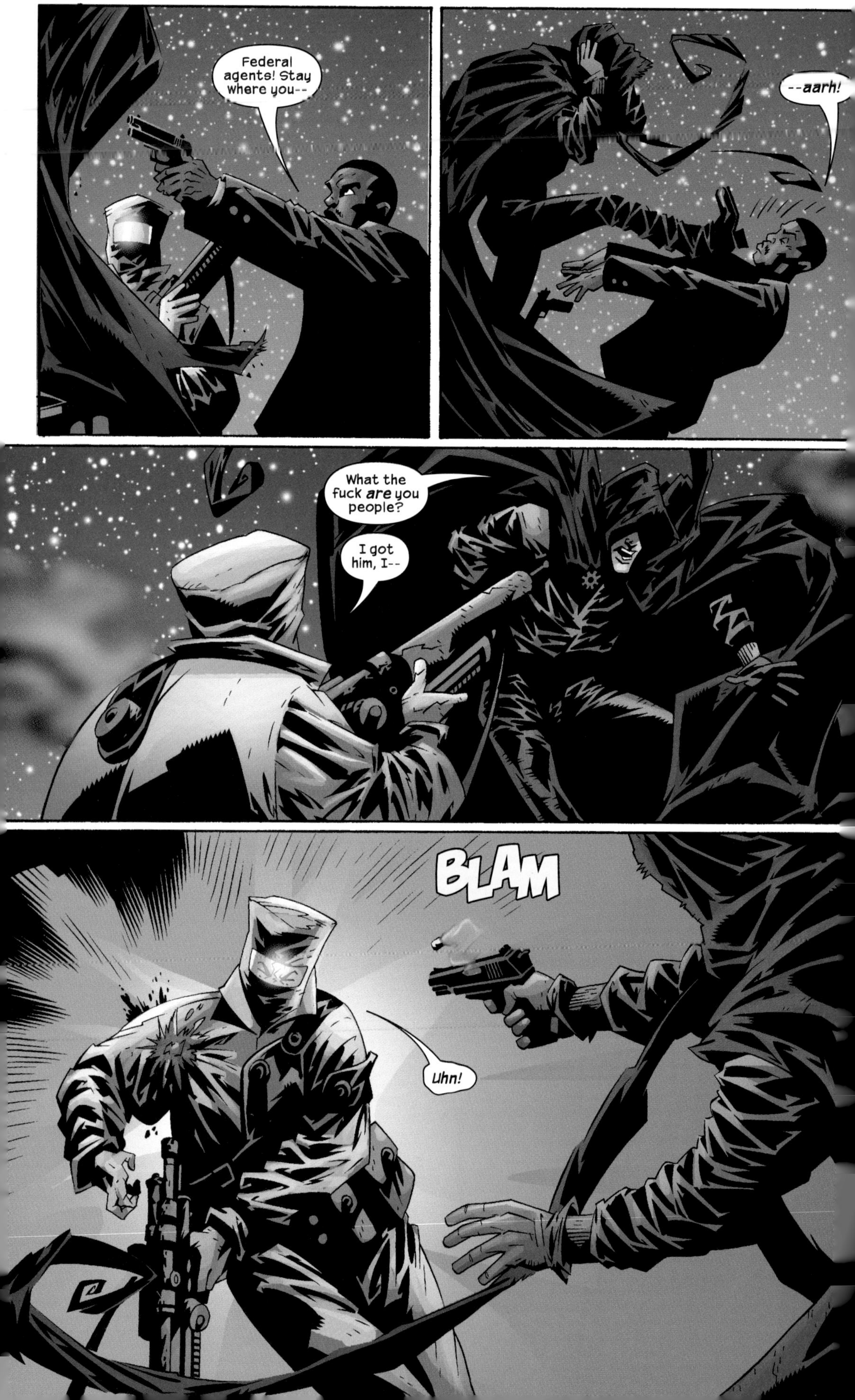
Federal agents! Stay where you--
--aarh!
What the fuck *are* you people?
I got him, I--
BLAM
Uhn!

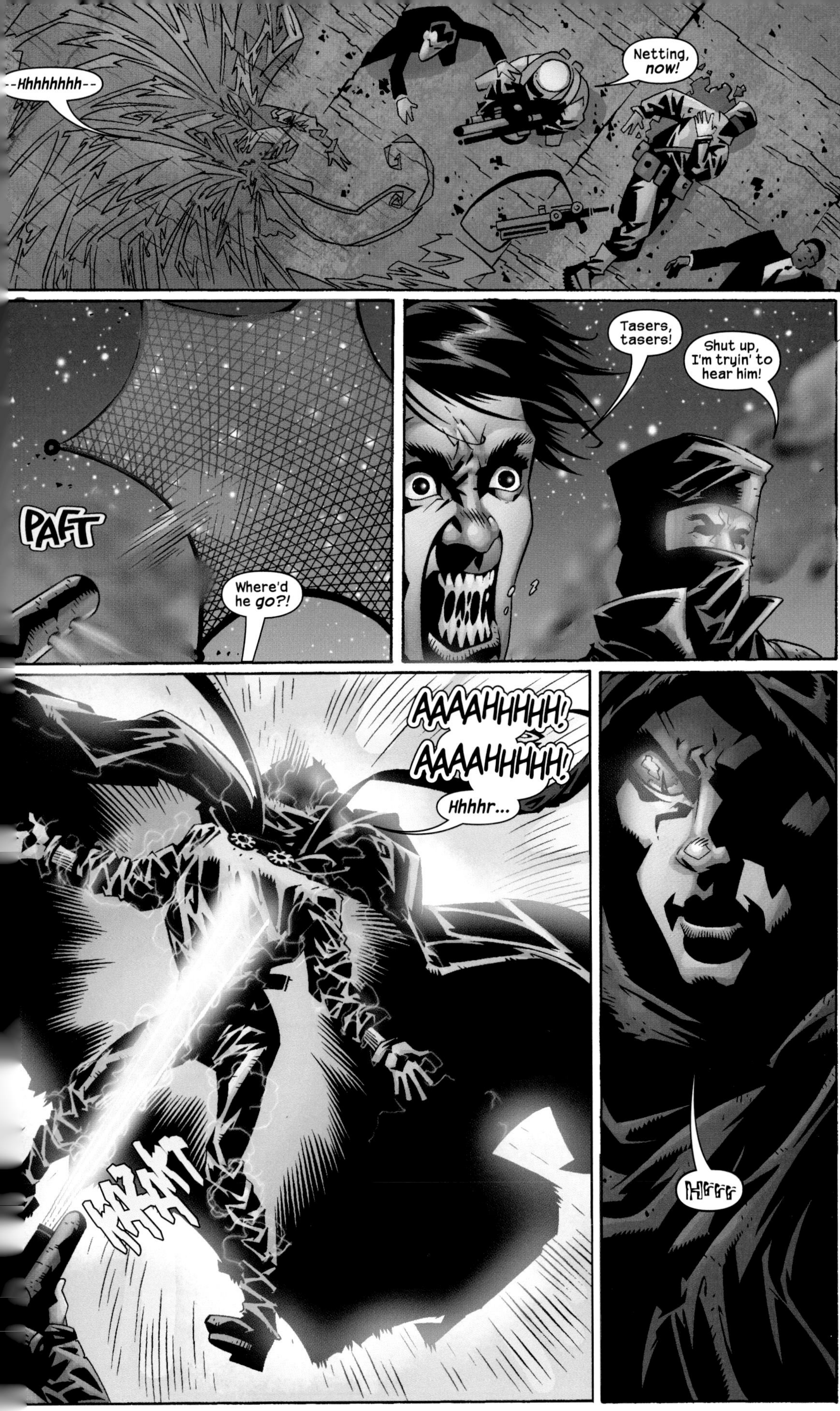
--Hhhhhhhh--
Netting, now!
PAFT
Where'd he go?!
Tasers, tasers!
Shut up, I'm tryin' to hear him!
AAAAHHHHH!
AAAAHHHHH!
Hhhhr...

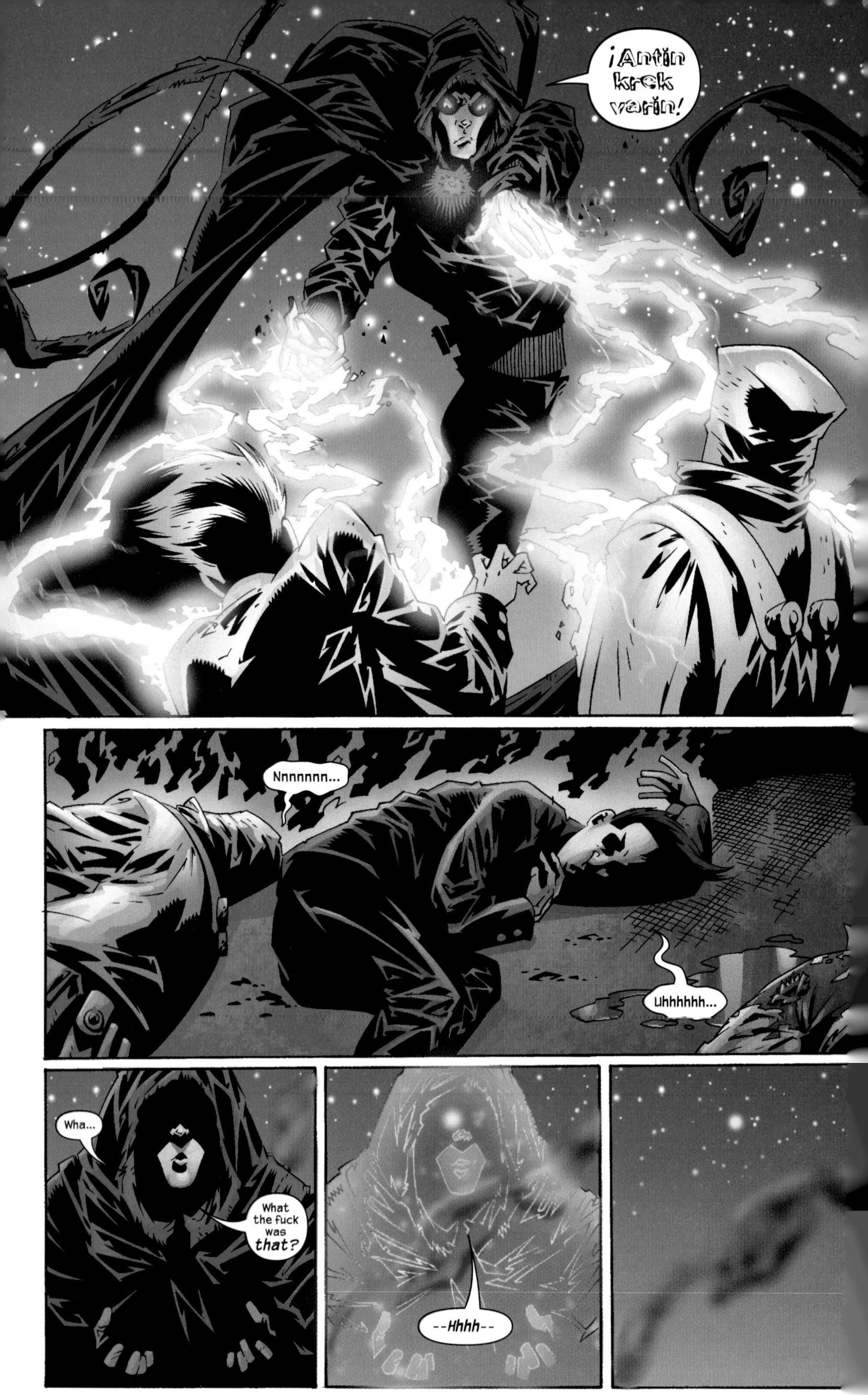
¡Antin krek varin!
Nnnnnnn...
Uhhhhhh...
Wha...
What the fuck was *that*?
--Hhhh--

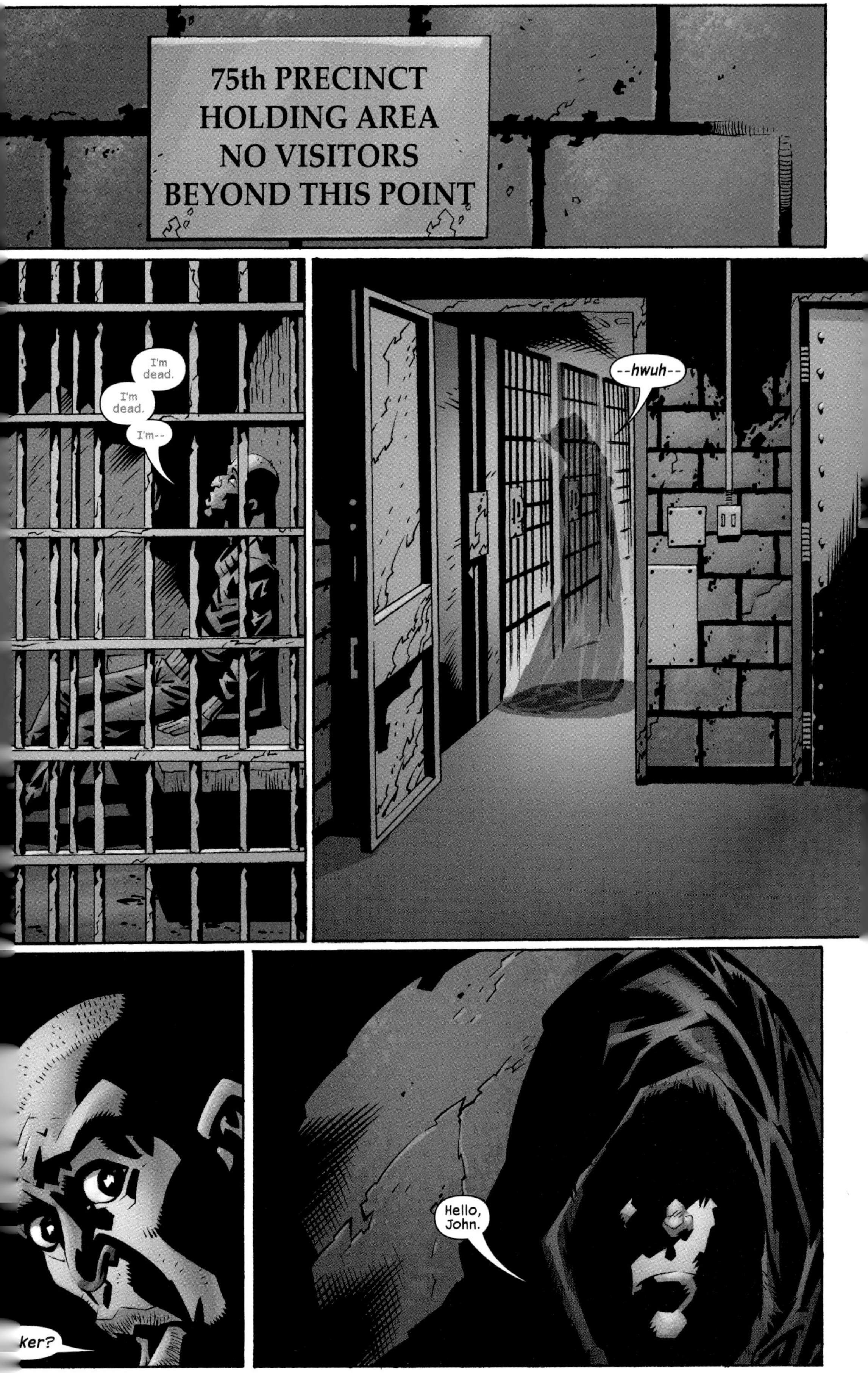

75th PRECINCT
HOLDING AREA
NO VISITORS
BEYOND THIS POINT
I'm dead.
I'm dead.
I'm--
--hwuh--
ker?
Hello, John.

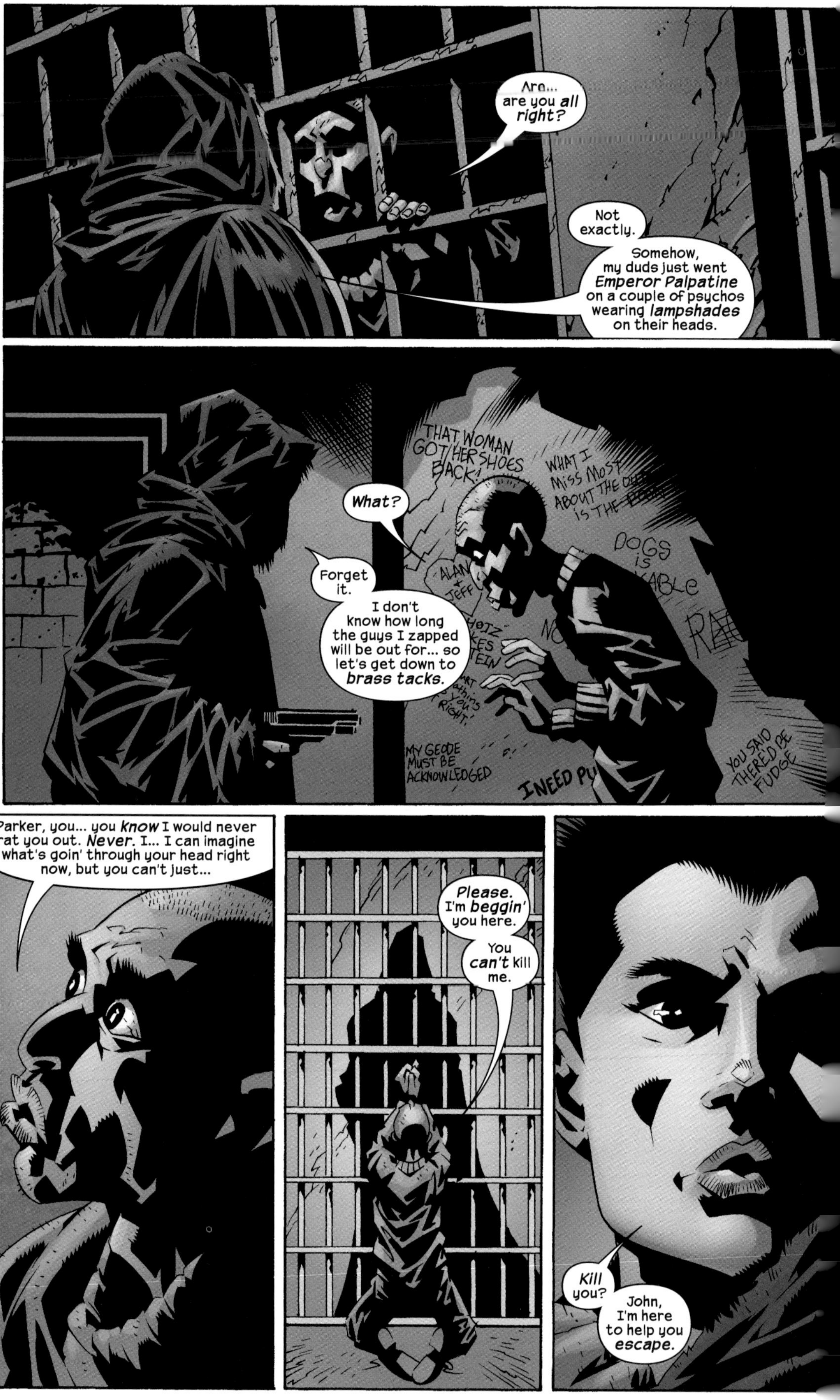
Are... are you *all* right?
Not exactly.
Somehow, my duds just went *Emperor Palpatine* on a couple of psychos wearing *lampshades* on their heads.
THAT WOMAN GOT HER SHOES BACK!
MY GEODE MUST BE ACKNOWLEDGED
YOU SAID THERE'D BE FUDGE
*What?*
Forget it.
I don't know how long the guys I zapped will be out for... so let's get down to *brass tacks.*
Parker, you... you *know* I would never rat you out. *Never.* I... I can imagine what's goin' through your head right now, but you can't just...
*Please.* I'm *beggin'* you here.
You *can't* kill me.
*Kill* you?
John, I'm here to help you *escape.*

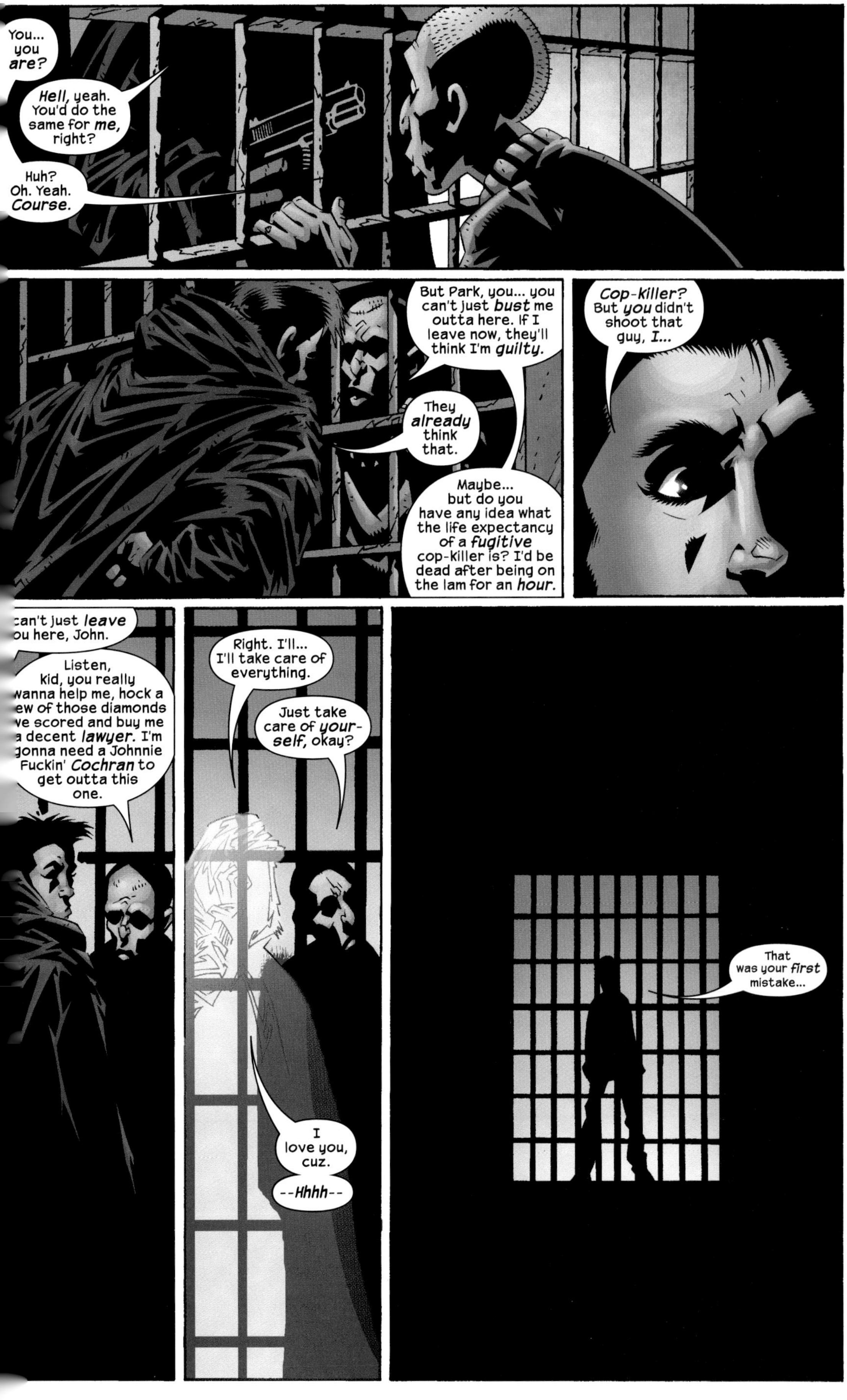
You... you are?
Hell, yeah. You'd do the same for me, right?
Huh? Oh. Yeah. Course.
But Park, you... you can't just bust me outta here. If I leave now, they'll think I'm guilty.
They already think that.
Maybe... but do you have any idea what the life expectancy of a fugitive cop-killer is? I'd be dead after being on the lam for an hour.
Cop-killer? But you didn't shoot that guy, I...
can't just leave ou here, John.
Listen, kid, you really wanna help me, hock a ew of those diamonds ve scored and buy me a decent lawyer. I'm gonna need a Johnnie Fuckin' Cochran to get outta this one.
Right. I'll... I'll take care of everything.
Just take care of yourself, okay?
I love you, cuz.
--Hhhh--
That was your first mistake...

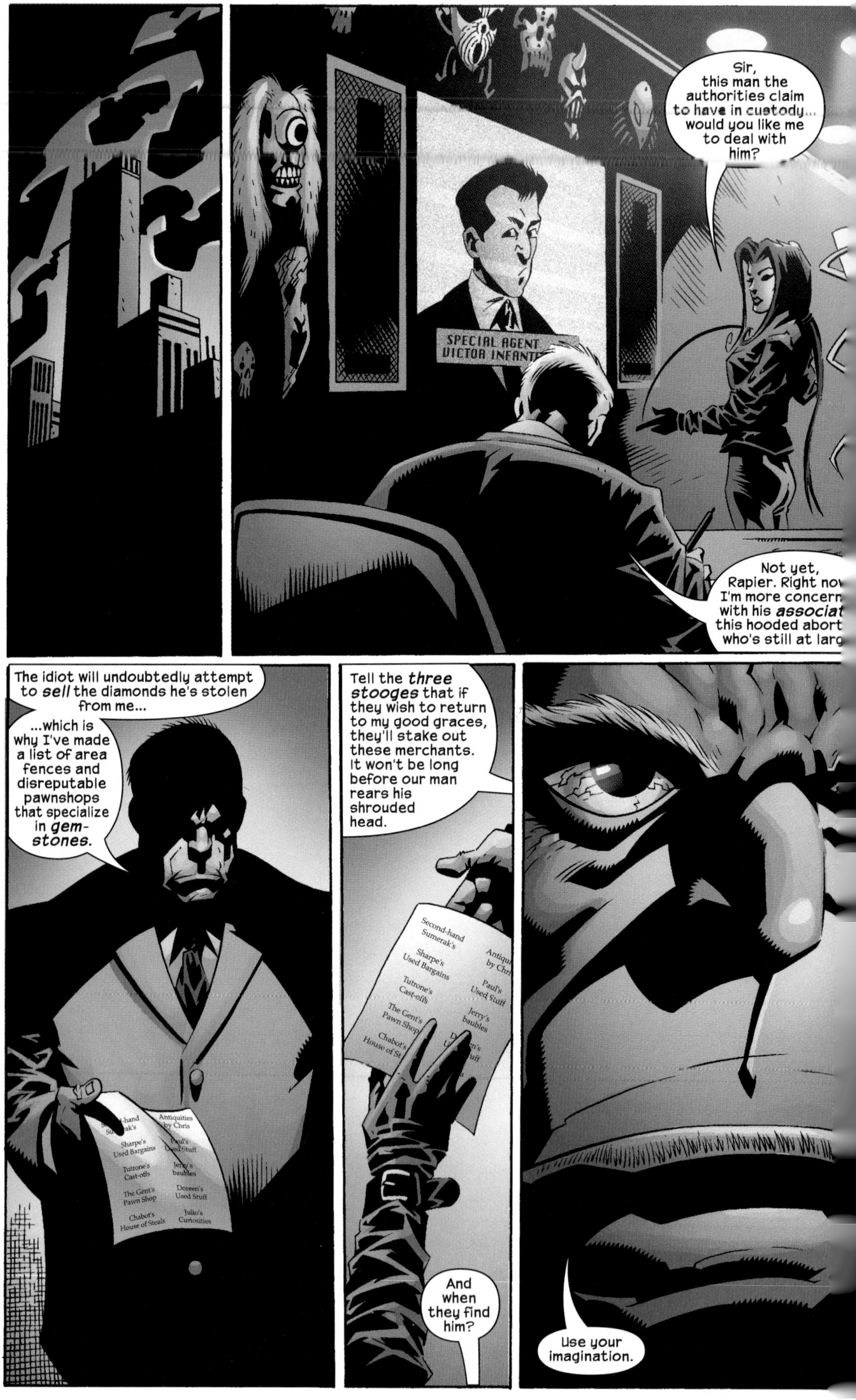

SPECIAL AGENT VICTOR INFANTE
Sir, this man the authorities claim to have in custody... would you like me to deal with him?
Not yet, Rapier. Right no I'm more concern with his *associat* this hooded abort who's still at larg
The idiot will undoubtedly attempt to *sell* the diamonds he's stolen from me...
...which is why I've made a list of area fences and disreputable pawnshops that specialize in *gem-stones.*
Antiquities by Chris
Sharpe's Used Bargains
Paul's Used Stuff
Tutrone's Cast-offs
Jerry's baubles
The Gent's Pawn Shop
Doreen's Used Stuff
Chabot's House of Steals
Julio's Curiosities
Second-hand Sumerak's
Tell the *three stooges* that if they wish to return to my good graces, they'll stake out these merchants. It won't be long before our man rears his shrouded head.
And when they find him?
Use your imagination.

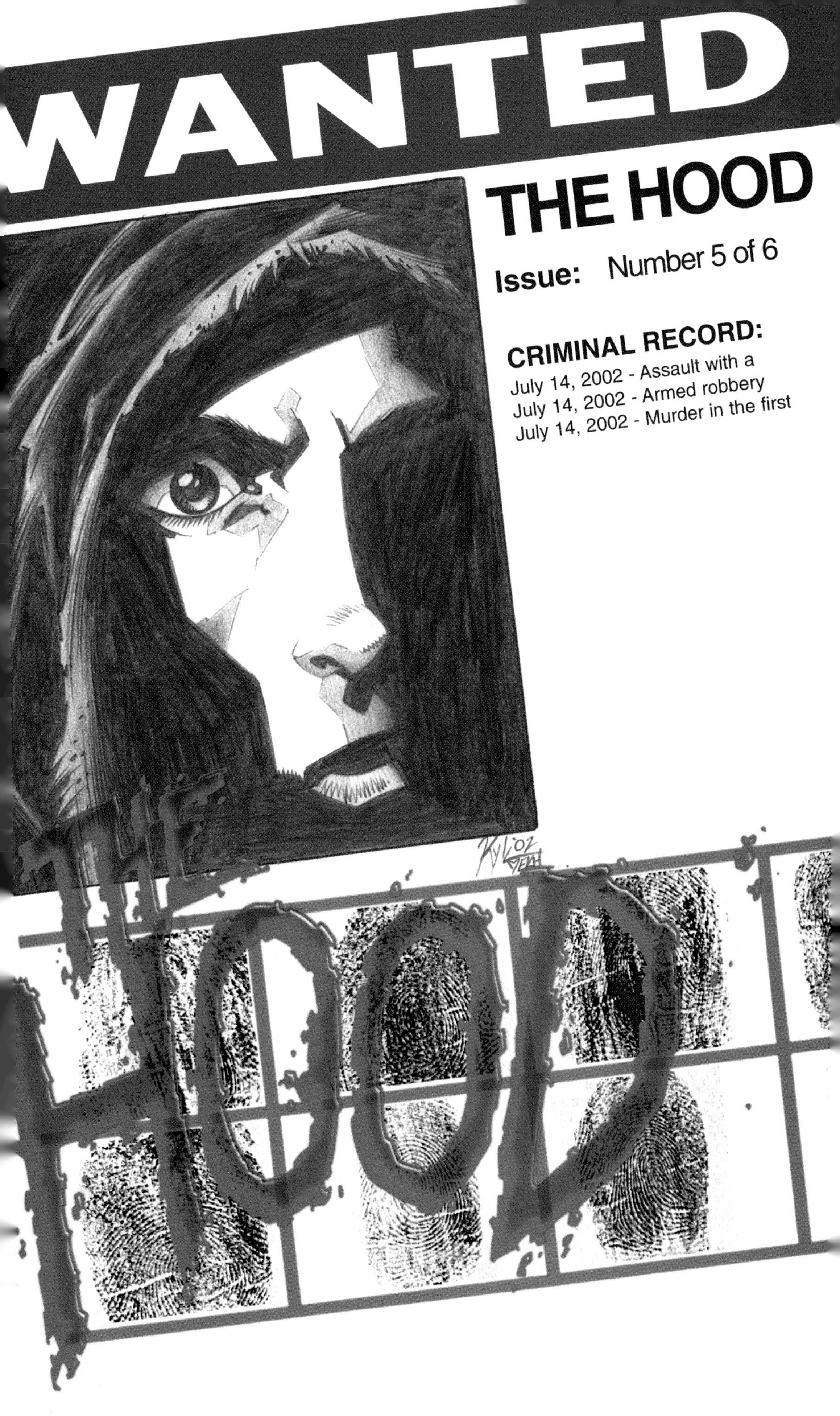
WANTED
THE HOOD
Issue: Number 5 of 6
CRIMINAL RECORD:
July 14, 2002 - Assault with a
July 14, 2002 - Armed robbery
July 14, 2002 - Murder in the first
THE HOOD

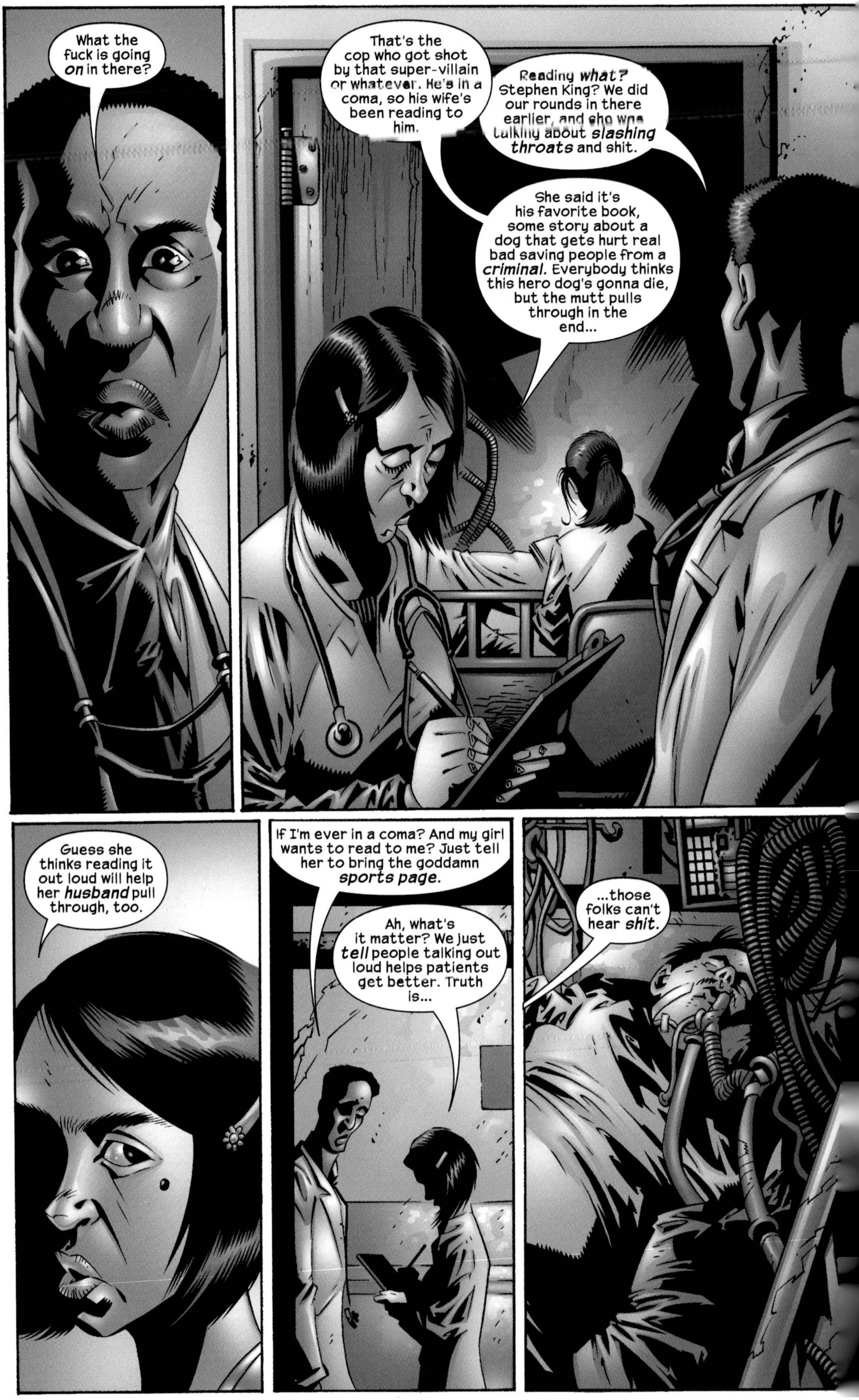
What the fuck is going on in there?
That's the cop who got shot by that super-villain or whatever. He's in a coma, so his wife's been reading to him.
Reading what? Stephen King? We did our rounds in there earlier, and she was talking about slashing throats and shit.
She said it's his favorite book, some story about a dog that gets hurt real bad saving people from a criminal. Everybody thinks this hero dog's gonna die, but the mutt pulls through in the end...
Guess she thinks reading it out loud will help her husband pull through, too.
If I'm ever in a coma? And my girl wants to read to me? Just tell her to bring the goddamn sports page.
Ah, what's it matter? We just tell people talking out loud helps patients get better. Truth is...
...those folks can't hear shit.

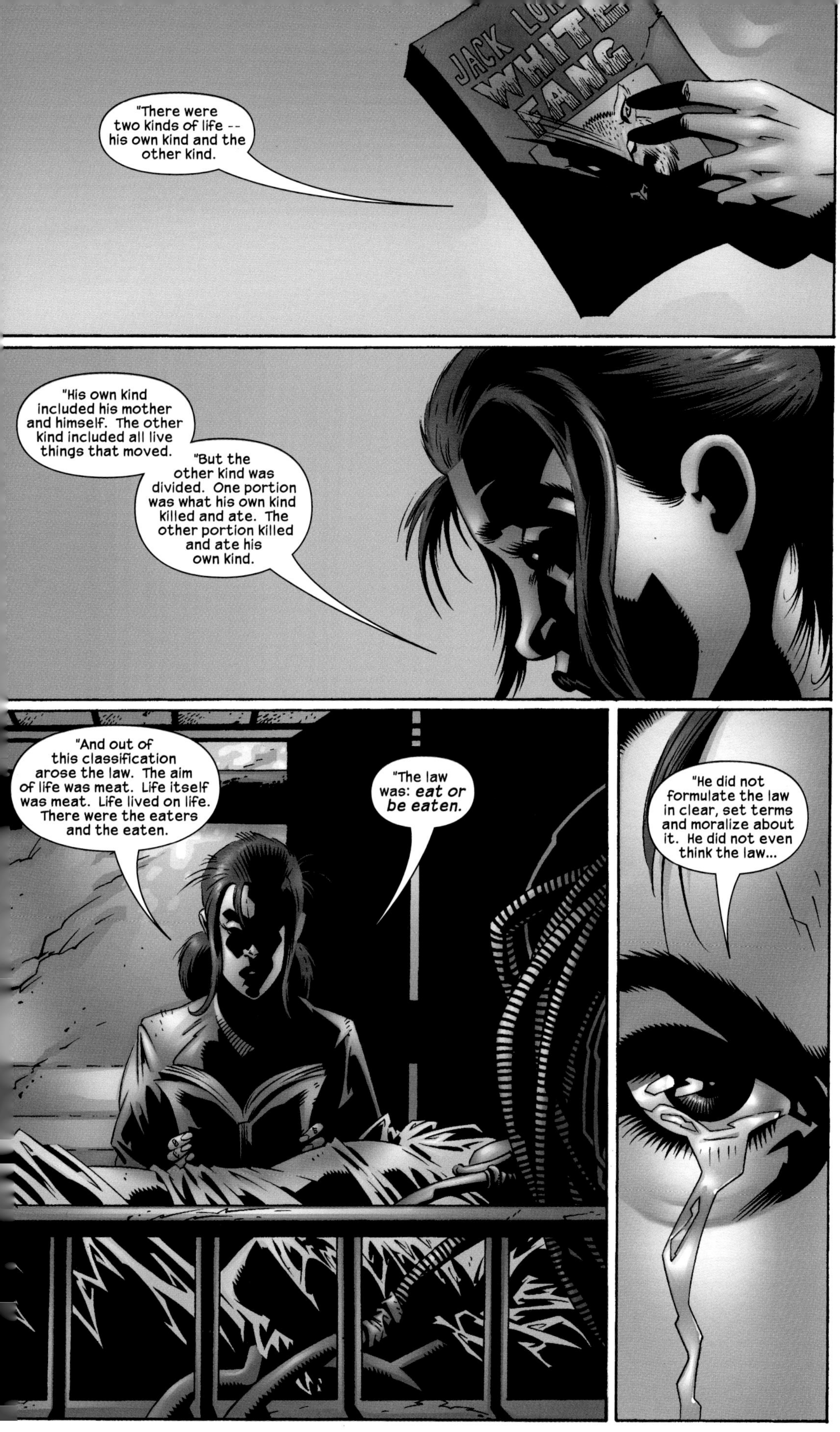
JACK LON[DON] WHITE FANG
"There were two kinds of life -- his own kind and the other kind.
"His own kind included his mother and himself. The other kind included all live things that moved.
"But the other kind was divided. One portion was what his own kind killed and ate. The other portion killed and ate his own kind.
"And out of this classification arose the law. The aim of life was meat. Life itself was meat. Life lived on life. There were the eaters and the eaten.
"The law was: *eat or be eaten.*
"He did not formulate the law in clear, set terms and moralize about it. He did not even think the law...

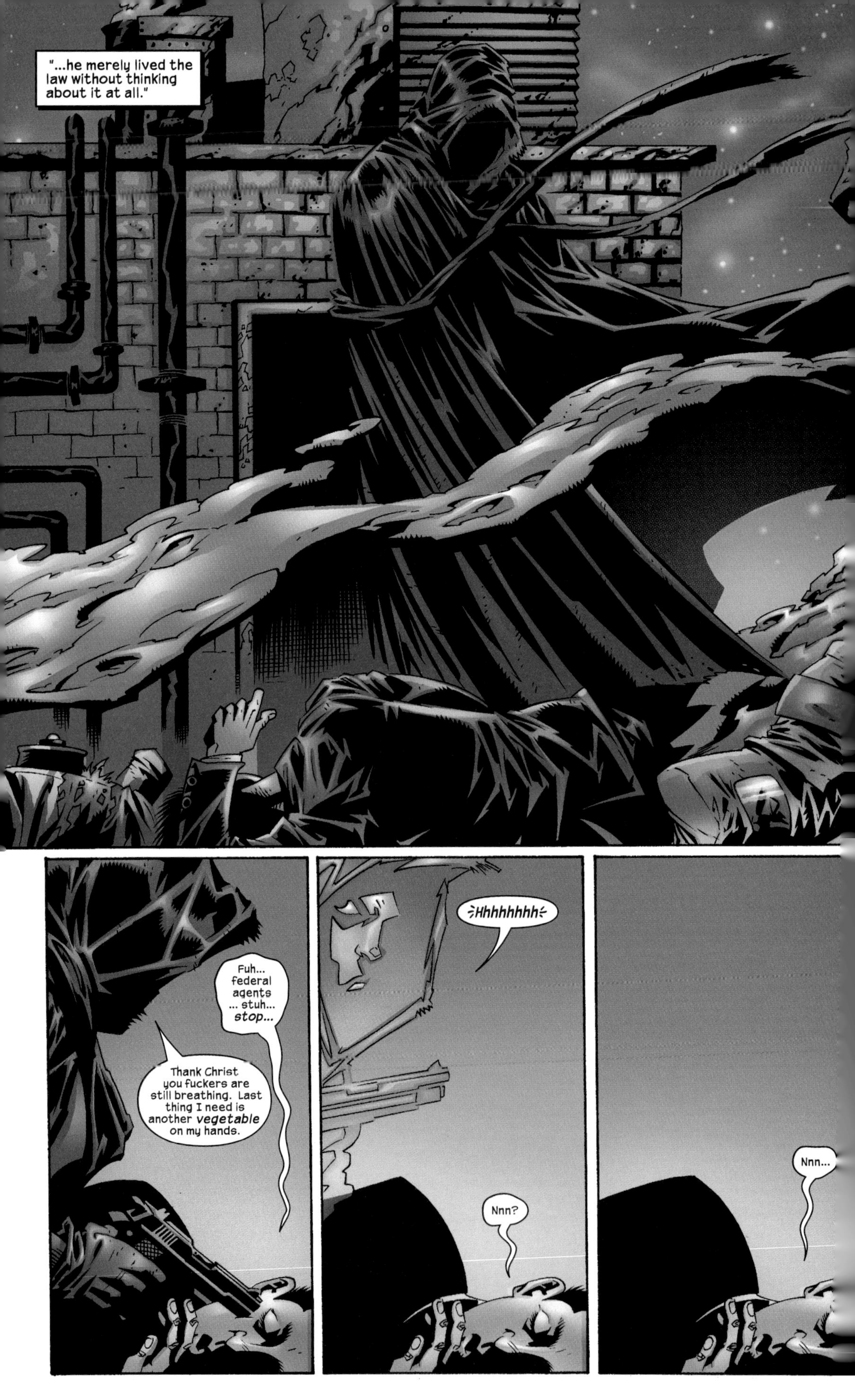
"...he merely lived the law without thinking about it at all."
Thank Christ you fuckers are still breathing. Last thing I need is another *vegetable* on my hands.
Fuh... federal agents ... stuh... *stop...*
Hhhhhhhh
Nnn?
Nnn...

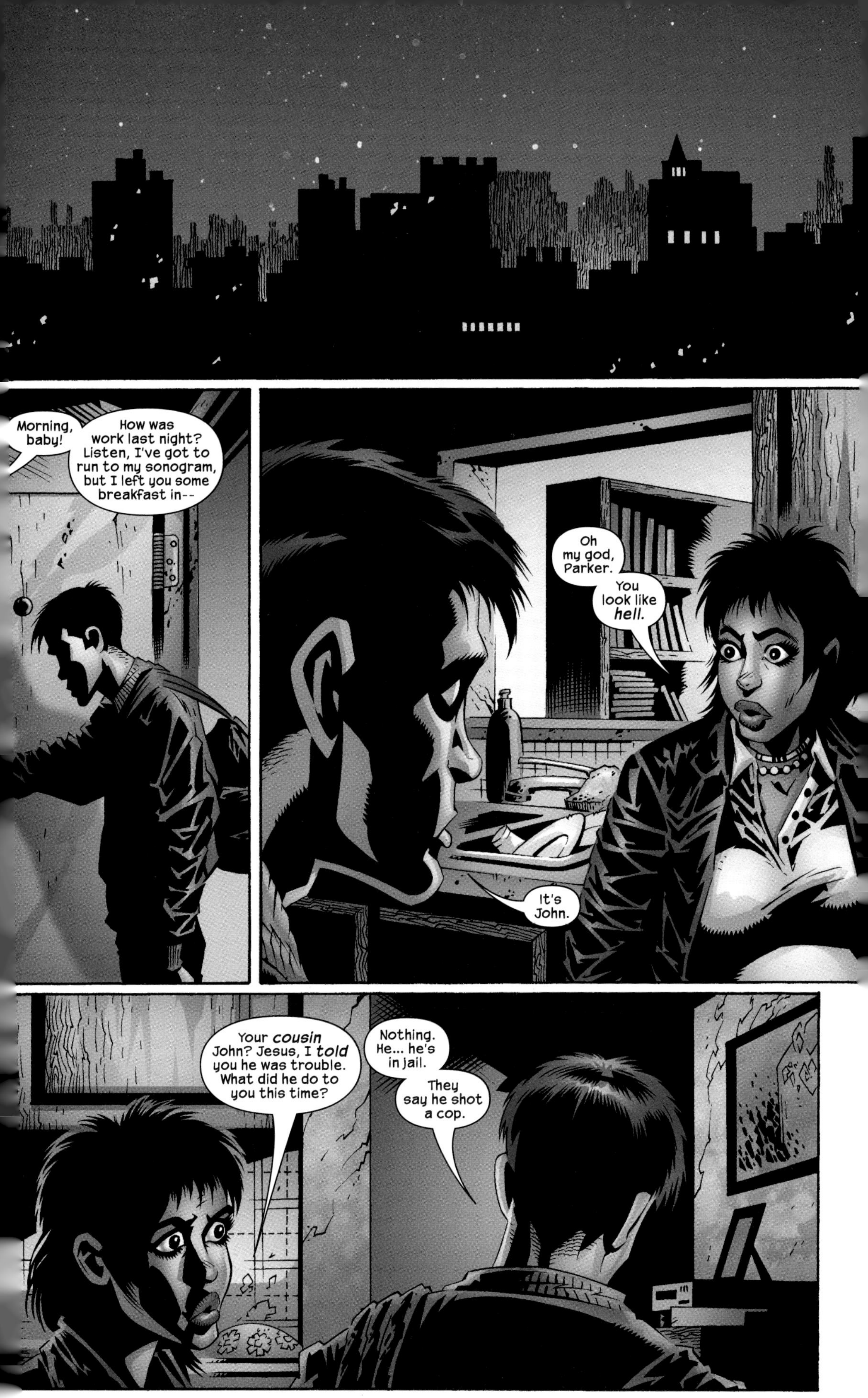
Morning, baby!
How was work last night? Listen, I've got to run to my sonogram, but I left you some breakfast in--
Oh my god, Parker.
You look like *hell.*
It's John.
Your *cousin* John? Jesus, I *told* you he was trouble. What did he do to you this time?
Nothing. He... he's in jail.
They say he shot a cop.

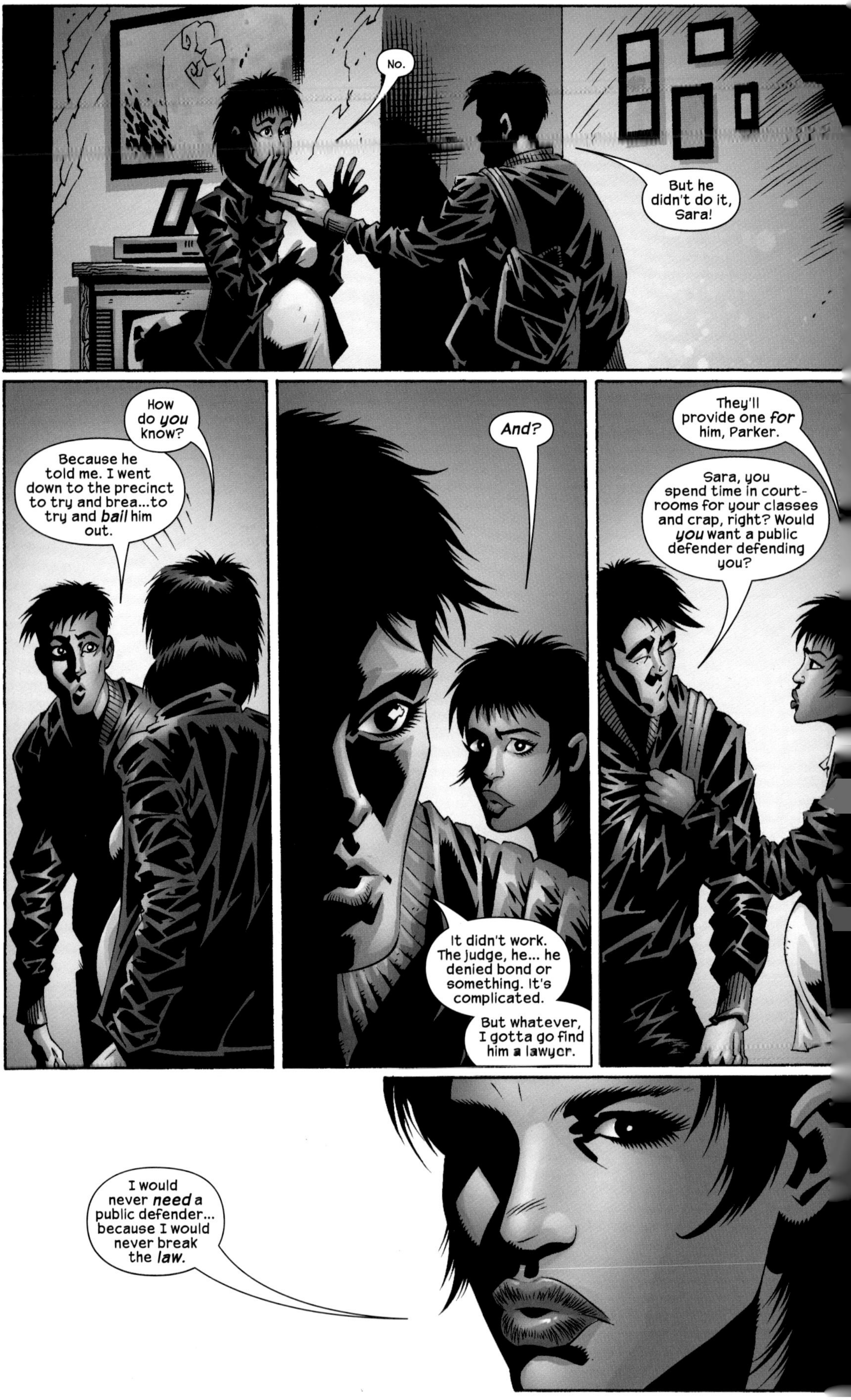
No.
But he didn't do it, Sara!
How do *you* know?
Because he told me. I went down to the precinct to try and brea...to try and *bail* him out.
*And?*
It didn't work. The judge, he... he denied bond or something. It's complicated.
But whatever, I gotta go find him a lawyer.
They'll provide one *for* him, Parker.
Sara, you spend time in court-rooms for your classes and crap, right? Would *you* want a public defender defending you?
I would never *need* a public defender... because I would never break the *law*.

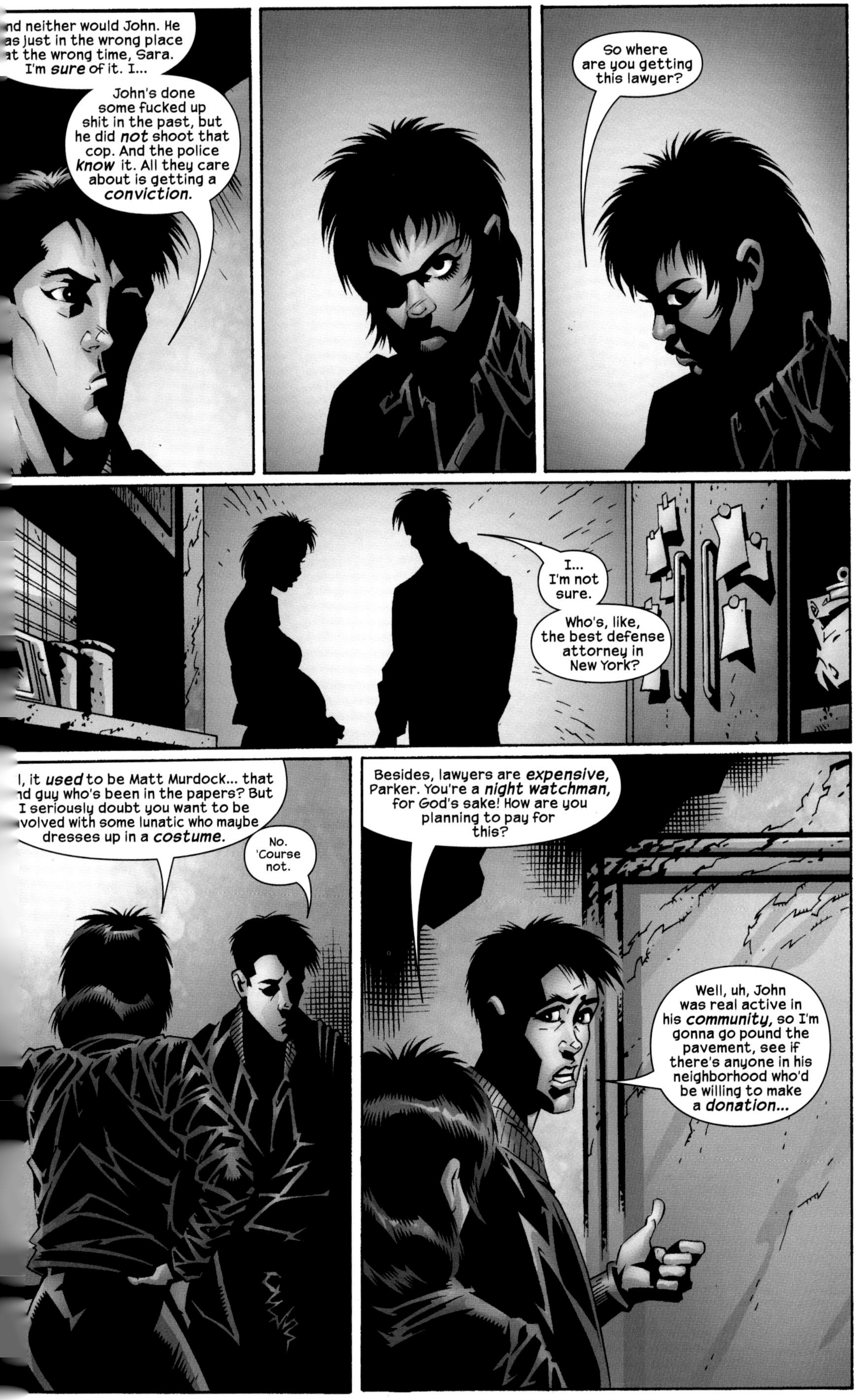
nd neither would John. He as just in the wrong place at the wrong time, Sara. I'm *sure* of it. I...
John's done some fucked up shit in the past, but he did *not* shoot that cop. And the police *know* it. All they care about is getting a *conviction.*
So where are you getting this lawyer?
I... I'm not sure.
Who's, like, the best defense attorney in New York?
l, it *used* to be Matt Murdock... that nd guy who's been in the papers? But I seriously doubt you want to be volved with some lunatic who maybe dresses up in a *costume.*
No. 'Course not.
Besides, lawyers are *expensive,* Parker. You're a *night watchman,* for God's sake! How are you planning to pay for this?
Well, uh, John was real active in his *community,* so I'm gonna go pound the pavement, see if there's anyone in his neighborhood who'd be willing to make a *donation...*

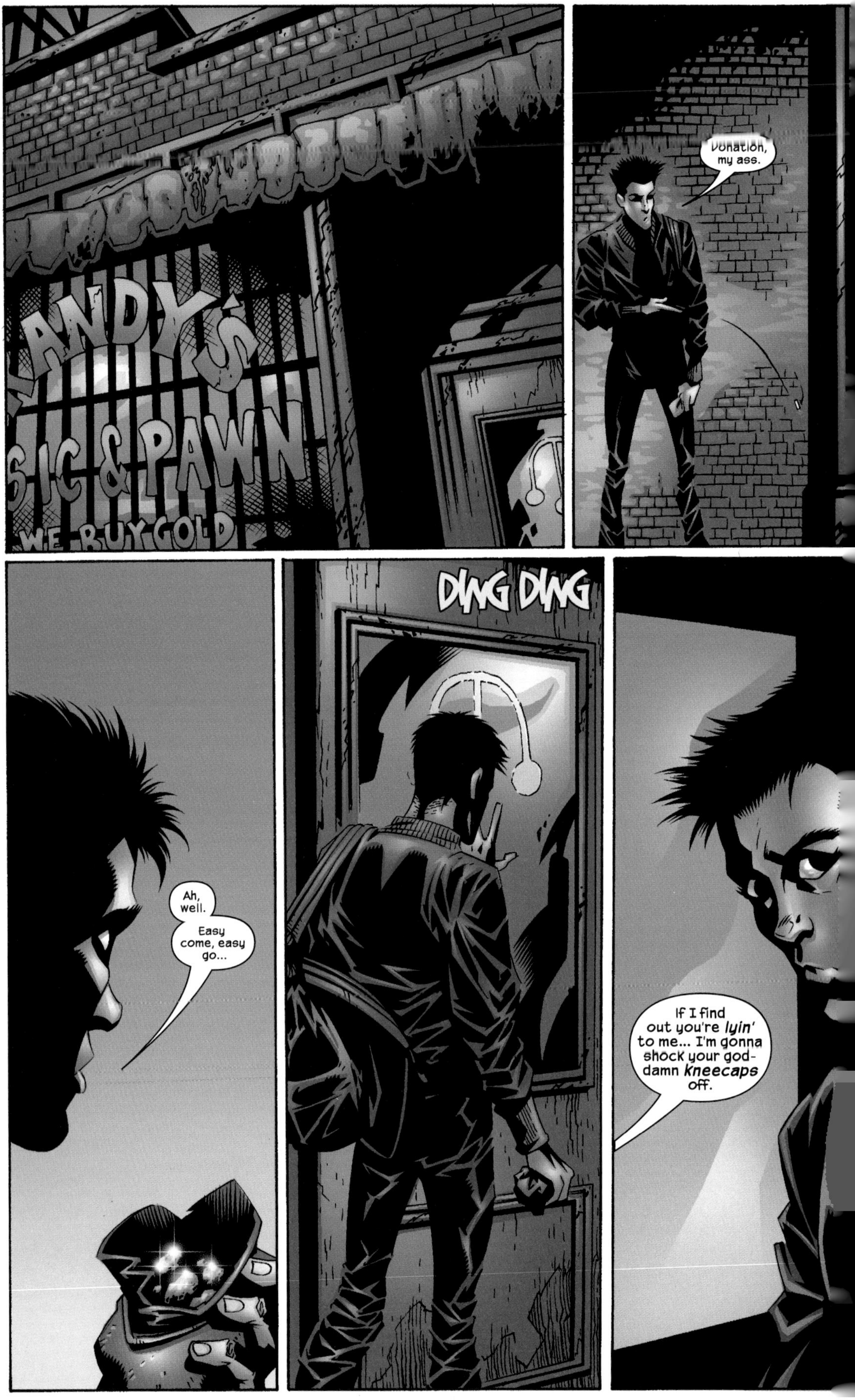
ANDY'S
SIC & PAWN
WE BUY GOLD
Donation, my ass.
Ah, well.
Easy come, easy go...
DING DING
If I find out you're *lyin'* to me... I'm gonna shock your god-damn *kneecaps* off.

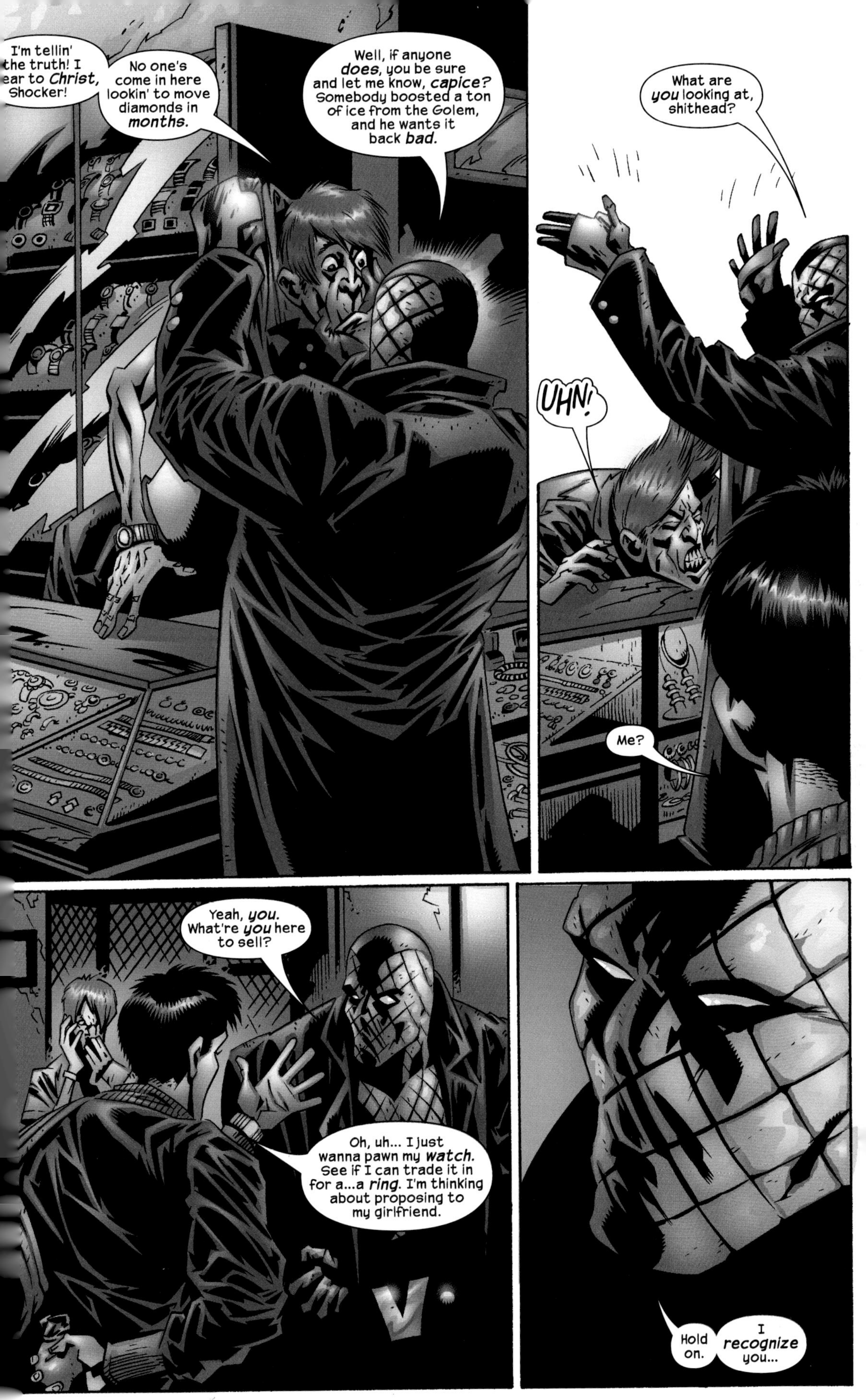
I'm tellin' the truth! I ear to Christ, Shocker!
No one's come in here lookin' to move diamonds in months.
Well, if anyone does, you be sure and let me know, capice? Somebody boosted a ton of ice from the Golem, and he wants it back bad.
What are you looking at, shithead?
UHN!
Me?
Yeah, you. What're you here to sell?
Oh, uh... I just wanna pawn my watch. See if I can trade it in for a...a ring. I'm thinking about proposing to my girlfriend.
Hold on.
I recognize you...

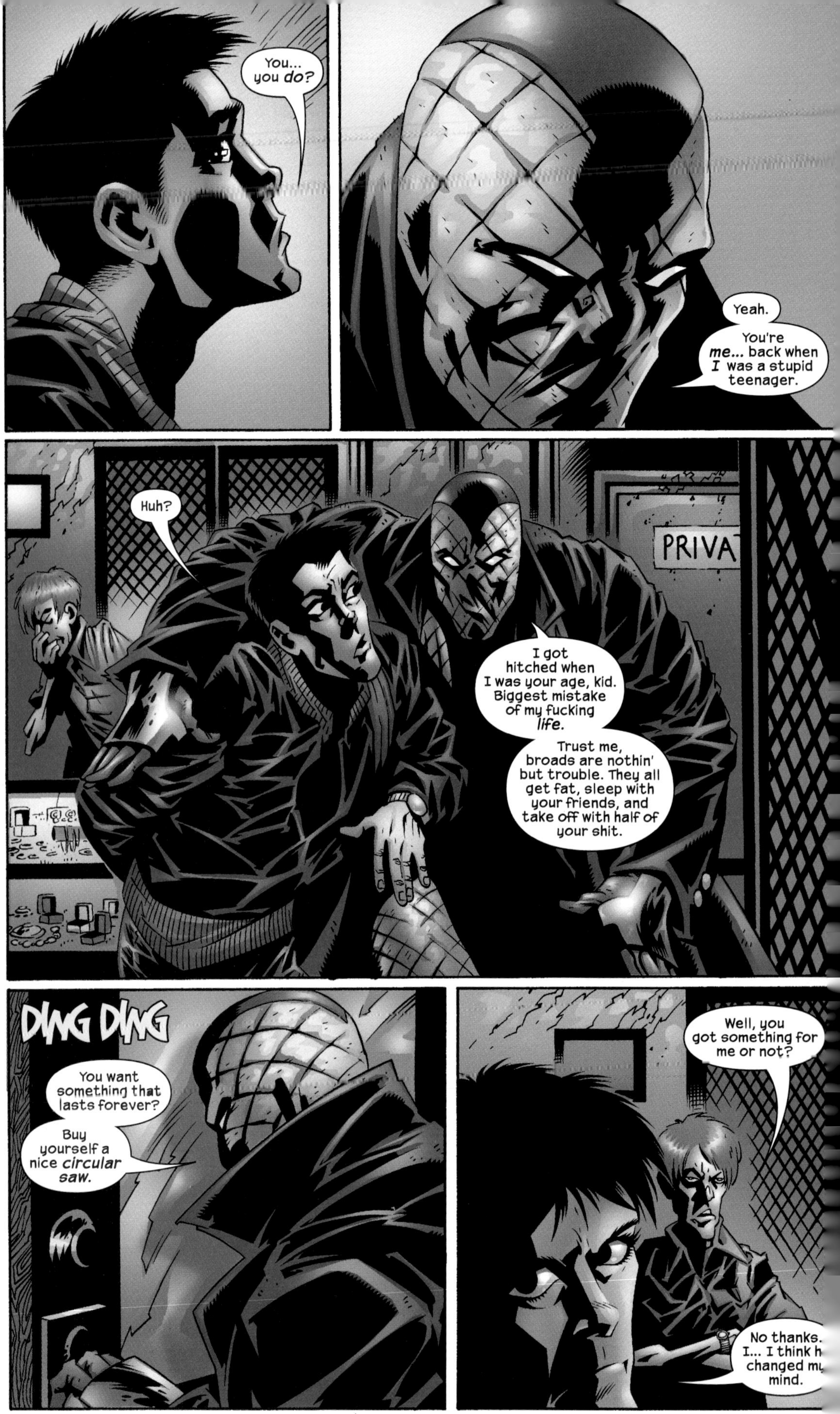
You... you do?
Yeah.
You're me... back when I was a stupid teenager.
Huh?
I got hitched when I was your age, kid. Biggest mistake of my fucking life.
Trust me, broads are nothin' but trouble. They all get fat, sleep with your friends, and take off with half of your shit.
PRIVA
DING DING
You want something that lasts forever?
Buy yourself a nice circular saw.
Well, you got something for me or not?
No thanks. I... I think h changed m mind.

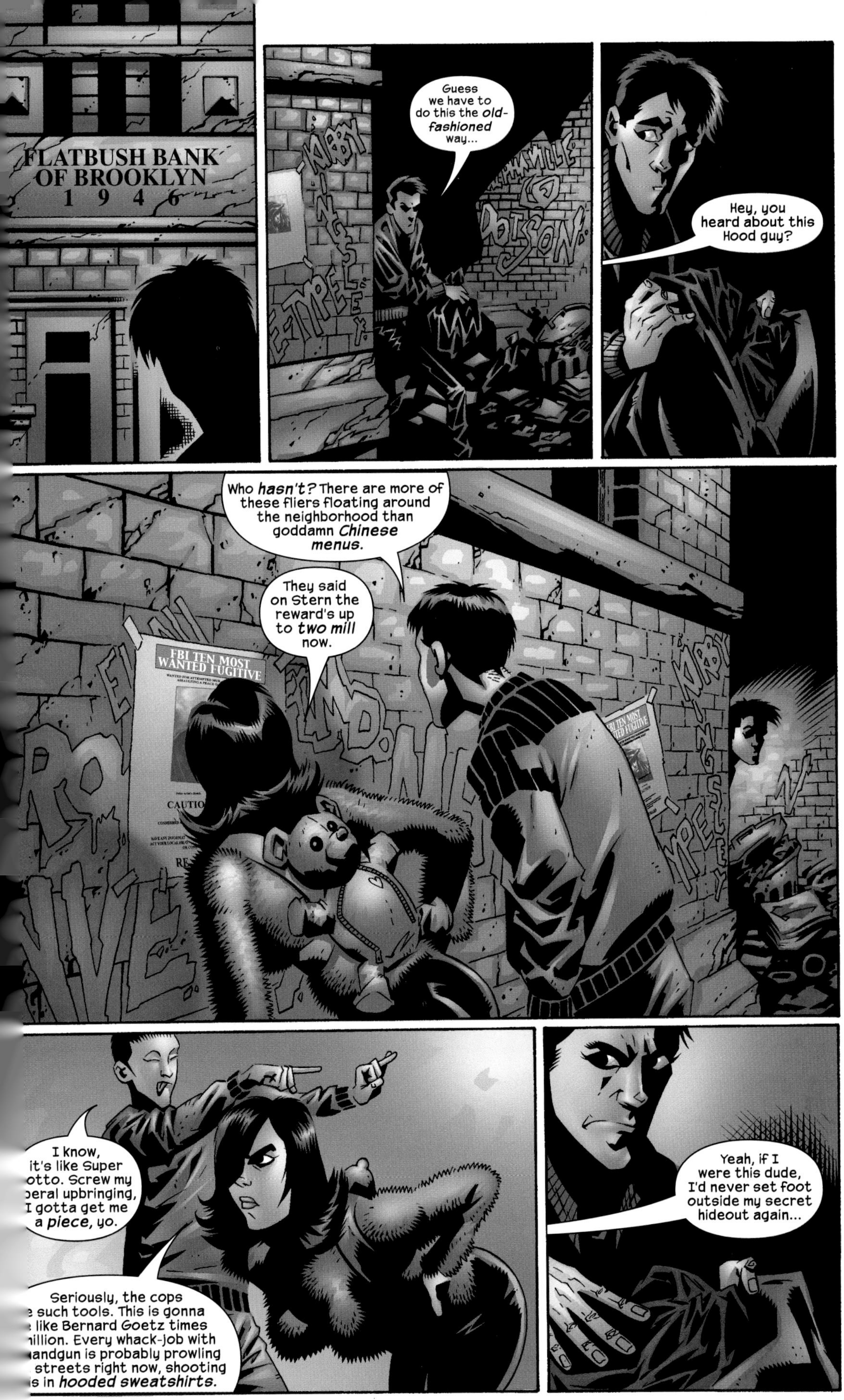
FLATBUSH BANK OF BROOKLYN 1946
Guess we have to do this the *old-fashioned* way...
Hey, you heard about this Hood guy?
Who ***hasn't?*** There are more of these fliers floating around the neighborhood than goddamn *Chinese menus.*
They said on Stern the reward's up to ***two mill*** now.
FBI TEN MOST WANTED FUGITIVE
CAUTION
I know, it's like Super otto. Screw my beral upbringing, I gotta get me a ***piece,*** yo.
Seriously, the cops e such tools. This is gonna e like Bernard Goetz times nillion. Every whack-job with handgun is probably prowling streets right now, shooting s in ***hooded sweatshirts.***
Yeah, if I were this dude, I'd never set foot outside my secret hideout again...

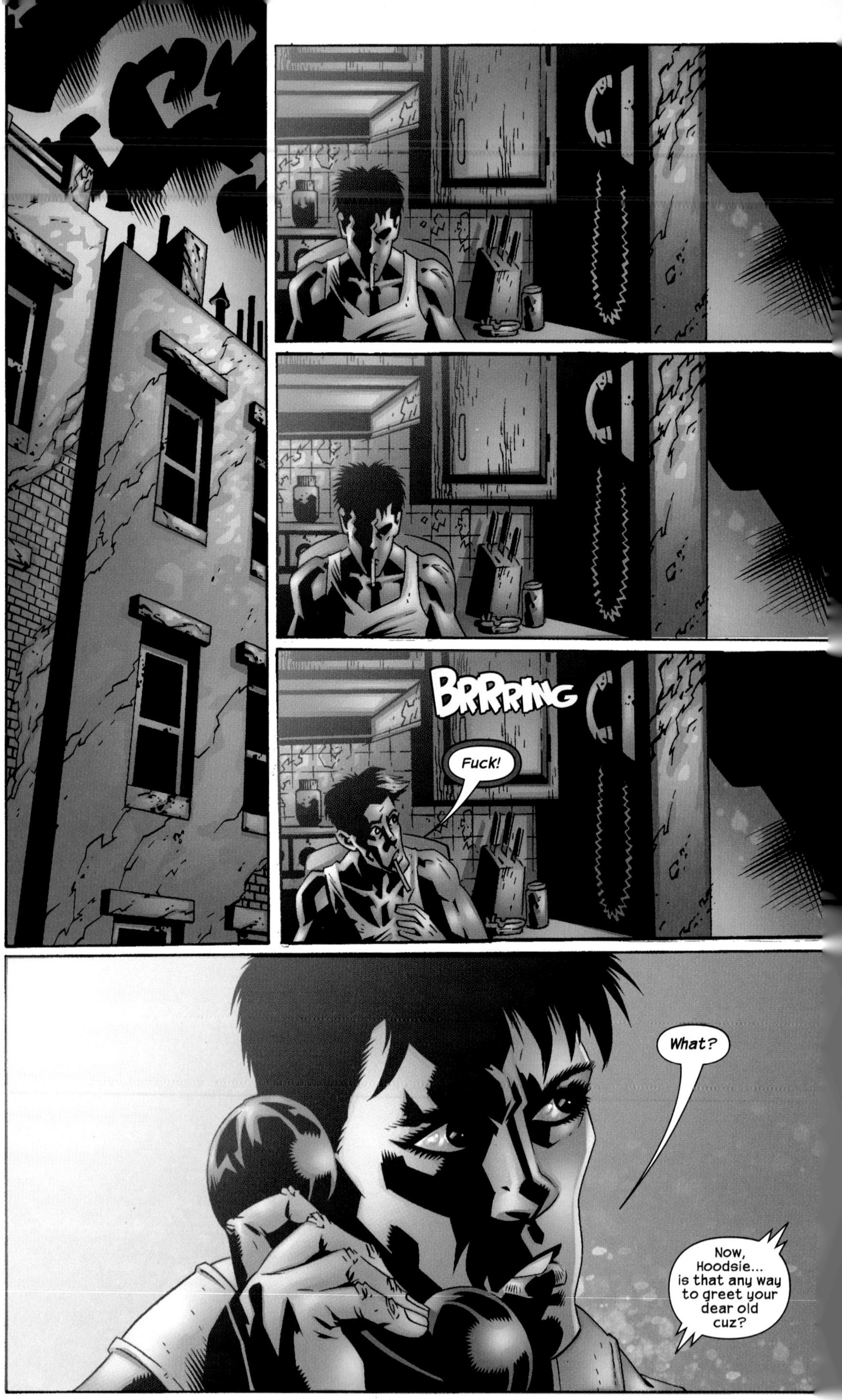
BRRRING
Fuck!
What?
Now, Hoodsie... is that any way to greet your dear old cuz?

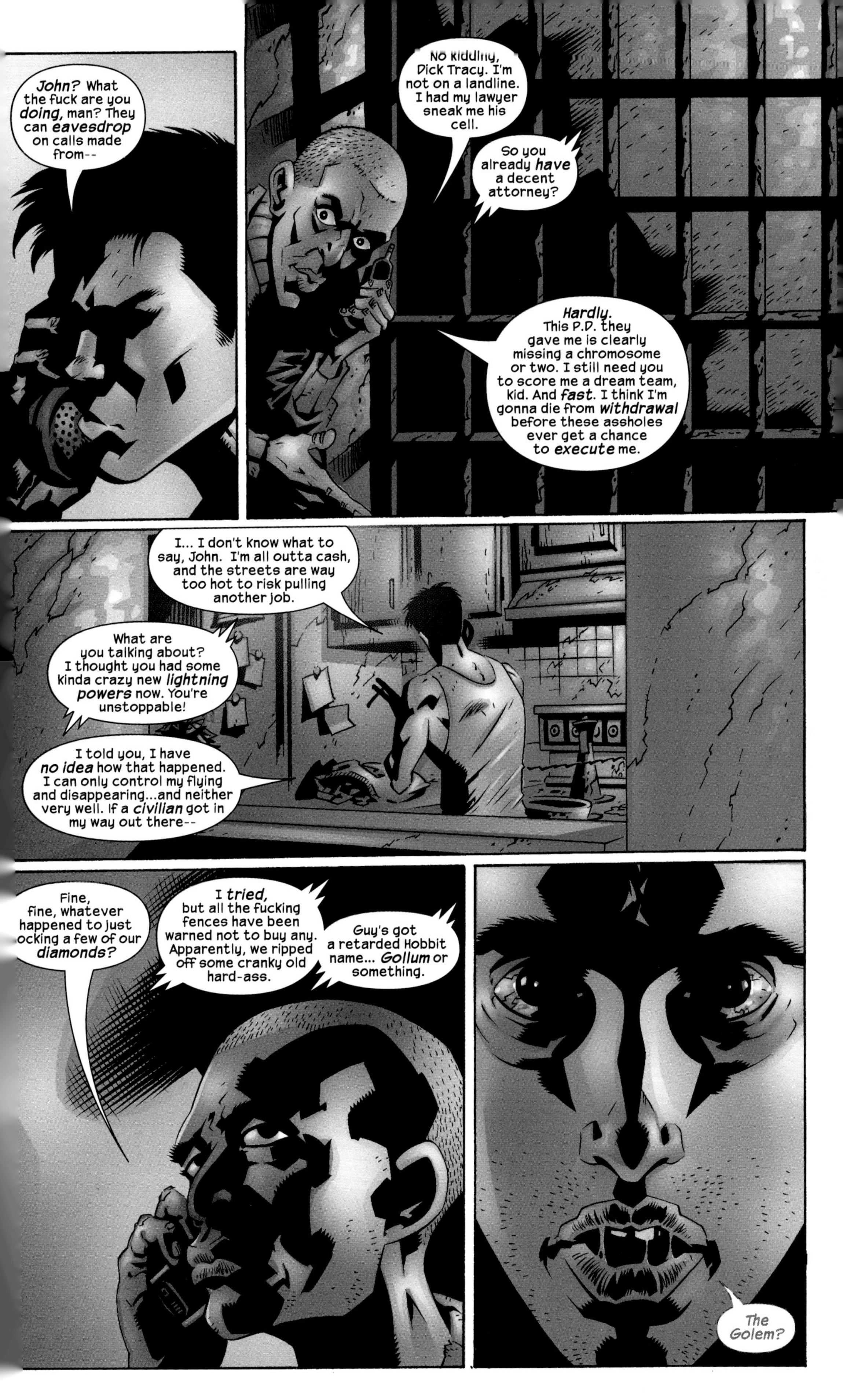
John? What the fuck are you doing, man? They can eavesdrop on calls made from--
No kidding, Dick Tracy. I'm not on a landline. I had my lawyer sneak me his cell.
So you already have a decent attorney?
Hardly. This P.D. they gave me is clearly missing a chromosome or two. I still need you to score me a dream team, kid. And fast. I think I'm gonna die from withdrawal before these assholes ever get a chance to execute me.
I... I don't know what to say, John. I'm all outta cash, and the streets are way too hot to risk pulling another job.
What are you talking about? I thought you had some kinda crazy new lightning powers now. You're unstoppable!
I told you, I have no idea how that happened. I can only control my flying and disappearing...and neither very well. If a civilian got in my way out there--
Fine, fine, whatever happened to just ocking a few of our diamonds?
I tried, but all the fucking fences have been warned not to buy any. Apparently, we ripped off some cranky old hard-ass.
Guy's got a retarded Hobbit name... Gollum or something.
The Golem?

Yeah, that's it. Why?

Your Dad never *told* you about him?

No, you know he never talked about work. Why, is this guy like Keyser Soze or something—

Park, the Golem makes Keyser Soze look like fuckin' *Paste Pot Pete.*

Real name's Golembuski, comes from a family of Polish freedom fighters or some shit. Supposedly whacked his first guy when he was *eight.*

He was an underboss back when our old men were soldiering for the Kingpin... but he quit the life.

You mean he turned state's?

No, I mean he *quit.* Left before he got ground down or bumped off like everybody else.

But nobody just *quits* working for the fucking *Kingpin.*

Well, this cat did. And for some reason, the fat man just let him go.

Nobody knows *who* Golembuski answers to now... the devil, Von Doom, little green men. Either way, he is *not* to be fucked with!

*Now* you tell me. This guy have an office in the city?

Why, you gonna send him a *fruit basket*? The Golem doesn't accept *apologies,* Parker! Face it, we're *both* dead!

Not necessarily. I know how these people think, John.

There might be a way to kill two birds with one bag of stones...

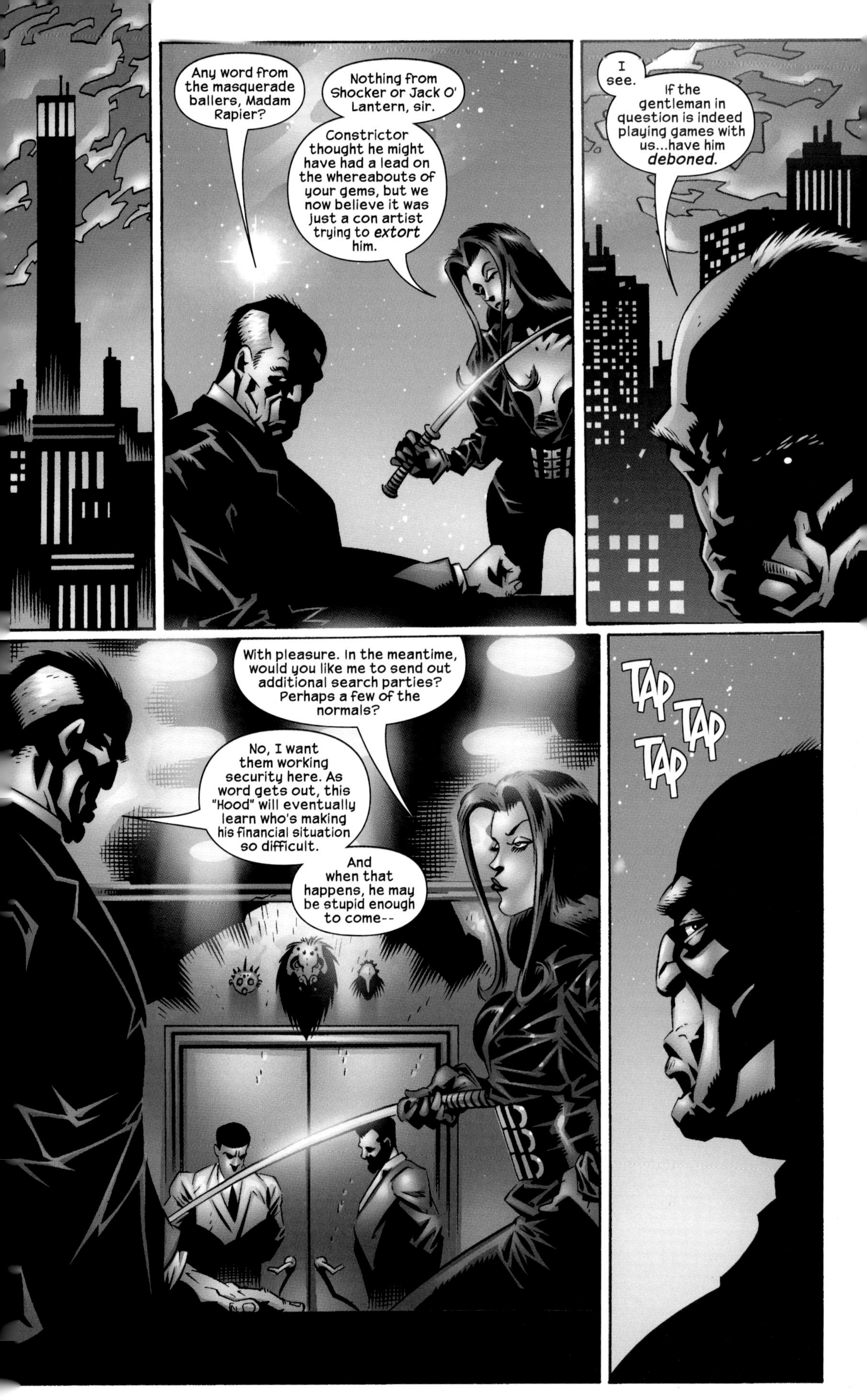
Any word from the masquerade ballers, Madam Rapier?
Nothing from Shocker or Jack O' Lantern, sir.
Constrictor thought he might have had a lead on the whereabouts of your gems, but we now believe it was just a con artist trying to *extort* him.
I see.
If the gentleman in question is indeed playing games with us...have him ***deboned.***
With pleasure. In the meantime, would you like me to send out additional search parties? Perhaps a few of the normals?
No, I want them working security here. As word gets out, this "Hood" will eventually learn who's making his financial situation so difficult.
And when that happens, he may be stupid enough to come--
TAP TAP TAP

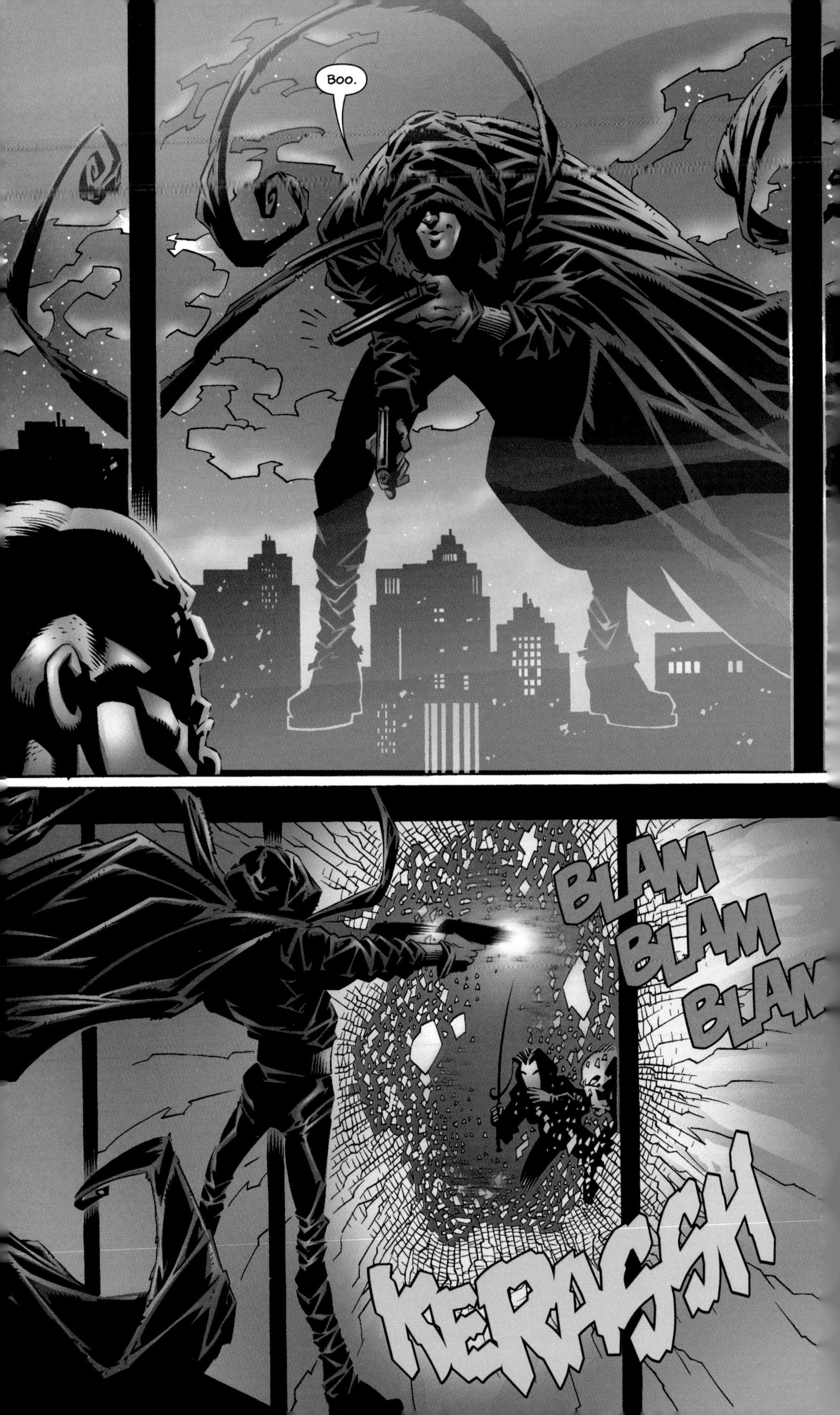
Boo.
BLAM
BLAM
BLAM
KERASSH

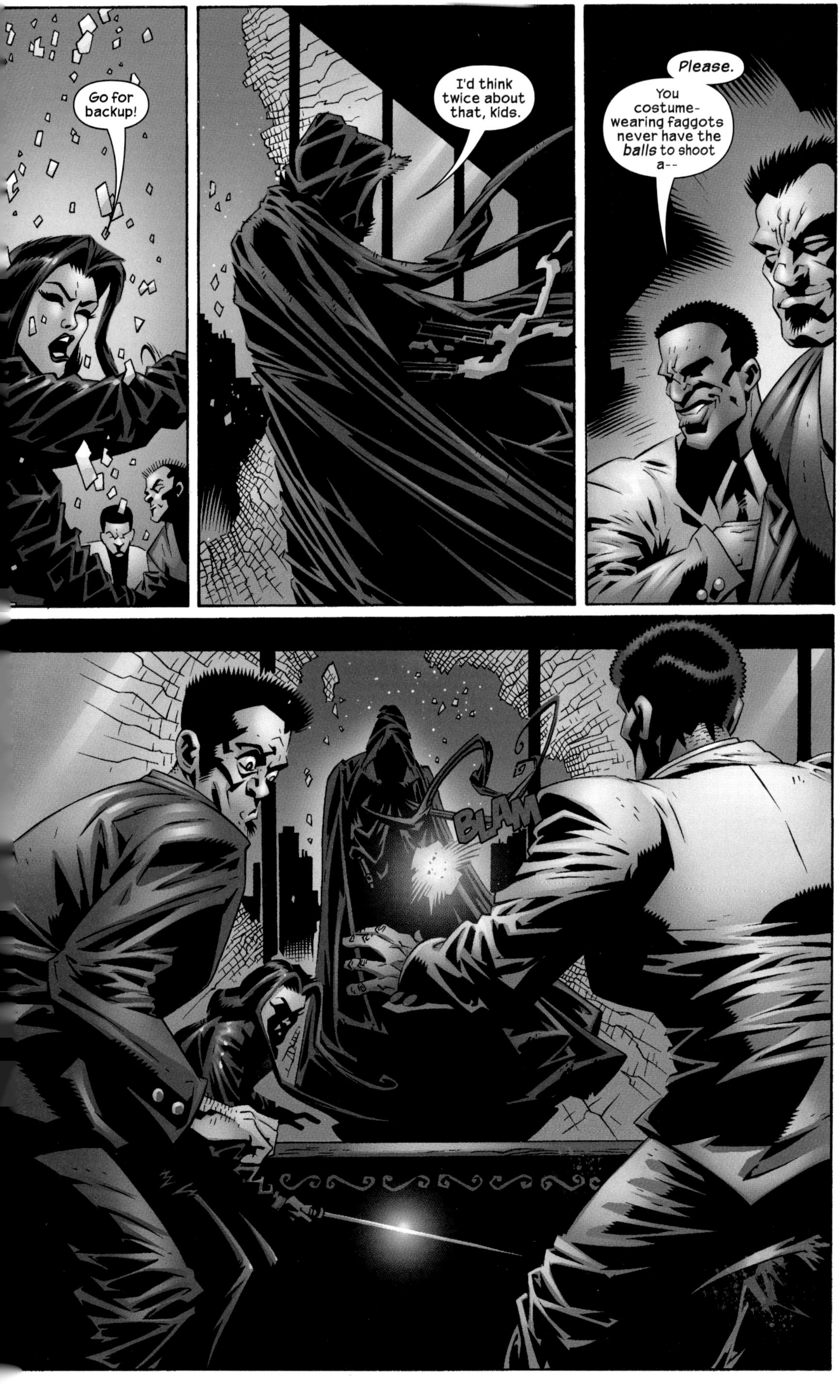
Go for backup!
I'd think twice about that, kids.
Please.
You costume-wearing faggots never have the *balls* to shoot a--
BLAM

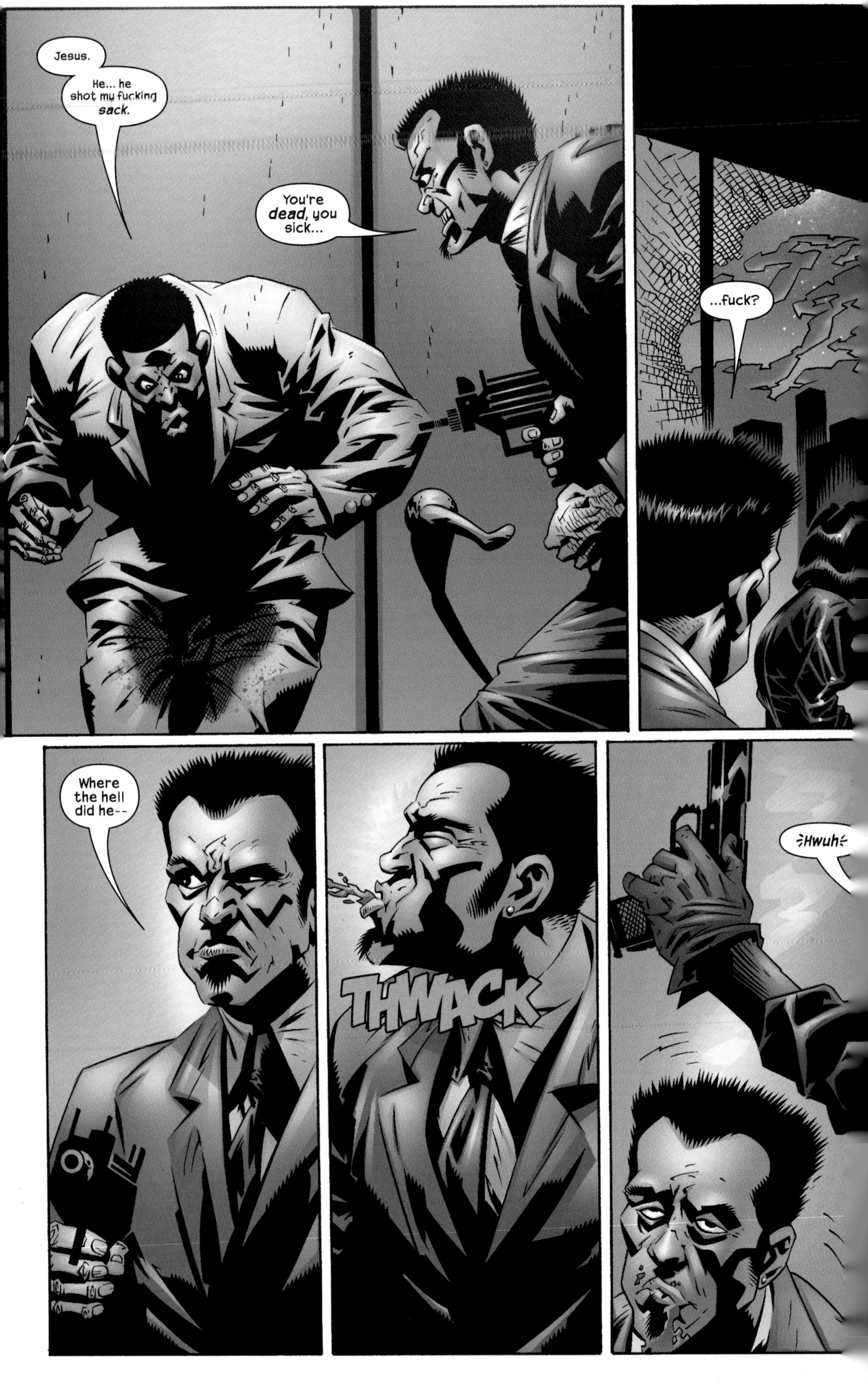
Jesus.
He... he shot my fucking *sack*.
You're *dead*, you sick...
...fuck?
Where the hell did he--
THWACK
*Hwuh*

Now then...
Call her off, Golem.
Kill me now and you'll never see your diamonds again.
If I wanted to kill you...
"...you'd already be dead"?
Yeah, that's what *I* was about to say.
Right.
Let's hear your pitch...

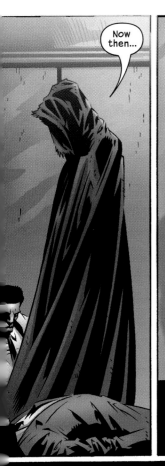

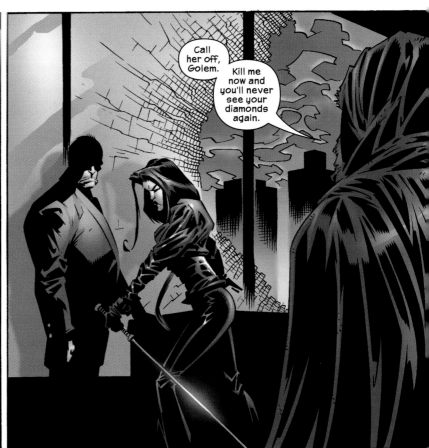

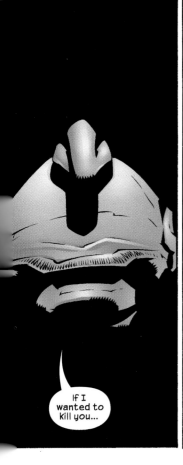

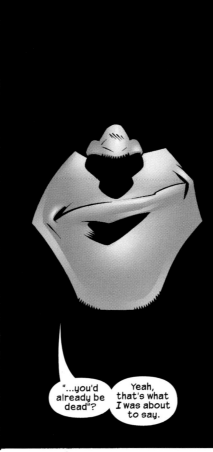

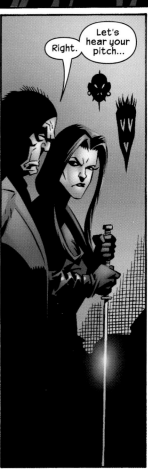

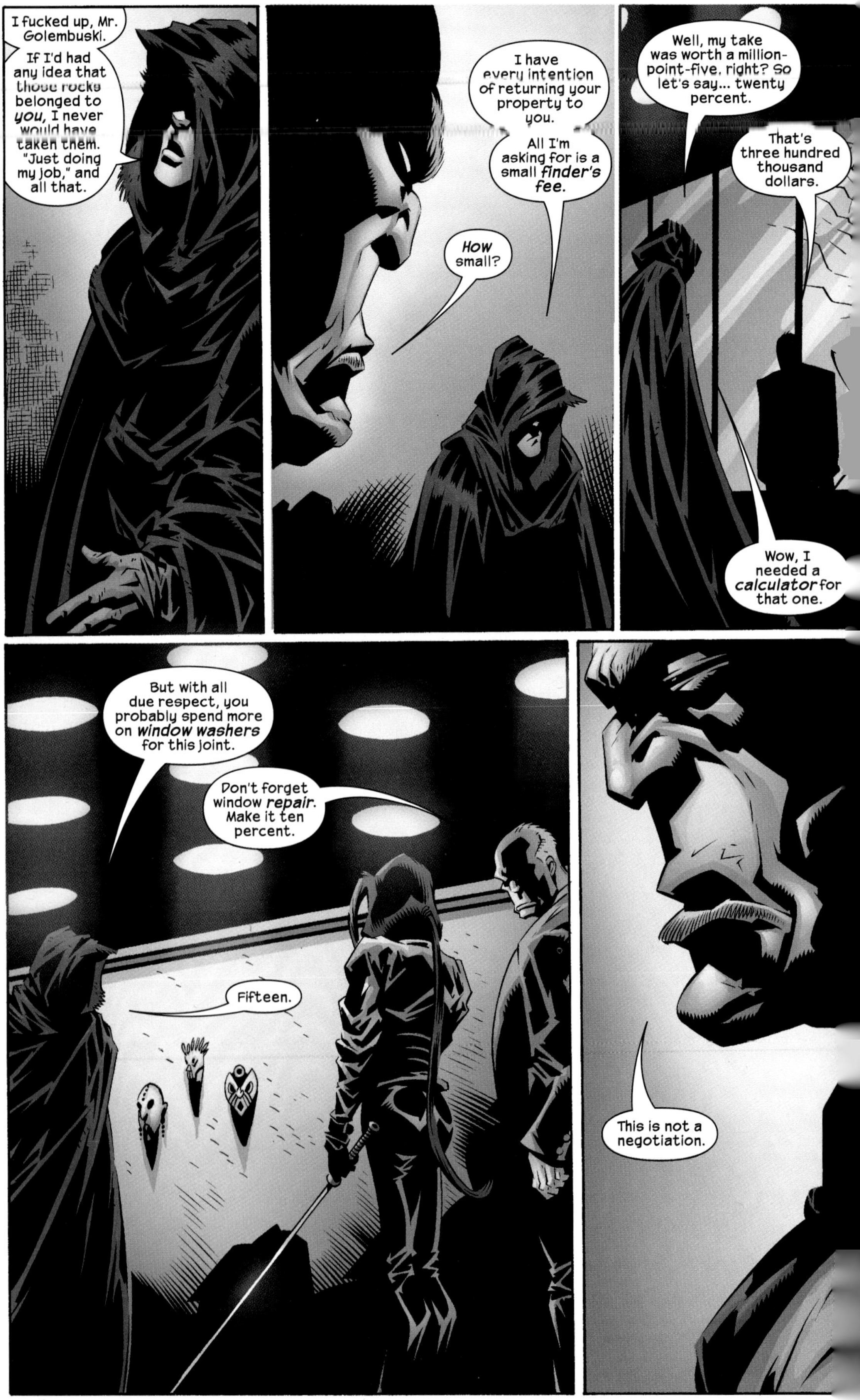
I fucked up, Mr. Golembuski.
If I'd had any idea that those rocks belonged to *you*, I never would have taken them. "Just doing my job," and all that.
I have every intention of returning your property to you.
All I'm asking for is a small *finder's fee.*
*How* small?
Well, my take was worth a million-point-five, right? So let's say... twenty percent.
That's three hundred thousand dollars.
Wow, I needed a *calculator* for that one.
But with all due respect, you probably spend more on *window washers* for this joint.
Don't forget window *repair*. Make it ten percent.
Fifteen.
This is not a negotiation.

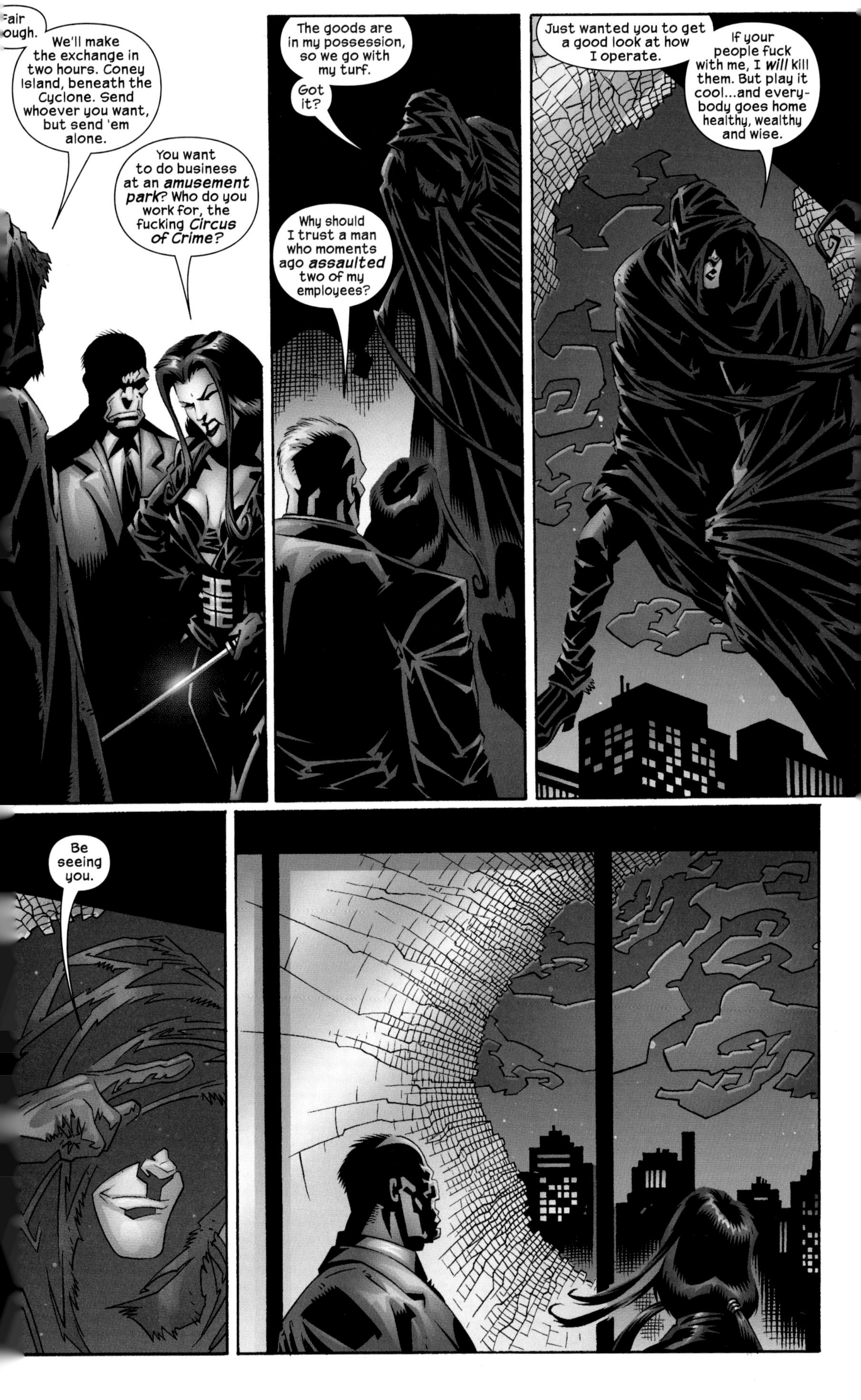

Fair ough.
We'll make the exchange in two hours. Coney Island, beneath the Cyclone. Send whoever you want, but send 'em alone.
You want to do business at an *amusement park*? Who do you work for, the fucking *Circus of Crime*?
The goods are in my possession, so we go with my turf.
Got it?
Why should I trust a man who moments ago *assaulted* two of my employees?
Just wanted you to get a good look at how I operate.
If your people fuck with me, I *will* kill them. But play it cool...and everybody goes home healthy, wealthy and wise.
Be seeing you.

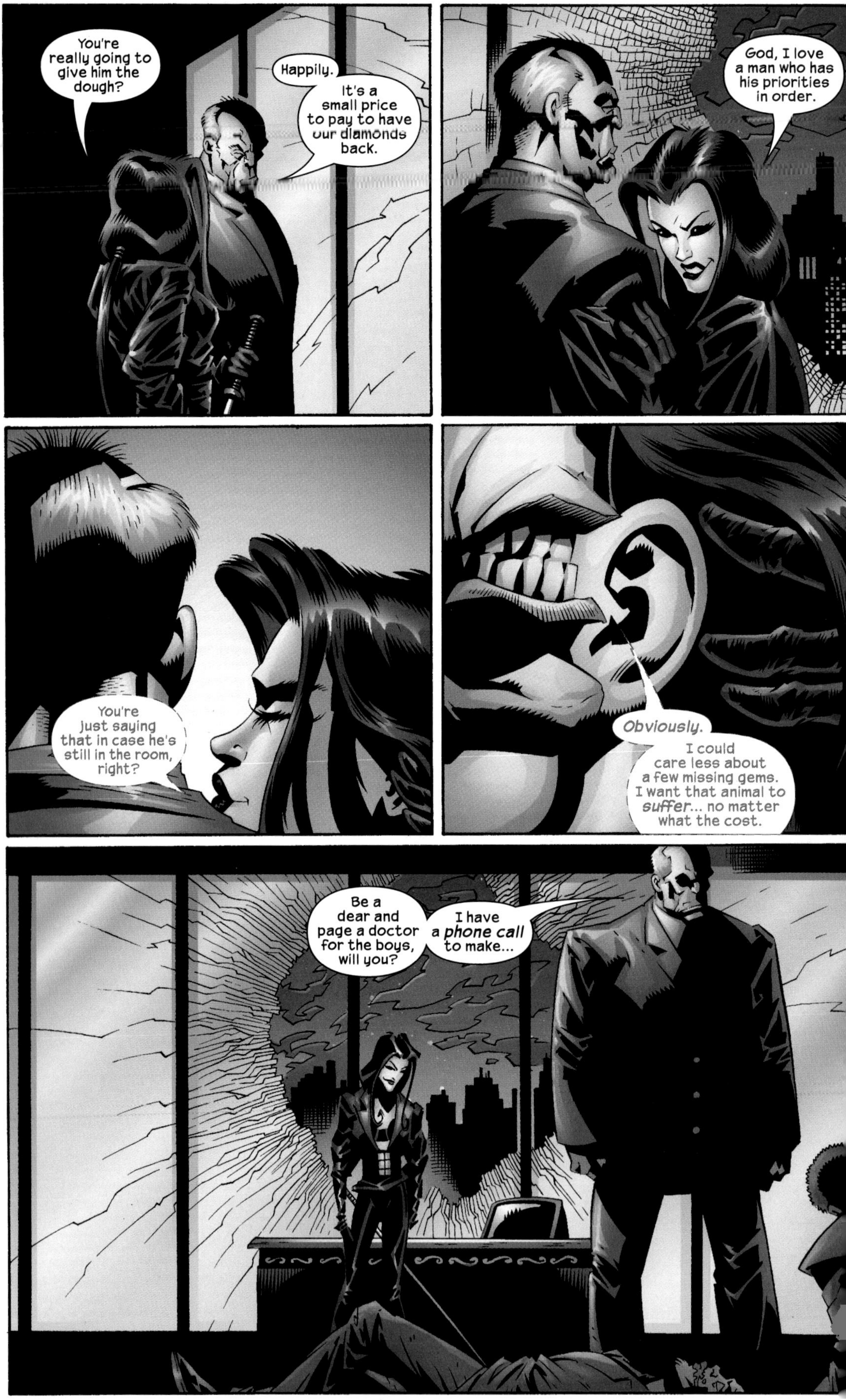
You're really going to give him the dough?
Happily.
It's a small price to pay to have our diamonds back.
God, I love a man who has his priorities in order.
You're just saying that in case he's still in the room, right?
Obviously.
I could care less about a few missing gems. I want that animal to suffer... no matter what the cost.
Be a dear and page a doctor for the boys, will you?
I have a phone call to make...

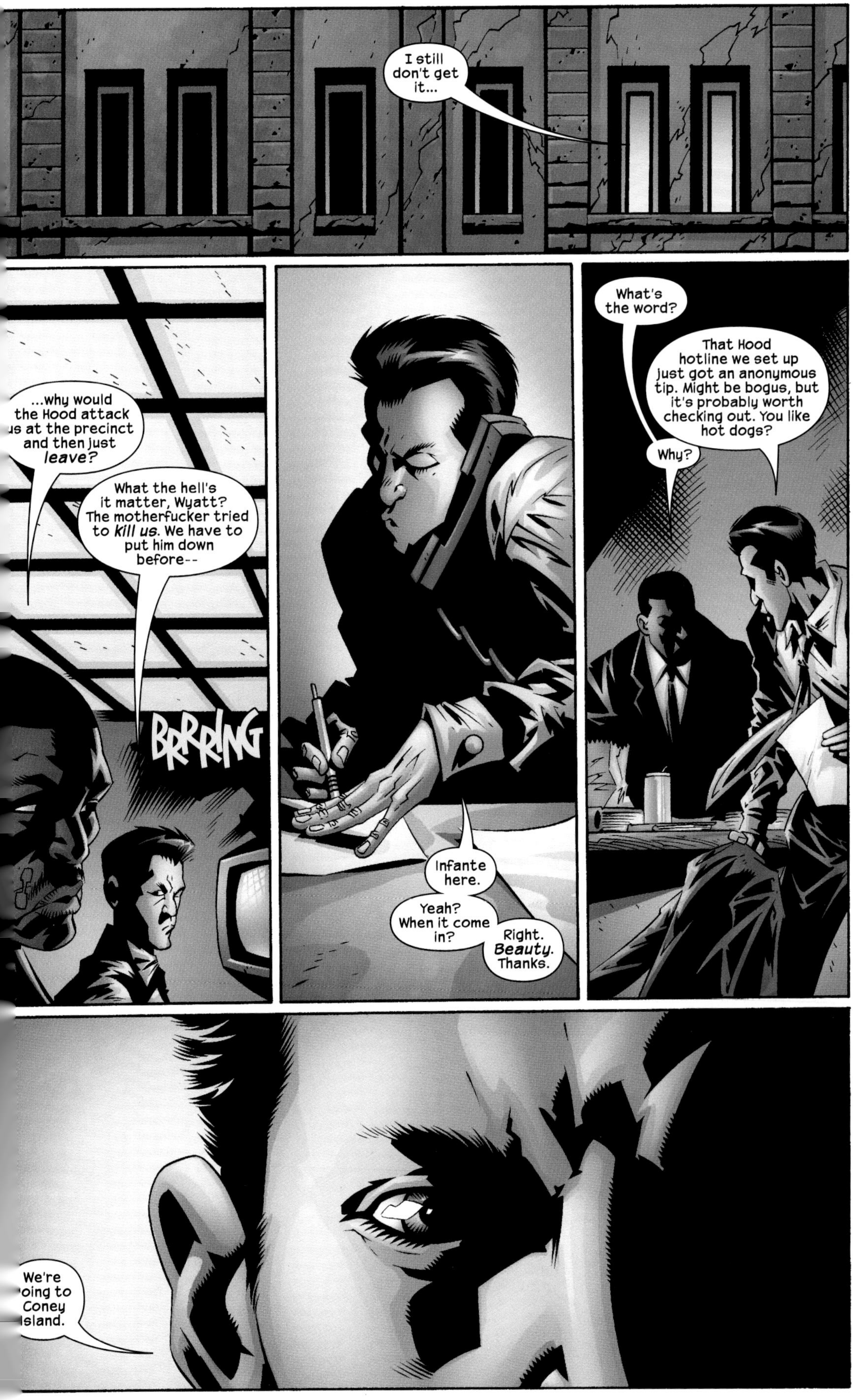
I still don't get it...
...why would the Hood attack s at the precinct and then just *leave?*
What the hell's it matter, Wyatt? The motherfucker tried to *kill us*. We have to put him down before--
BRRRING
Infante here.
Yeah? When it come in?
Right. *Beauty*. Thanks.
What's the word?
That Hood hotline we set up just got an anonymous tip. Might be bogus, but it's probably worth checking out. You like hot dogs?
Why?
We're oing to Coney sland.

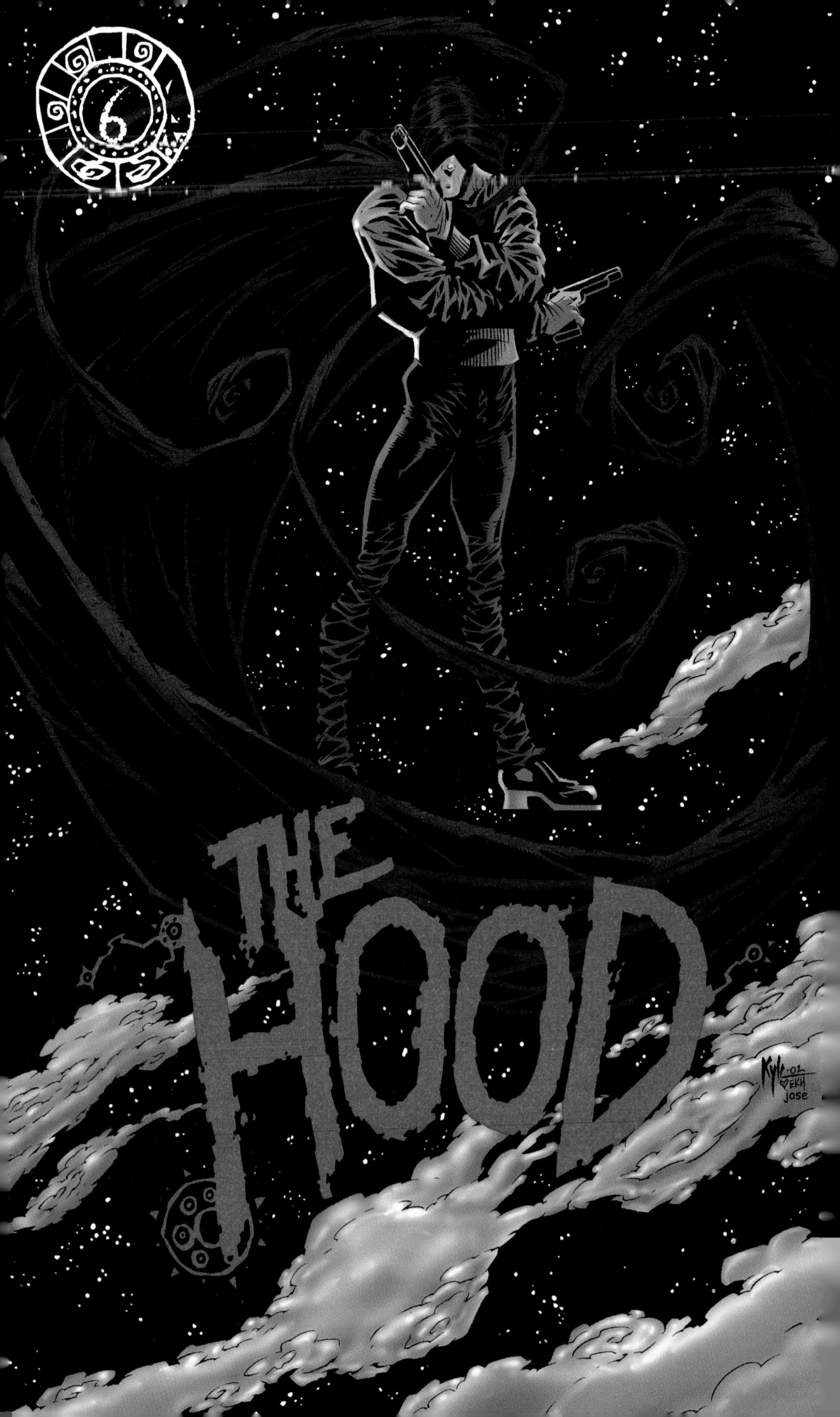
6
THE HOOD

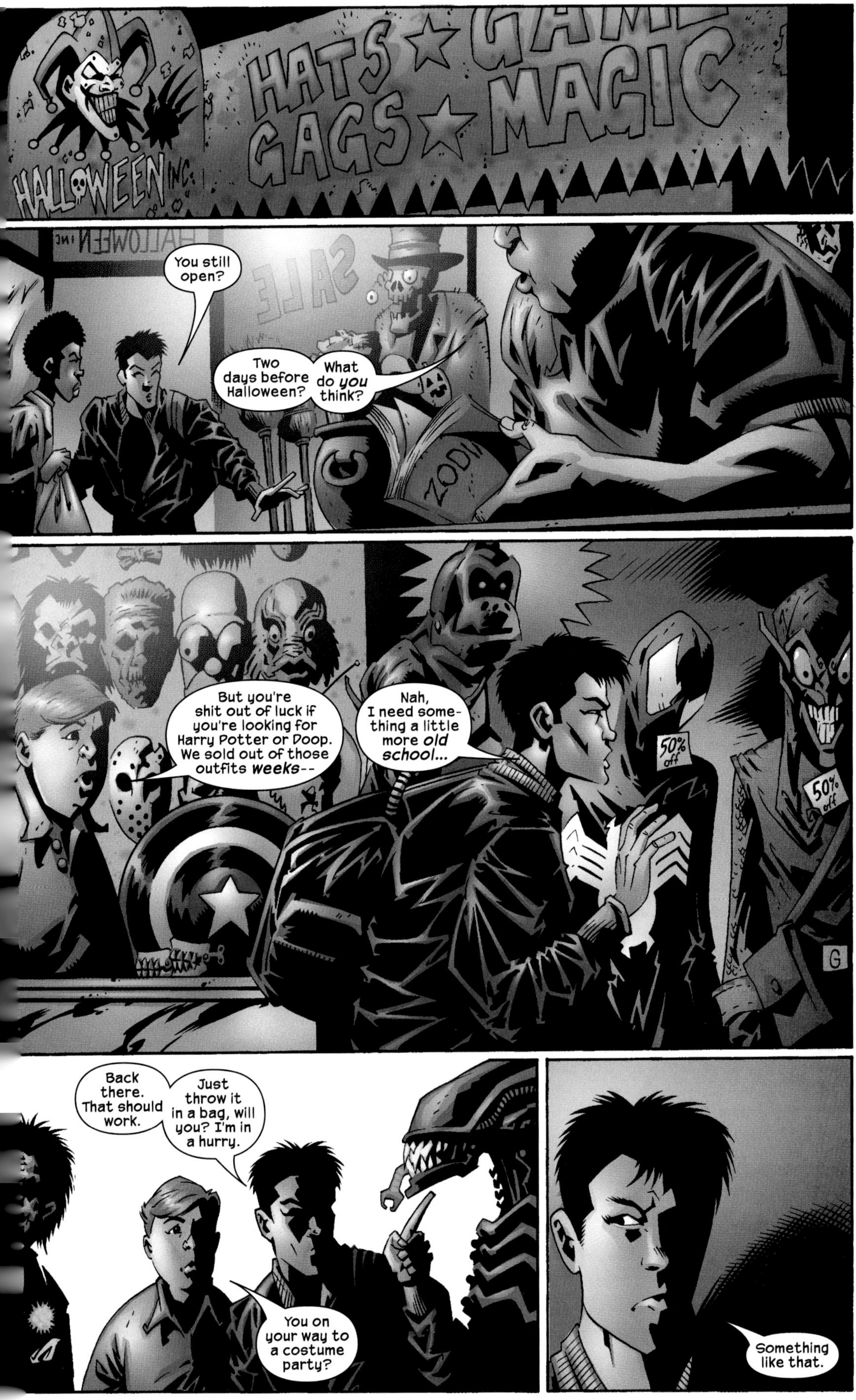
HATS ★ GAME
GAGS ★ MAGIC
HALLOWEEN INC.
You still open?
SALE
Two days before Halloween?
What do *you* think?
ZODI
But you're shit out of luck if you're looking for Harry Potter or Doop. We sold out of those outfits *weeks*--
Nah, I need something a little more *old school*...
50% off
50% off
Back there. That should work.
Just throw it in a bag, will you? I'm in a hurry.
You on your way to a costume party?
Something like that.

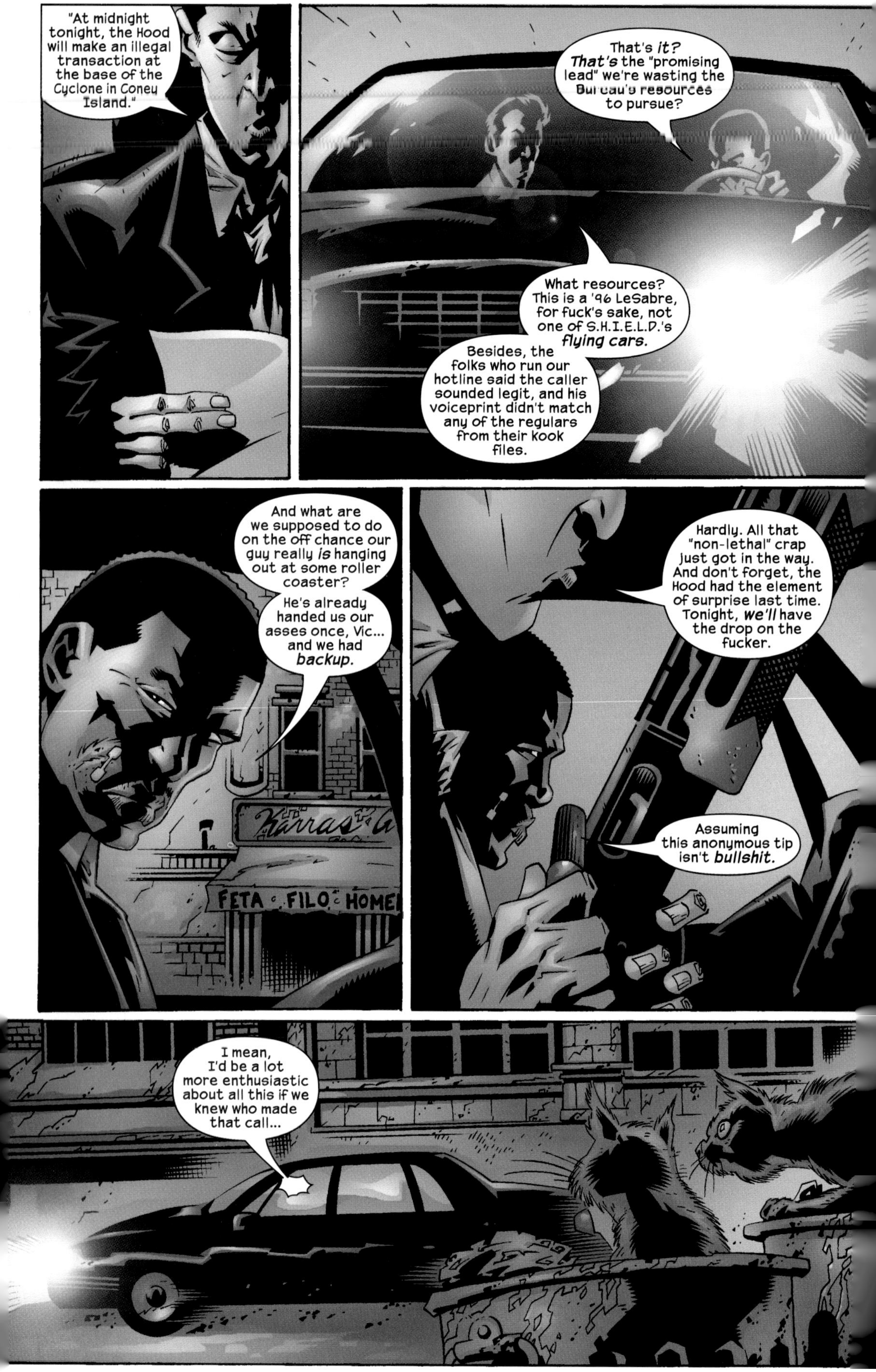
"At midnight tonight, the Hood will make an illegal transaction at the base of the Cyclone in Coney Island."
That's *it?* *That's* the "promising lead" we're wasting the Bureau's resources to pursue?
What resources? This is a '96 LeSabre, for fuck's sake, not one of S.H.I.E.L.D.'s *flying cars.*
Besides, the folks who run our hotline said the caller sounded legit, and his voiceprint didn't match any of the regulars from their kook files.
And what are we supposed to do on the off chance our guy really *is* hanging out at some roller coaster?
He's already handed us our asses once, Vic... and we had *backup.*
FETA FILO HOME
Hardly. All that "non-lethal" crap just got in the way. And don't forget, the Hood had the element of surprise last time. Tonight, *we'll* have the drop on the fucker.
Assuming this anonymous tip isn't *bullshit.*
I mean, I'd be a lot more enthusiastic about all this if we knew who made that call...

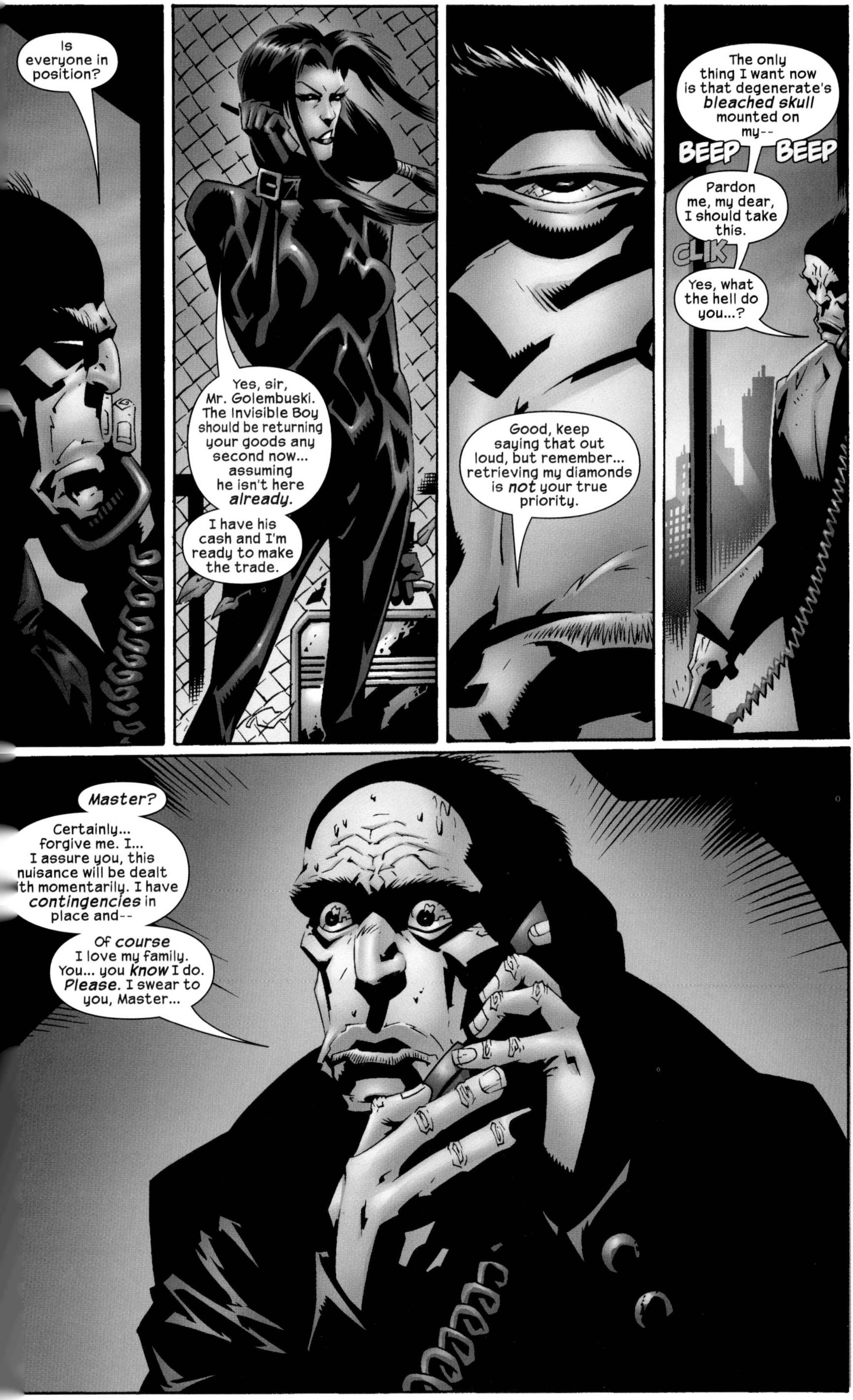
Is everyone in position?
Yes, sir, Mr. Golembuski. The Invisible Boy should be returning your goods any second now... assuming he isn't here *already.*
I have his cash and I'm ready to make the trade.
Good, keep saying that out loud, but remember... retrieving my diamonds is *not* your true priority.
The only thing I want now is that degenerate's *bleached skull* mounted on my--
BEEP BEEP
Pardon me, my dear, I should take this.
CLIK
Yes, what the hell do you...?
*Master?*
Certainly... forgive me. I... I assure you, this nuisance will be dealt ith momentarily. I have *contingencies* in place and--
Of *course* I love my family. You... you *know* I do. *Please.* I swear to you, Master...

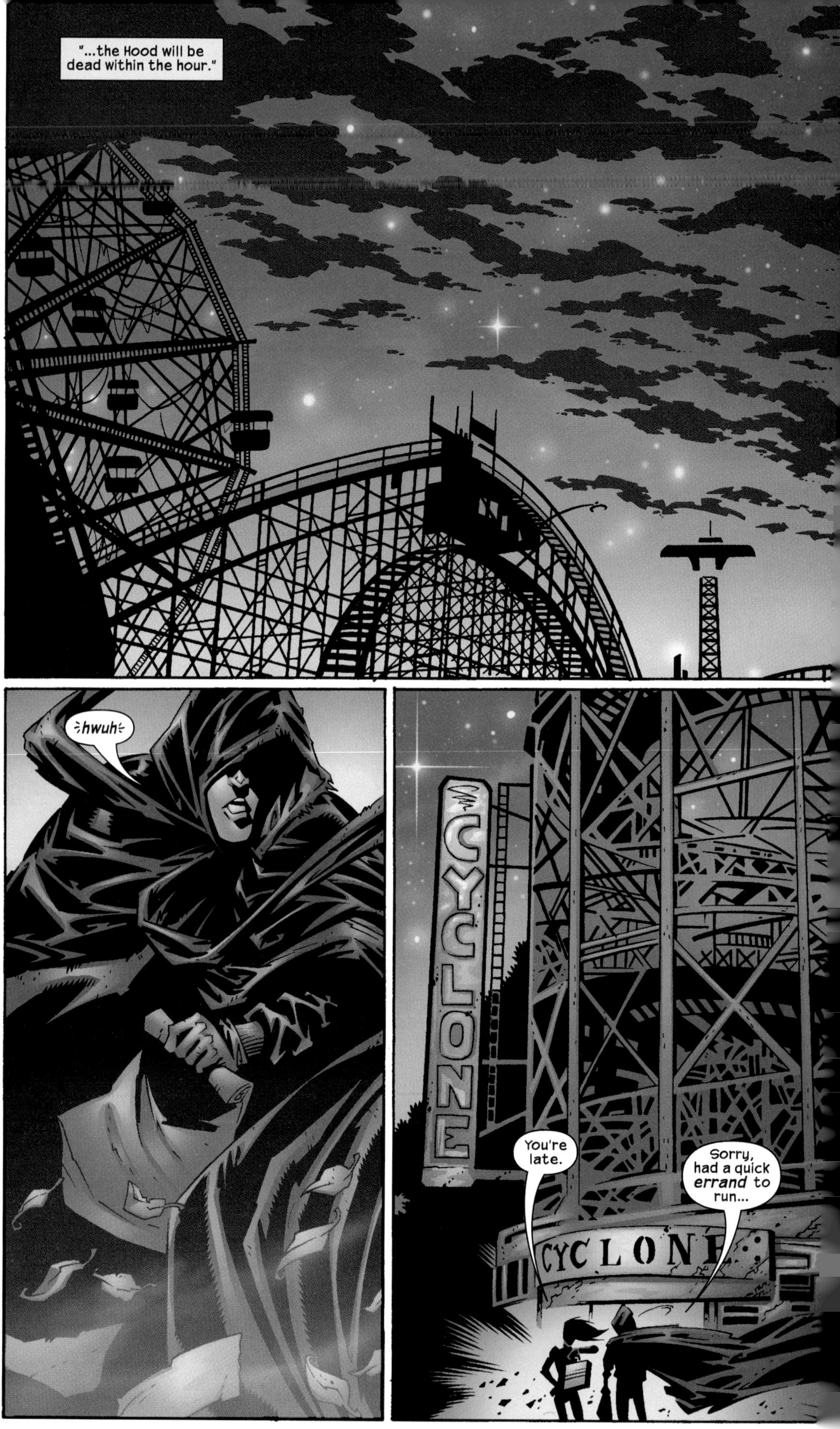
"...the Hood will be dead within the hour."
hwuh
CYCLONE
You're late.
Sorry, had a quick *errand* to run...
CYCLONE

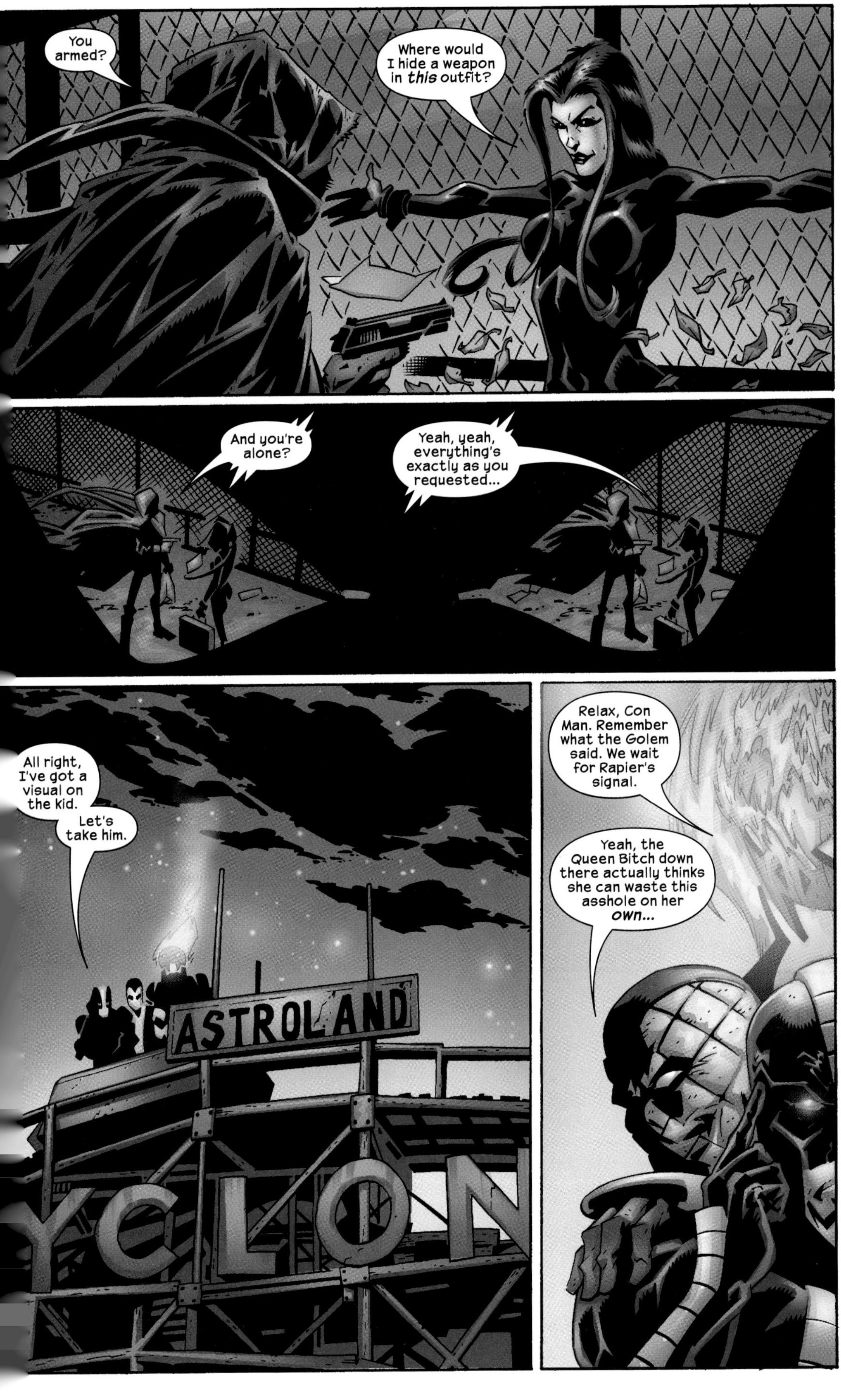
You armed?
Where would I hide a weapon in *this* outfit?
And you're alone?
Yeah, yeah, everything's exactly as you requested...
All right, I've got a visual on the kid.
Let's take him.
ASTROLAND
YCLON
Relax, Con Man. Remember what the Golem said. We wait for Rapier's signal.
Yeah, the Queen Bitch down there actually thinks she can waste this asshole on her *own*...

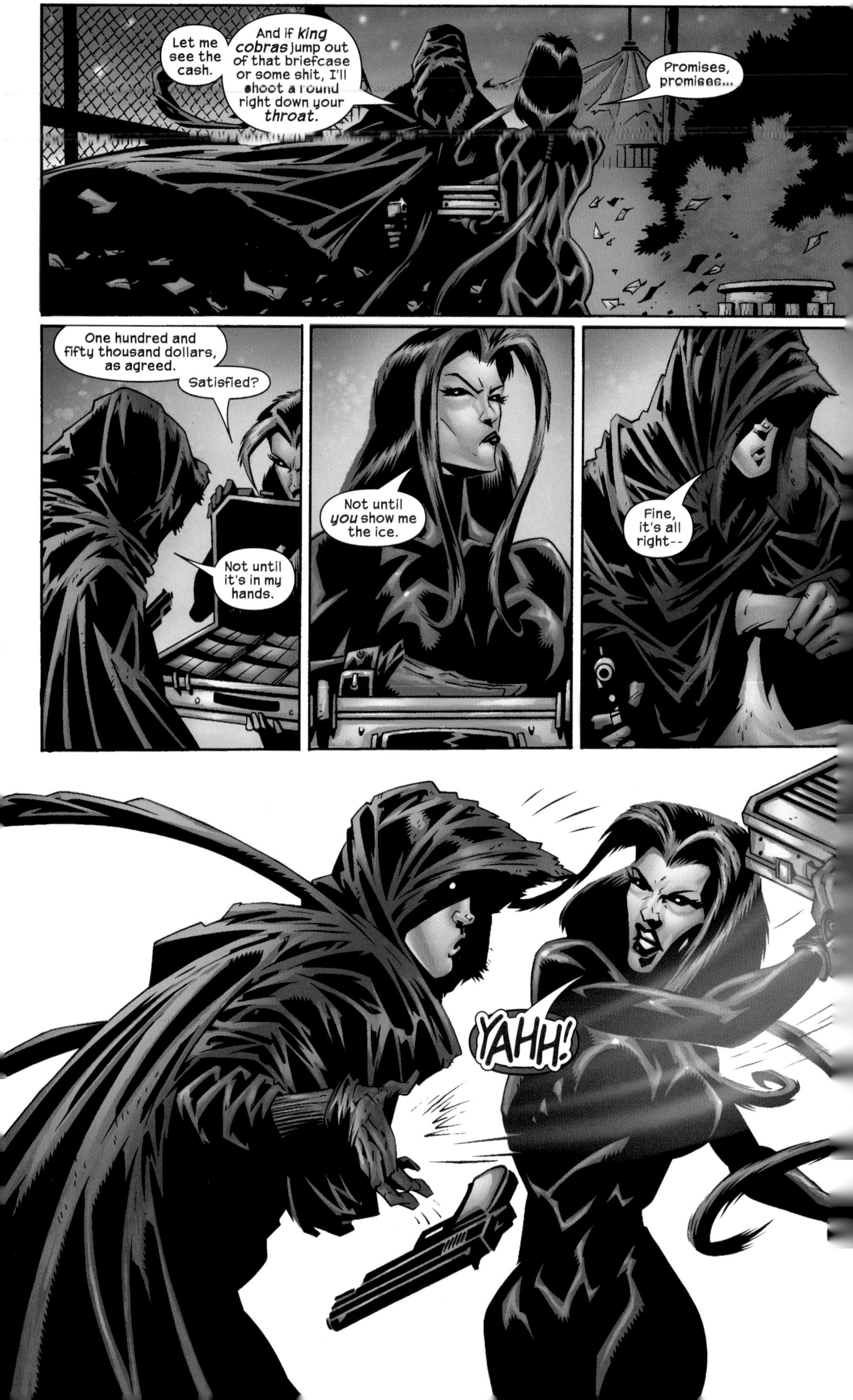
Let me see the cash.
And if king cobras jump out of that briefcase or some shit, I'll shoot a round right down your throat.
Promises, promises...
One hundred and fifty thousand dollars, as agreed.
Satisfied?
Not until it's in my hands.
Not until you show me the ice.
Fine, it's all right--
YAHH!

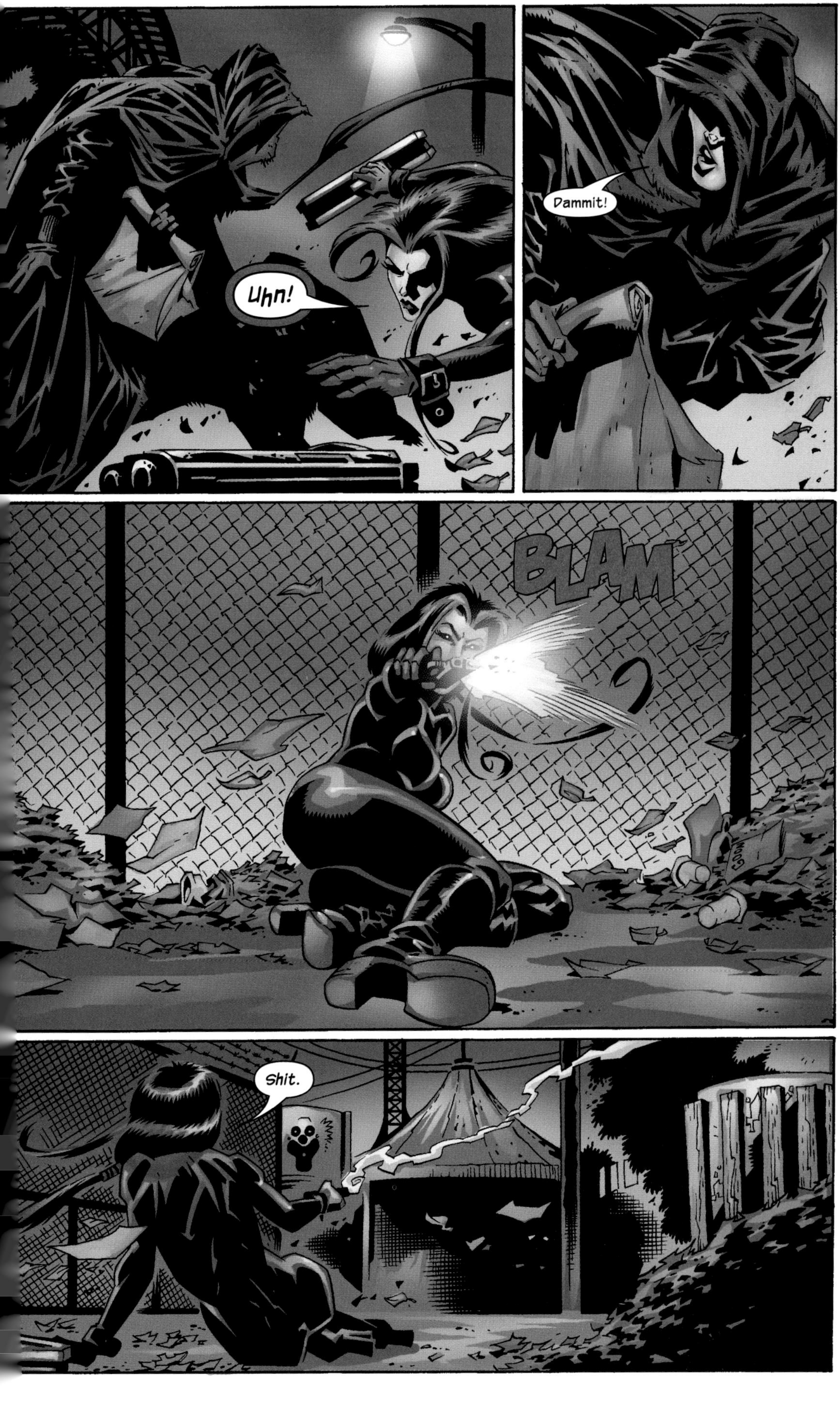
Uhn!
Dammit!
BLAM
Shit.

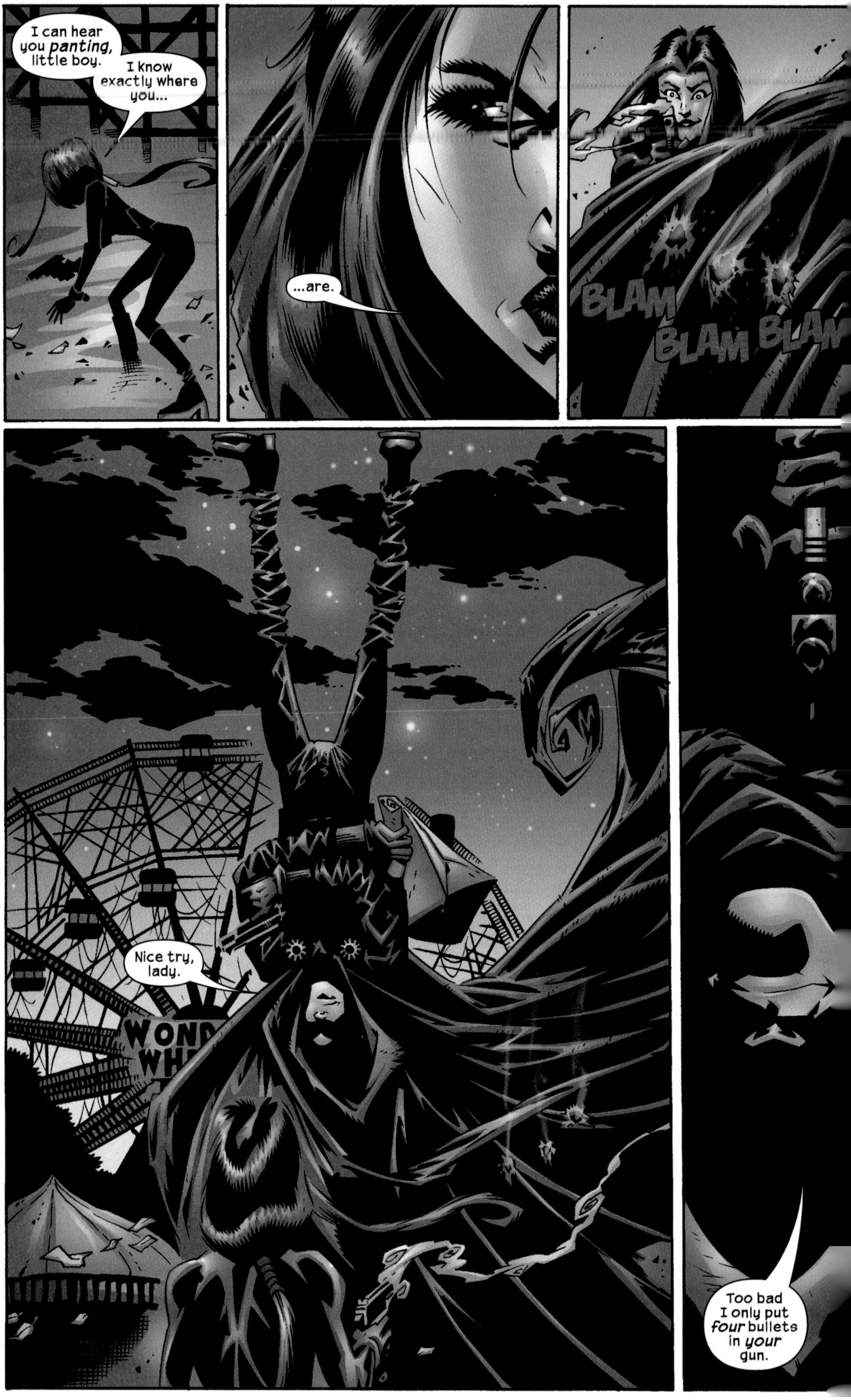
I can hear you *panting*, little boy.
I know exactly where you...
...are.
BLAM
BLAM BLAM BLAM
Nice try, lady.
WOND
WHE
Too bad I only put *four* bullets in *your* gun.

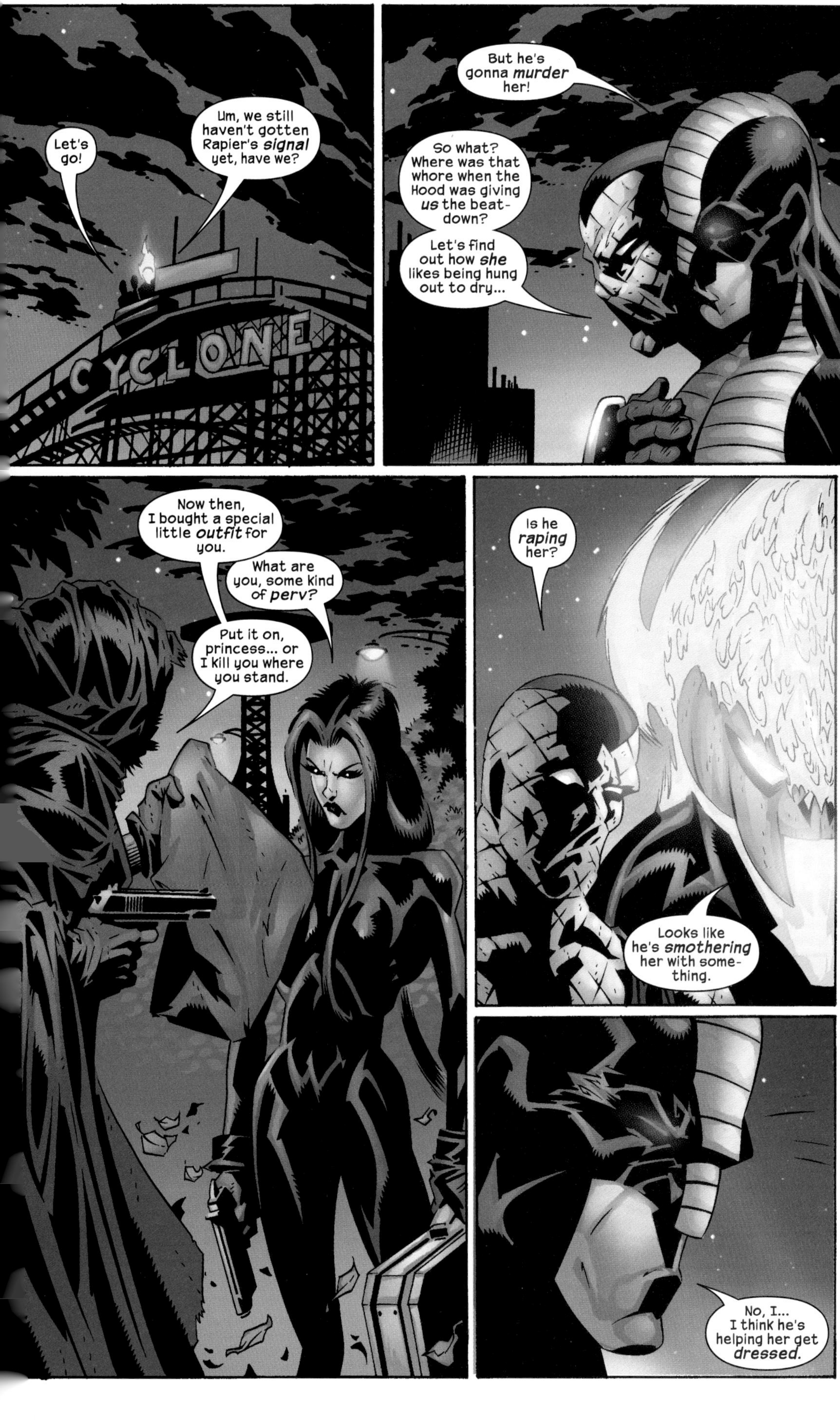
Let's go!
Um, we still haven't gotten Rapier's *signal* yet, have we?
CYCLONE
But he's gonna *murder* her!
So what? Where was that whore when the Hood was giving *us* the beat-down?
Let's find out how *she* likes being hung out to dry...
Now then, I bought a special little *outfit* for you.
What are you, some kind of *perv?*
Put it on, princess... or I kill you where you stand.
Is he *raping* her?
Looks like he's *smothering* her with some-thing.
No, I... I think he's helping her get *dressed.*

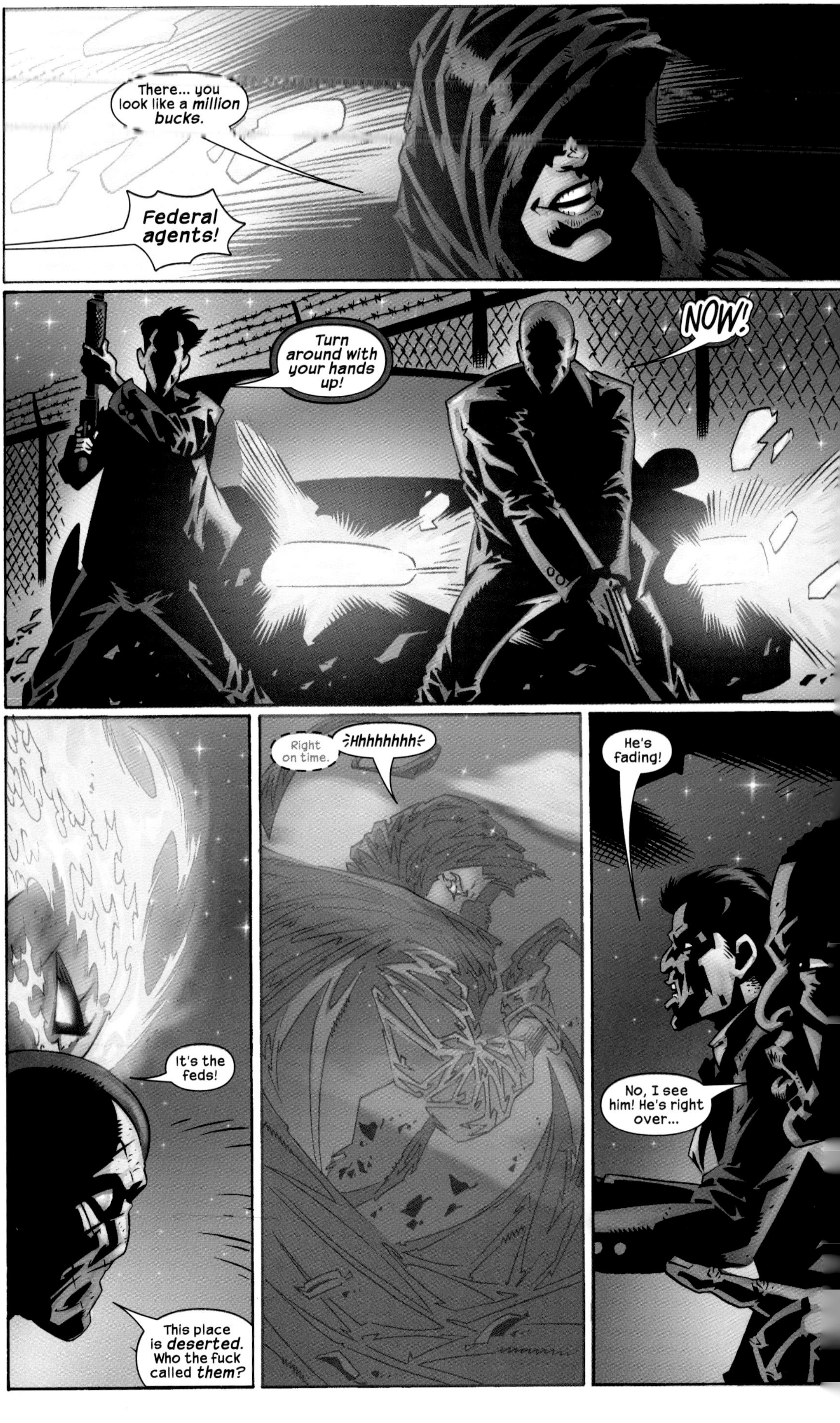

There... you look like a *million* bucks.
*Federal agents!*
*Turn around with your hands up!*
*NOW!*
It's the feds!
This place is *deserted*. Who the fuck called *them*?
Right on time.
Hhhhhhhh
He's fading!
No, I see him! He's right over...

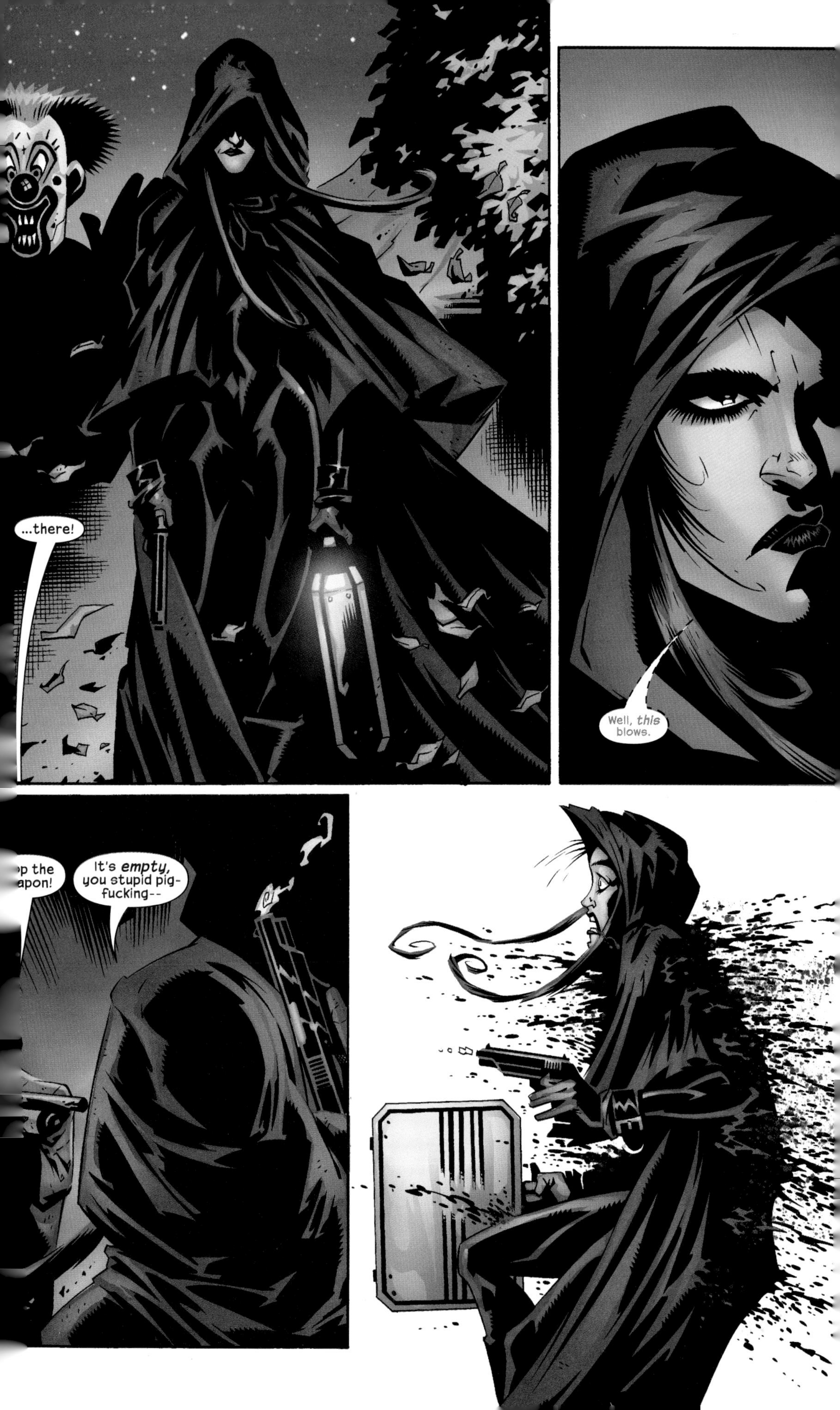
...there!
Well, *this* blows.
p the apon!
It's *empty*, you stupid pig-fucking--

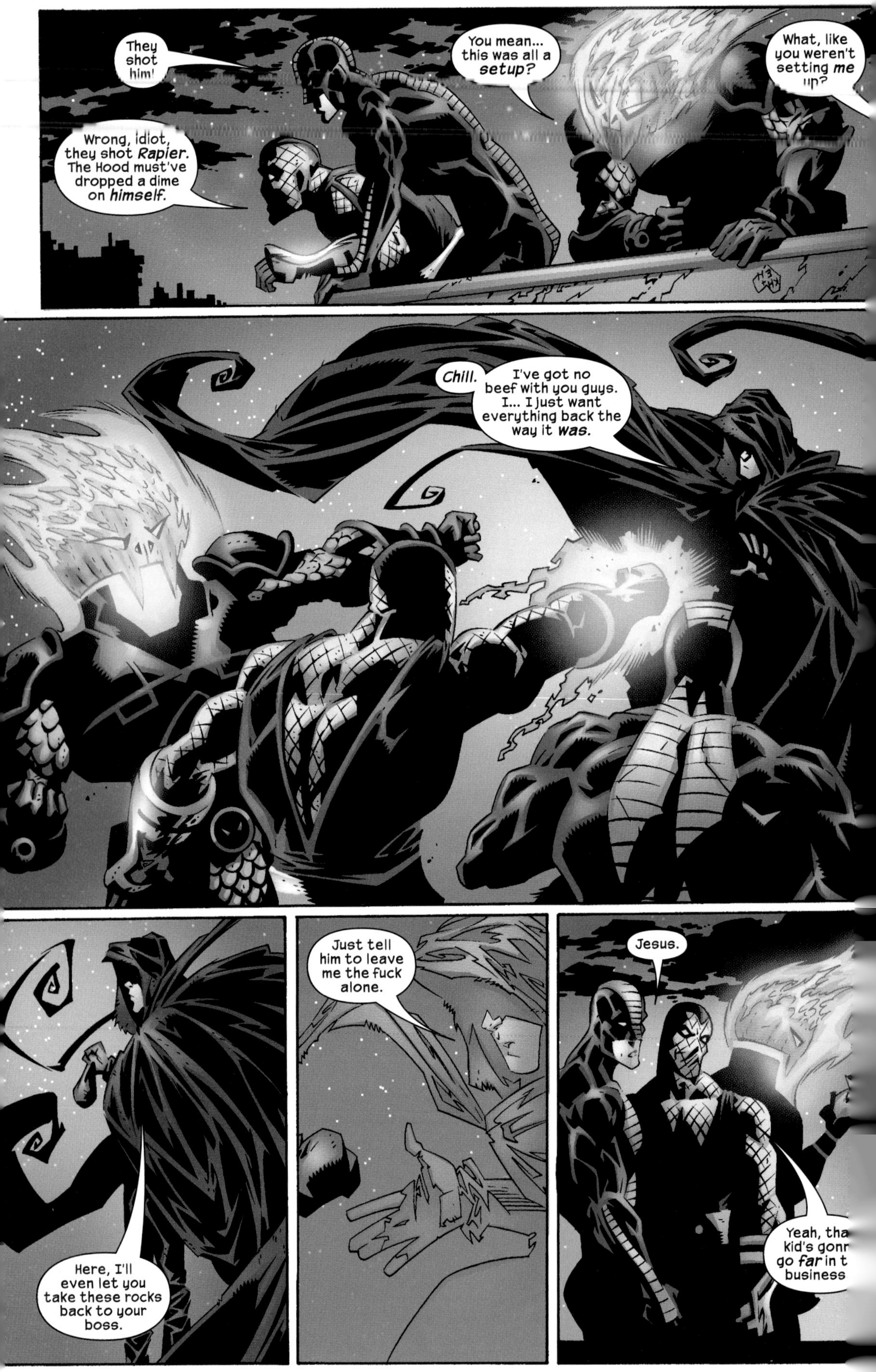
They shot him!
Wrong, idiot, they shot Rapier. The Hood must've dropped a dime on himself.
You mean... this was all a setup?
What, like you weren't setting me up?
Chill.
I've got no beef with you guys. I... I just want everything back the way it was.
Here, I'll even let you take these rocks back to your boss.
Just tell him to leave me the fuck alone.
Jesus.
Yeah, tha kid's gonn go far in t business

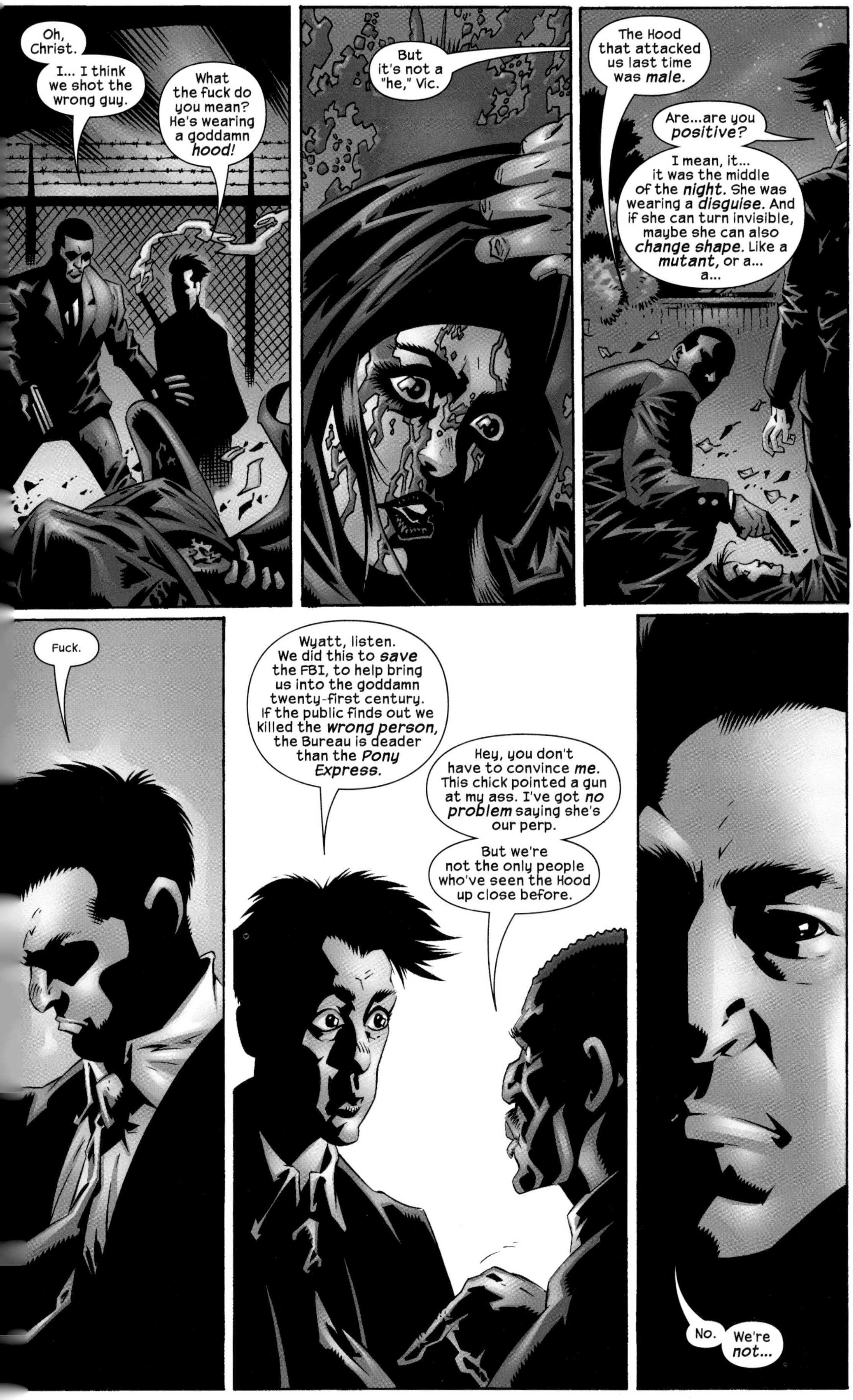
Oh, Christ.
I... I think we shot the wrong guy.
What the fuck do you mean? He's wearing a goddamn *hood!*
But it's not a "he," Vic.
The Hood that attacked us last time was *male.*
Are...are you *positive?*
I mean, it... it was the middle of the *night.* She was wearing a *disguise.* And if she can turn invisible, maybe she can also *change shape.* Like a *mutant,* or a... a...
Fuck.
Wyatt, listen. We did this to *save* the FBI, to help bring us into the goddamn twenty-first century. If the public finds out we killed the *wrong person,* the Bureau is deader than the *Pony Express.*
Hey, you don't have to convince *me.* This chick pointed a gun at my ass. I've got *no problem* saying she's our perp.
But we're not the only people who've seen the Hood up close before.
No.
We're *not...*

Hello, John.

You two. What is it, time for me to get beaten with a phone book?

We think there's been a mistake, sir.

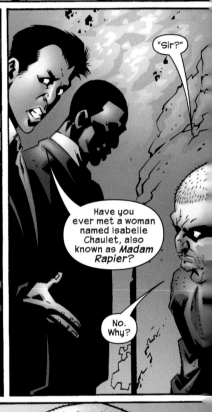

"Sir?"

Have you ever met a woman named Isabelle Chaulet, also known as *Madam Rapier*?

No. Why?

She tried to shoot us a few hours ago. We killed her.

Ms. Chaulet was wearing a cloak and carrying a briefcase filled with thousands of dollars in non-sequential bills.

Ballistics tie the .45 she aimed at us to the bullets pulled from *Officer Bondi's* neck wound.

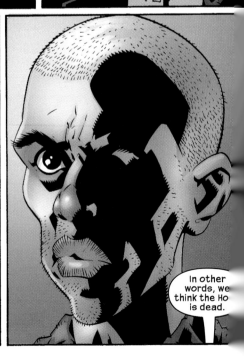

In other words, we think the Ho is dead.

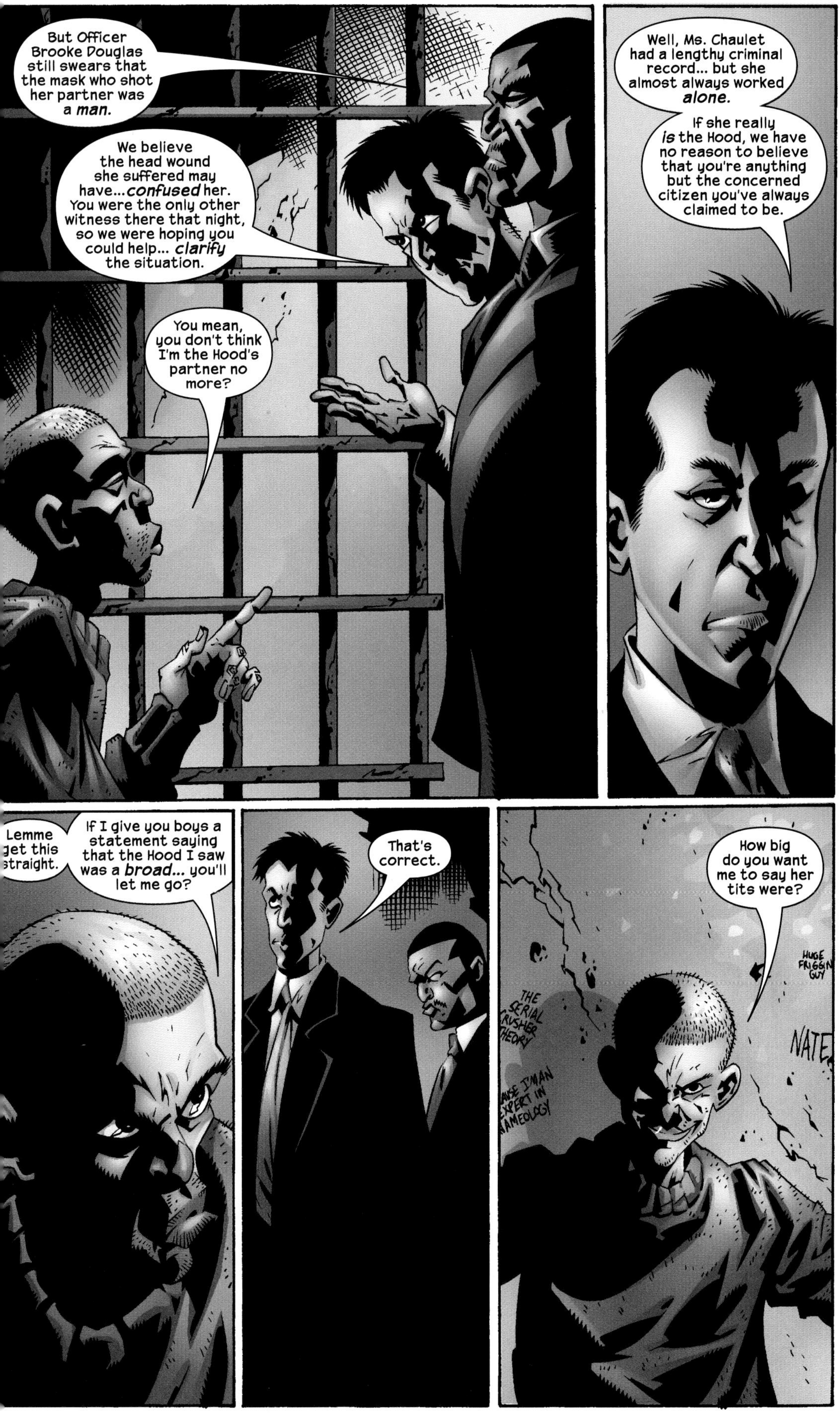

But Officer Brooke Douglas still swears that the mask who shot her partner was a *man.*
We believe the head wound she suffered may have...*confused* her. You were the only other witness there that night, so we were hoping you could help... *clarify* the situation.
You mean, you don't think I'm the Hood's partner no more?
Well, Ms. Chaulet had a lengthy criminal record... but she almost always worked *alone.*
If she really *is* the Hood, we have no reason to believe that you're anything but the concerned citizen you've always claimed to be.
Lemme get this straight.
If I give you boys a statement saying that the Hood I saw was a *broad...* you'll let me go?
That's correct.
How big do you want me to say her tits were?
HUGE FRIGGIN GUY
NATE
THE SERIAL CRUSHER THEORY

On behalf of the FBI, I'm here to inform you that one of our most wanted fugitives, an individual known as the Hood, was killed last night in an encounter with federal agents.

We hope this incident will serve as a reminder to the nation that the FBI is *committed* to ridding our communities of the scourge of masked crime.

Special Agent Infante went on to say that Mr. John King, a man once believed to be the Hood's *accomplice*, has been cleared of all charges and released...

Oh my god. He really *was* inno--

Sara, I'm *hooooome!*

Hope you don't mind a guest. You remember my cousin John, right?

Hello, ma'am.

John's landlord sold his place while he was, you know, *unjustly imprisoned*... so I thought he could crash here for a few nights.

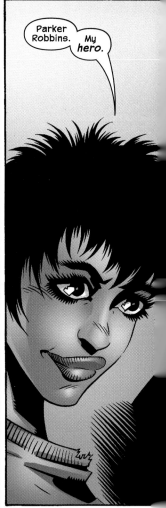

Parker Robbins. *My hero.*

d, you're azing. I'm orry I ever oted you, baby.

Don't worry, you weren't alone. Parker was the only dude *alive* who believed I didn't have nothing to do with that costumed *nutball*. He saved my--

⇁Oof.⇐

I'm just glad everything worked out the way it was supposed to.

Yeah, though I do feel terrible for that police officer's widow.

"Widow?"

It was just on the news. That cop the Hood shot slipped out of his coma last night.

He's dead.

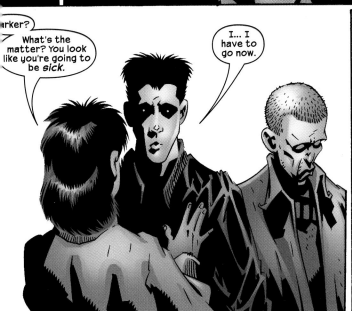

rker? What's the matter? You look like you're going to be *sick*.

I... have to go now.

Wait!

Where the hell are you *going*?

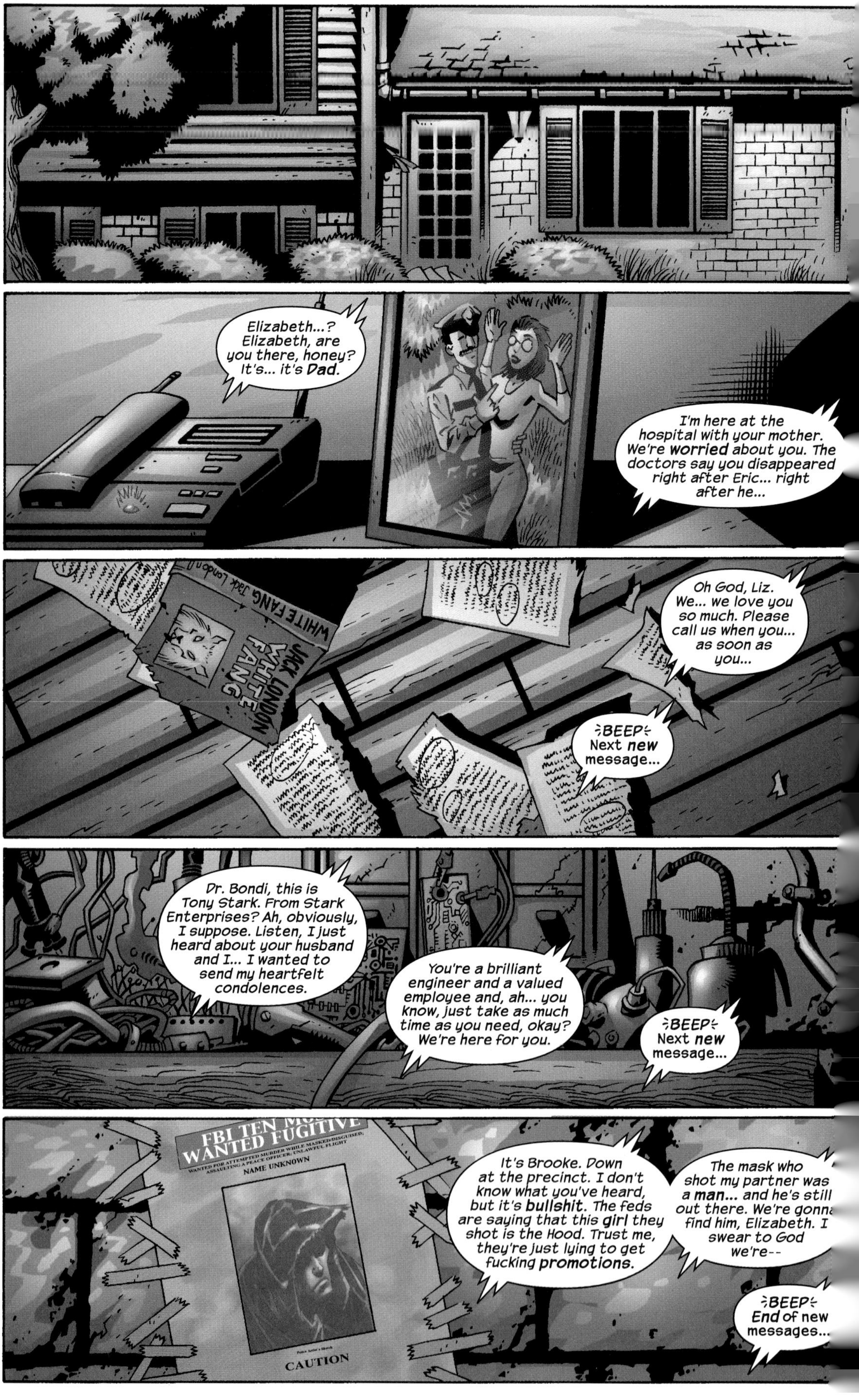

Elizabeth...? Elizabeth, are you there, honey? It's... it's Dad.
I'm here at the hospital with your mother. We're worried about you. The doctors say you disappeared right after Eric... right after he...
WHITE FANG Jack London
JACK LONDON WHITE FANG
Oh God, Liz. We... we love you so much. Please call us when you... as soon as you...
BEEP Next new message...
Dr. Bondi, this is Tony Stark. From Stark Enterprises? Ah, obviously, I suppose. Listen, I just heard about your husband and I... I wanted to send my heartfelt condolences.
You're a brilliant engineer and a valued employee and, ah... you know, just take as much time as you need, okay? We're here for you.
BEEP Next new message...
FBI TEN MOST WANTED FUGITIVE
WANTED FOR ATTEMPTED MURDER WHILE MASKED/DISGUISED, ASSAULTING A PEACE OFFICER, UNLAWFUL FLIGHT
NAME UNKNOWN
CAUTION
It's Brooke. Down at the precinct. I don't know what you've heard, but it's bullshit. The feds are saying that this girl they shot is the Hood. Trust me, they're just lying to get fucking promotions.
The mask who shot my partner was a man... and he's still out there. We're gonna find him, Elizabeth. I swear to God we're--
BEEP End of new messages...

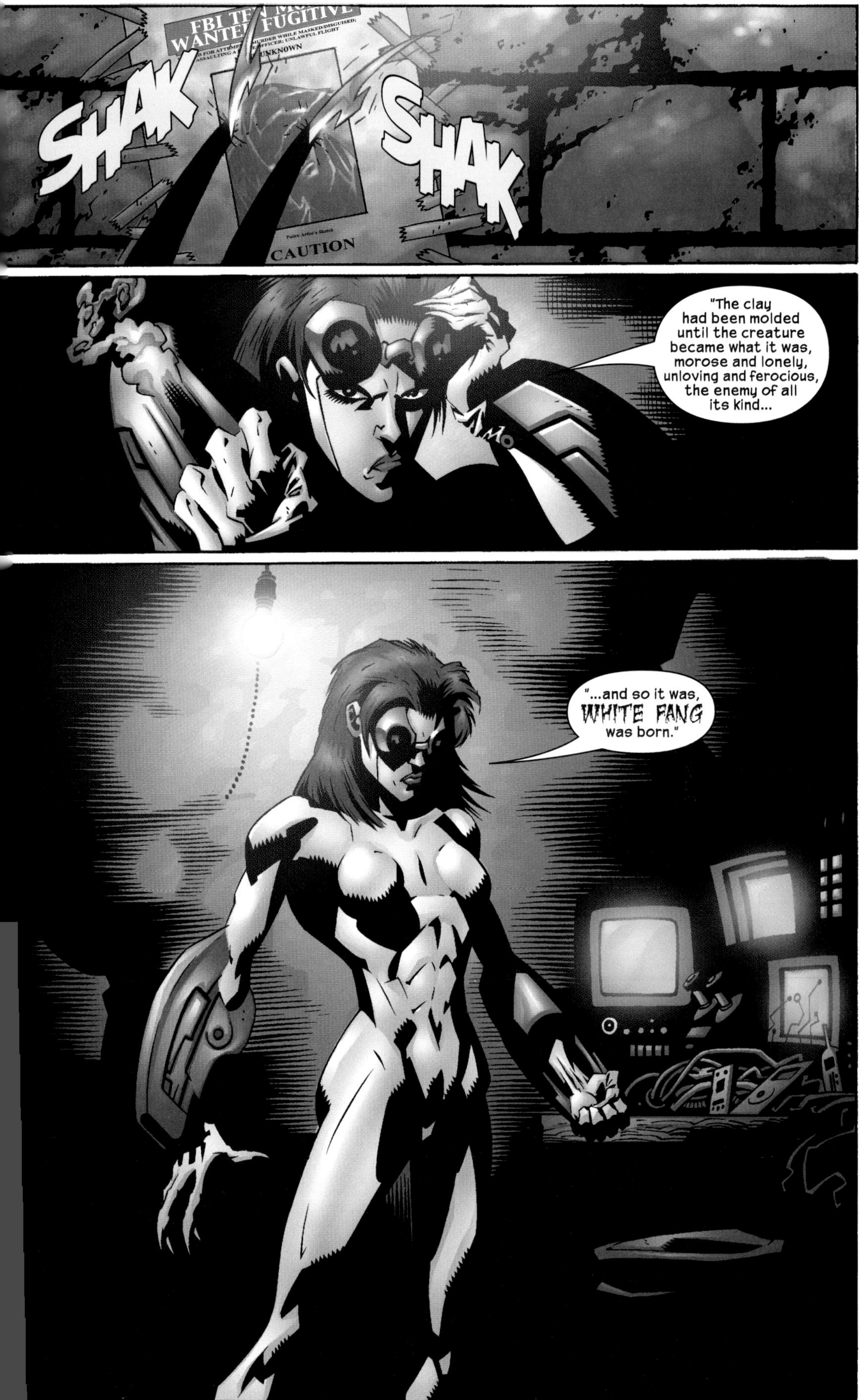
FUGITIVE
UNKNOWN
SHAK
SHAK
CAUTION
"The clay had been molded until the creature became what it was, morose and lonely, unloving and ferocious, the enemy of all its kind...
"...and so it was, WHITE FANG was born."

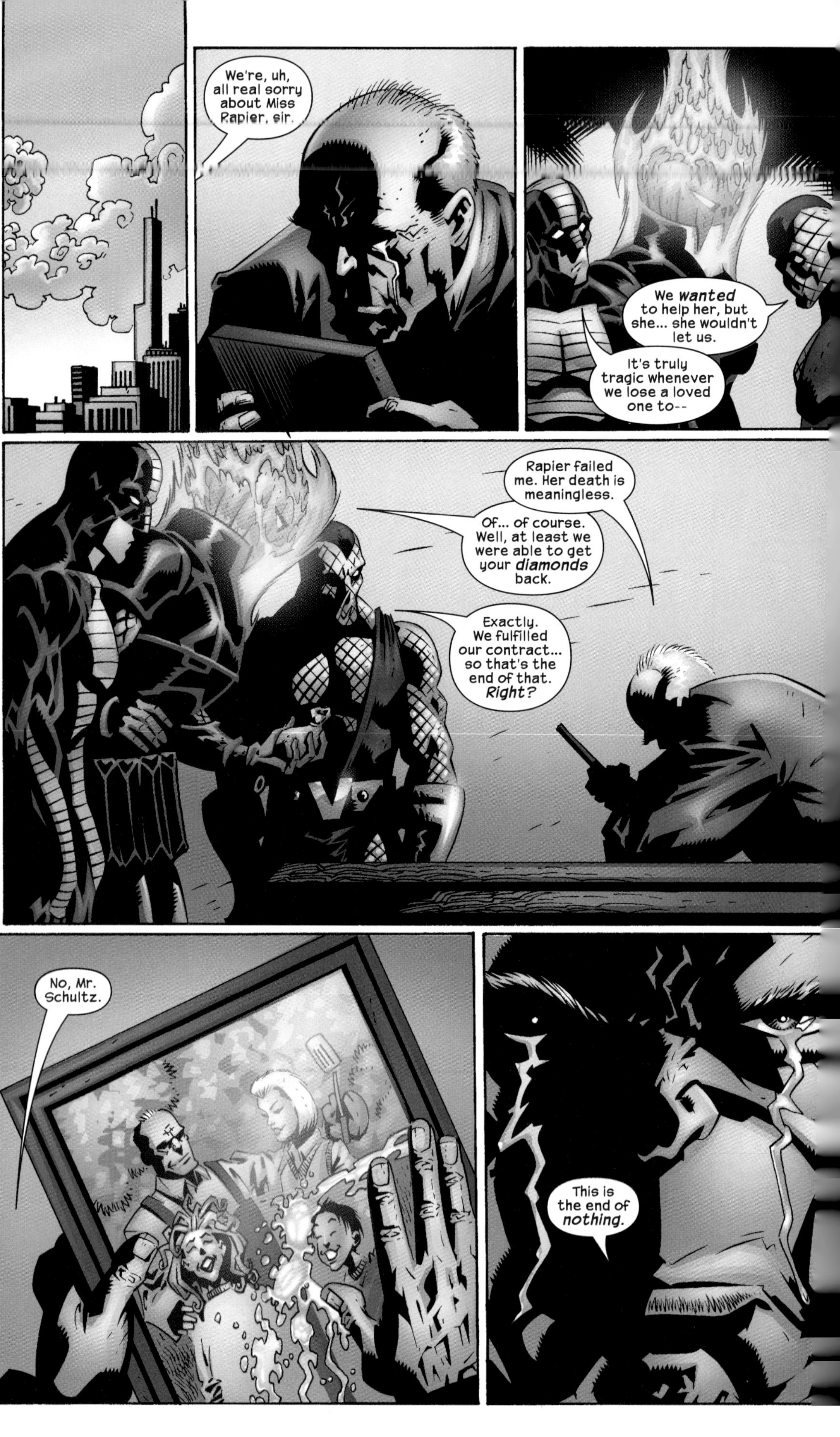
We're, uh, all real sorry about Miss Rapier, sir.
We *wanted* to help her, but she... she wouldn't let us.
It's truly tragic whenever we lose a loved one to--
Rapier failed me. Her death is meaningless.
Of... of course. Well, at least we were able to get your *diamonds* back.
Exactly. We fulfilled our contract... so that's the end of that. *Right?*
No, Mr. Schultz.
This is the end of *nothing*.

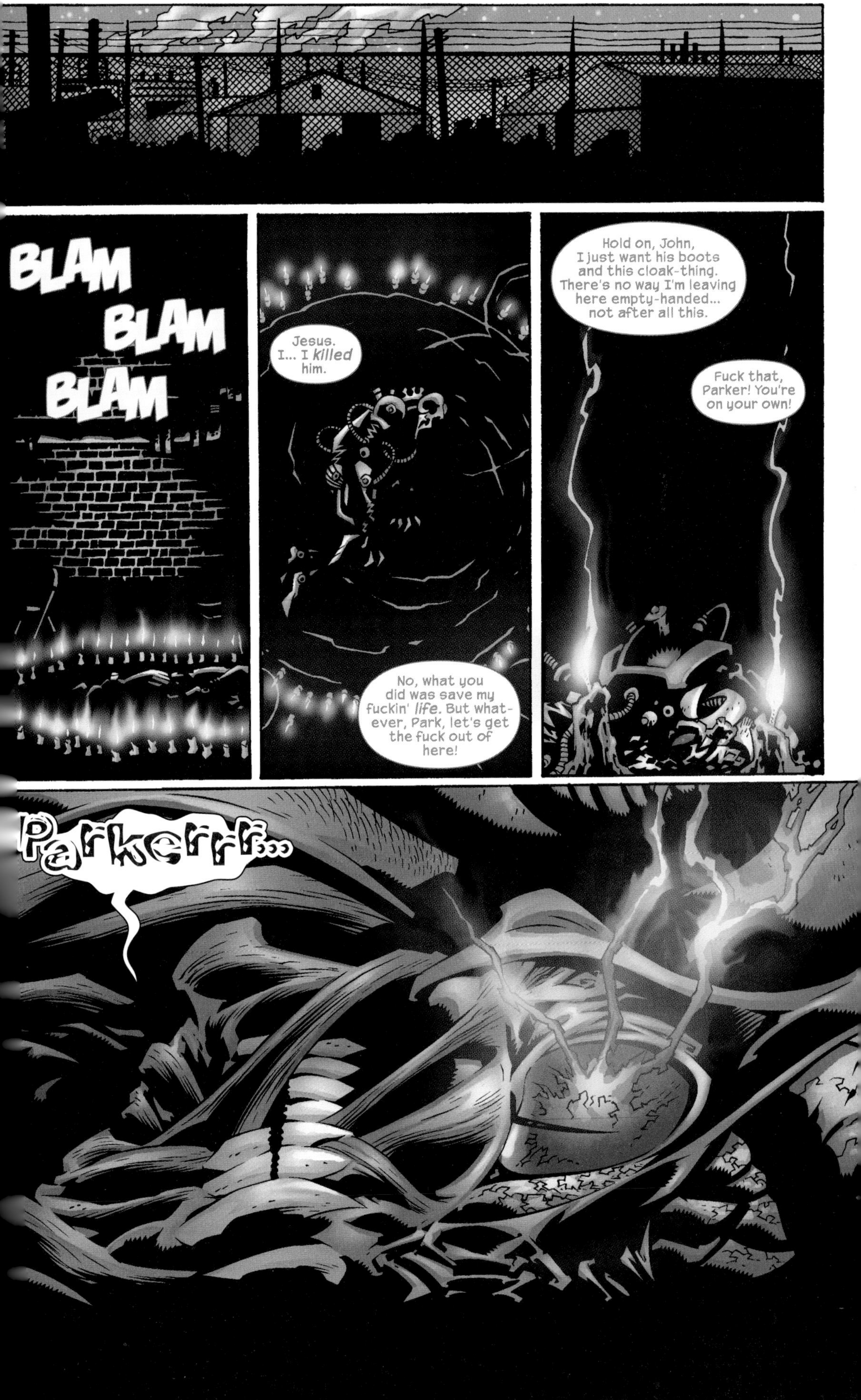
BLAM BLAM BLAM
Jesus. I... I *killed* him.
No, what you did was save my fuckin' *life.* But whatever, Park, let's get the fuck out of here!
Hold on, John, I just want his boots and this cloak-thing. There's no way I'm leaving here empty-handed... not after all this.
Fuck that, Parker! You're on your own!
Parkerrr...

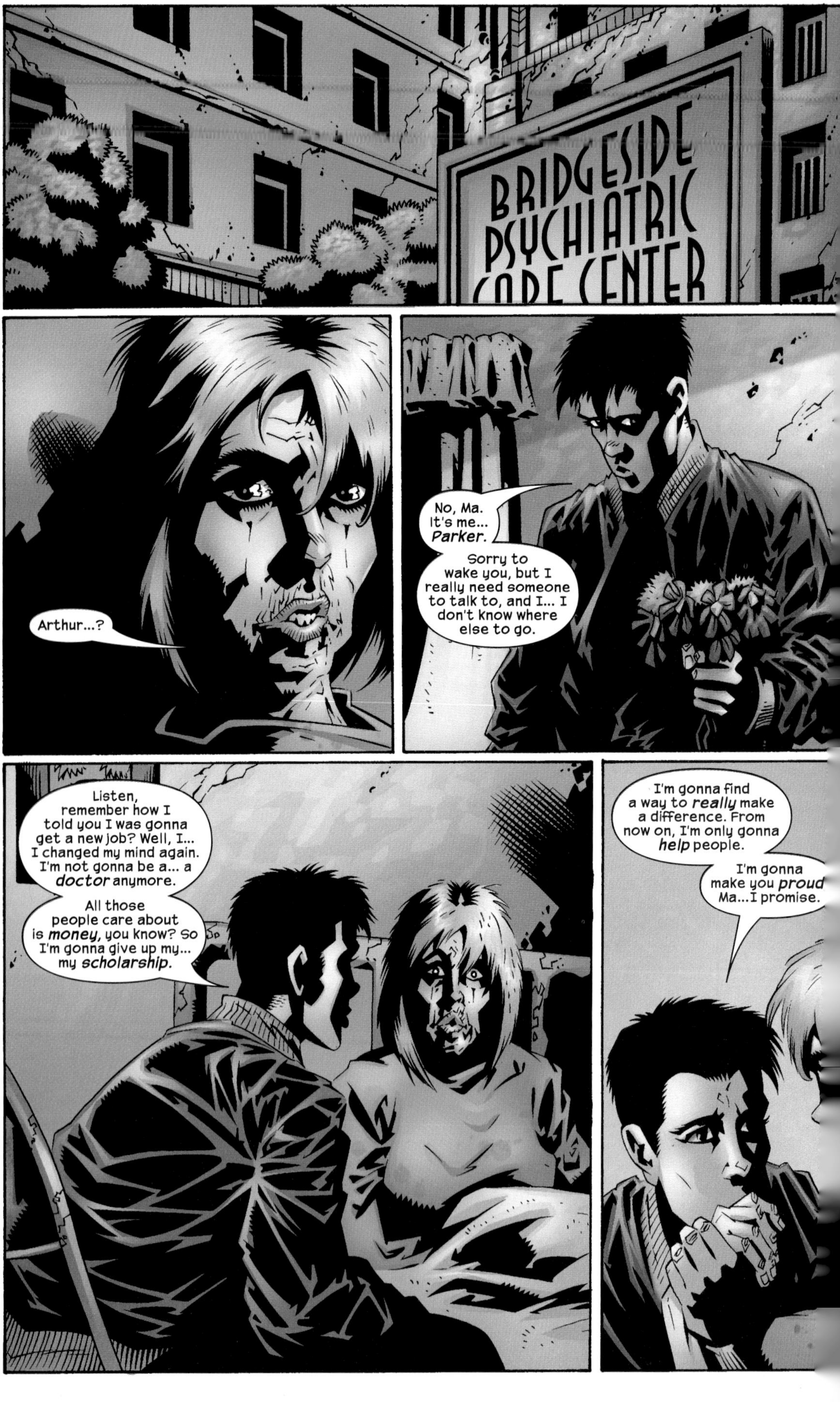
BRIDGESIDE PSYCHIATRIC CARE CENTER
Arthur...?
No, Ma. It's me... *Parker.*
Sorry to wake you, but I really need someone to talk to, and I... I don't know where else to go.
Listen, remember how I told you I was gonna get a new job? Well, I... I changed my mind again. I'm not gonna be a... a *doctor* anymore.
All those people care about is *money*, you know? So I'm gonna give up my... my *scholarship.*
I'm gonna find a way to *really* make a difference. From now on, I'm only gonna *help* people.
I'm gonna make you *proud* Ma...I promise.

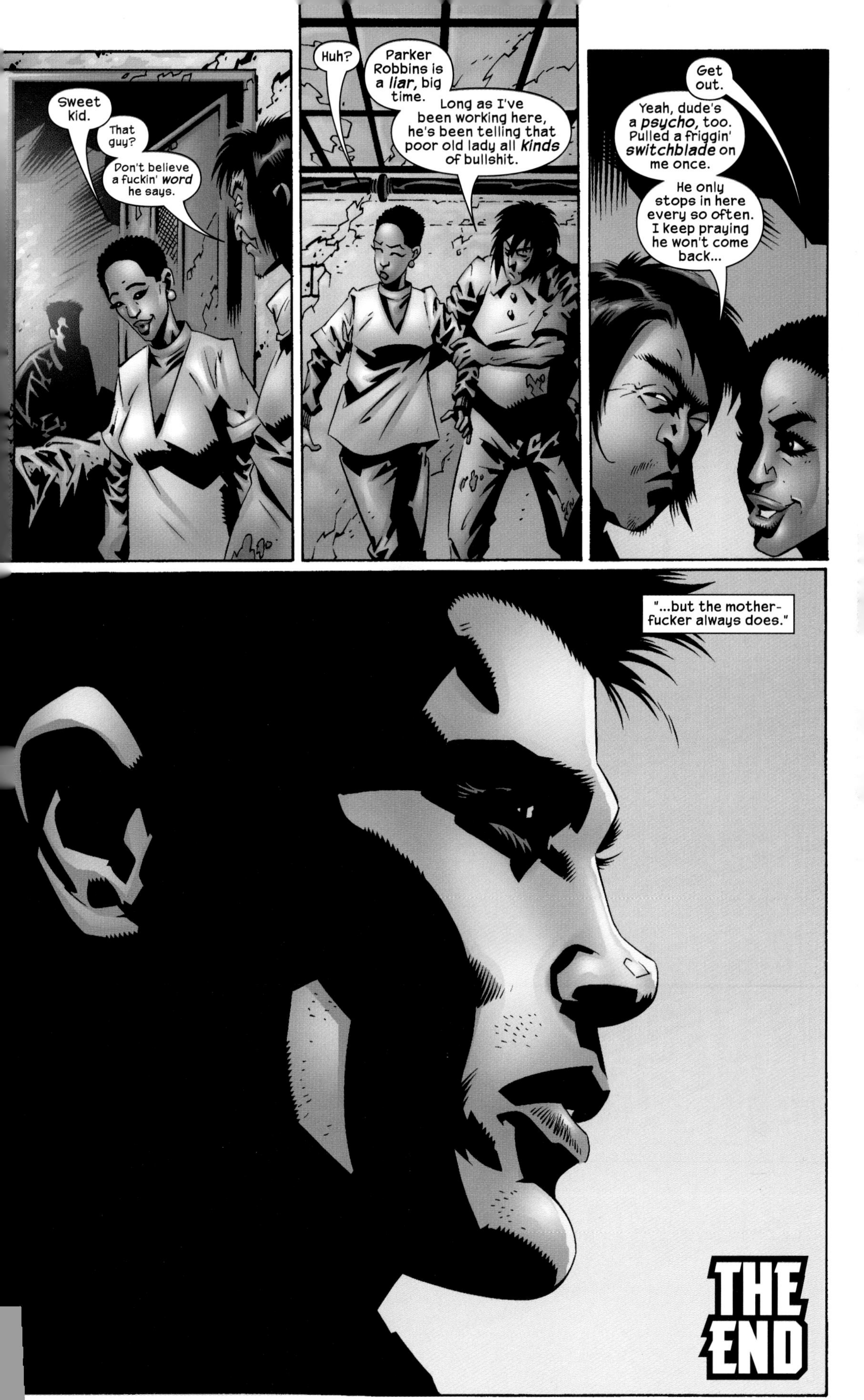

Sweet kid.
That guy?
Don't believe a fuckin' *word* he says.
Huh?
Parker Robbins is a *liar,* big time.
Long as I've been working here, he's been telling that poor old lady all *kinds* of bullshit.
Get out.
Yeah, dude's a *psycho,* too. Pulled a friggin' *switchblade* on me once.
He only stops in here every so often. I keep praying he won't come back...
"...but the mother-fucker always does."
THE END